High-Performance C5 Corvette Builder's Guide

WALT THURN

CarTech®

Copyright © 2007 Walt Thurn

All rights reserved. All text and photographs in this publication are the property of the author, unless otherwise noted or credited. It is unlawful to reproduce – or copy in any way – resell, or redistribute this information without the express written permission of the publisher.

All text, photographs, drawings, and other artwork (hereafter referred to as information) contained in this publication is sold without any warranty as to its usability or performance. In all cases, original manufacturer's recommendations, procedures, and instructions supersede and take precedence over descriptions herein. Specific component design and mechanical procedures – and the qualifications of individual readers – are beyond the control of the publisher, therefore the publisher disclaims all liability, either expressed or implied, for use of the information in this publication. All risk for its use is entirely assumed by the purchaser/user. In no event will CarTech®, Inc., or the author, be liable for any indirect, special, or consequential damages, including but not limited to personal injury or any other damages, arising out of the use or misuse of any information in this publication.

This book is an independent publication, and the author(s) and/or publisher thereof are not in any way associated with, and are not authorized to act on behalf of, any of the manufacturers included in this book. All registered trademarks are the property of their owners. The publisher reserves the right to revise this publication or change its content from time to time without obligation to notify any persons of such revisions or changes.

Edited By: Josh Brown

ISBN 978-1-61325-026-6
Item No. SA127P

Printed in USA

CarTech®
39966 Grand Avenue
North Branch, MN 55056
Telephone (651) 277-1200 • (800) 551-4754 • Fax: (651) 277-1203
www.cartechbooks.com

Cover:
The fifth-generation Corvette was a "clean sheet" design, meaning it does not share components with the previous generation models.

Title Page:
This 550-horsepower Callaway Z06 is able to produce spectacular burnouts.

Back Cover, Top:
Chuck Mallett put this attention-getting slime-green paint on his car before a Super Tuner shootout.

Back Cover, Middle:
MTI Racing has just removed the complete drivetrain out of the bottom of this 2000 C5.

Back Cover, Bottom:
When a driver is able to master a tight corner like this, they know they have the right setup to miss pylons in a real race.

TABLE OF CONTENTS

Chapter 1: Introduction to the C5 7

Chapter 2: Buying a C5 That is Right for You 15

Chapter 3: Suspension Upgrades 30

Chapter 4: Wheels and Tires 43

Chapter 5: Brakes 53

Chapter 6: Driveline 65

Chapter 7: Basic Engine Bolt-ons 77

Chapter 8: Serious Engine Modifications 92

Chapter 9: Drag Racing 107

Chapter 10: Autocrossing 121

Chapter 11: Road Racing 134

ABOUT THE AUTHOR

Walt has been involved with the Corvette hobby since 1963 and has been a Corvette owner since 1965. He has written many how-to articles on street Corvettes and has covered many Corvette racing events. During the early 1970s, Walt was responsible for providing public relations coverage for the Toye English Rebel L-88 Corvette Racing team. Team drivers Bob Johnson and Dave Heinz finished fourth overall in 1972 at the 12 Hours of Sebring. Only two Ferraris and one Alfa Romeo prototype finished in front of the thundering L-88 hardtop. This Corvette record stood until 2004, when a Pratt & Miller C5-R matched the team's finish. During his time with this team, Walt spent time with Corvette Chief Engineer Zora Duntov and Lead Corvette Engineer Gib Hufsteader. Zora and Gib provided valuable behind-the-scenes support to the English Racing team, especially at the 1972 24 Hours of Le Mans. This private team finished fifteenth overall at that year's race, which was the first finish for Corvette since 1960. English Racing went on to finish third overall at the 1973 24 Hours of Daytona. Walt was there to record and document this important part of Corvette's racing history.

During the early 1990s, Walt wrote many articles about the Morrison Motorsports ZR-1 team. While he was with that team, he met many of today's leading Corvette personalities. Some of these people are: John Heinricy, Jim Minneker, Boris Said, Andy Pilgrim, Stu Hayner, Reese Cox, and Chuck and Lance Mallett. In May 1997, he shadowed the Mallett Motorsports team in a brand-new, black C5 Corvette in the One Lap of America. His articles about this wild experience gave readers a first-hand insight about the reliability of the fifth-generation Corvette. In 2000, Walt joined the Pratt & Miller C5-R team as a writer. Walt spent one year with the factory Corvette team, covering the 2000 season. He accompanied the C5/C6 Corvette Registry on three Le Mans trips and wrote stories in their quarterly magazine. He has been published in *VETTE*, *Corvette Fever*, *Corvette Quarterly*, *Corvette Enthusiast*, and Corvette Magazine.com magazines. Along with his racing coverage, he has written a number of how-to tech articles about C3, C4, C5, and C6 Corvettes. He traveled to Europe to document the construction and building of the C6 Z06 R with Callaway Competition. The Z06 R currently competes in the European FIA GT3 championship. Walt and his wife Dianne currently live in Florida.

ACKNOWLEDGMENTS

Writing a book is a time-consuming but fascinating opportunity to revisit your past experiences. I could not have completed this task without the help and support of my wife, Dianne, who encouraged me all along the way. I am grateful to all of the General Motors (GM) engineers, managers, and designers who shared their experiences with me about building and testing the C5. I especially want to thank GM Engineers John Heinricy and Jim Minneker. This also includes designer John Cafaro, Corvette Assembly Plant manager Wil Cooksey, and Chief Engineer David Hill. A special tip of the hat goes to Pratt & Miller Engineering for allowing me to be part of their team in 2000 and witness their first C5-R victory in Texas. A heartfelt thanks goes to the Mallett family, owners of Mallett Cars Ltd. in Berea, Ohio. They invited me into their inner sanctum to let me watch the inside workings of a top tuner. They also trusted me with a brand-new C5 Corvette to drive for the 7,000-mile, 1997 One Lap of America. Reeves Callaway and his team at Callaway Cars, Inc., in Old Lyme, Connecticut, were also very helpful to me during this writing journey. They were always willing to answer my questions and provide me with their outstanding products to include in this book. Thanks to Reese Cox and his MTI Racing team in Marietta, Georgia, for sharing their knowledge on how they modify the C5 and C6 into the best sports car in the world. I appreciate their patience in allowing me to photograph and document their top-quality work. In my opinion, MTI Racing is one of the top Corvette tuners in the United States. Thanks also goes to Mid-America Motorworks, Chief Cheerleader Mike Yager and his team, for providing product support to me while writing this book. Vette Brakes and Products in St. Petersburg, Florida, was an immense help and a special thanks goes to private Corvette race team owner Danny Kellermeyer of DJ Racing. A big "C5" thank you to Dan Adovasio and Jake Drennon, Directors of the C5/C6 Registry, for being my friends and allowing me to use their extensive database for this book. Another thanks goes to Bill Palicka and his service team at Maher Chevrolet for their technical assistance while writing this book. Finally, I want to thank Paul Lesinski and Danny Popp for teaching me about C5 handling and competitive autocross racing. Whew! I am also grateful to all of the people who helped me who I am sure I have forgotten to mention.

This was a fun experience for me, and I feel very fortunate to have been offered the opportunity by CarTech to take this C5 journey. My fingers are crossed that you buy the book, read it, keep it for future reference, and enjoy your C5 journey as much as I have mine.

C5ya!
Walt Thurn

INTRODUCTION

Corvettes have been a big part of my life since the 1950s. My most important treasure is not the car, but the people who I have met and have become friends with all over the country and abroad. It seems like I have been involved in the Corvette hobby most of my life, and my close friends call me a Corvette junkie. Four generations of Corvettes have spent time in my garage, and every one holds a special place in my memories, but the C5 is my favorite. That is probably why I gladly accepted the invitation to write this book. Most importantly, I hope you have fun with your car. Corvettes are great to drive and a blast to work on.

INTRODUCTION

The Corvette hobby is not just about the car, it's about the people who share the same passion that you do about the car. Having fun with a C5 includes taking it to major Corvette shows like Corvettes at Carlisle or the National Corvette Museum. It also includes going to the Saturday night drags, autocrossing it on Sunday, or driving it to work during the week. Corvette ownership is all about fun and friends.

The C5 is a Corvette that almost wasn't built. It was scheduled for introduction in 1993 and came close to being axed several times during its development. But support for Corvette inside and outside GM was huge, and the Corvette was not allowed to die. I was fortunate to drive one of the first 6-speed C5s built in 1997. The serial number ended in 854. I drove it for 7,000 trouble-free miles in one week and I was hooked. I have watched tuners make the fifth-generation cars faster each year. It has been amazing to watch them completely dismantle a C5, modify it, and successfully put it back together again in a very short timeframe. My hope is to share with you some insights about the C5 that I have learned during the car's eight years of production.

I have had the good fortune to spend time with C5 Chief Engineer Dave Hill, Corvette Plant Manager Will Cooksey, and C5 Chief Designer John Cafaro. Each one was very dedicated during the C5's production run to building the best Corvette yet. They knew how important the success of this car was to the future of Corvette. Thanks to their hard work, the C5 gained worldwide acceptance and today Corvette is a shining star within GM. The new C6 continues to build on the legacy the C5 started in 1997. Every Corvette engineer I have talked to plans on keeping it this way. Remember, deep down the C6 is a re-bodied C5. This is not a bad thing, because after all the C5 is a very good car. This book is designed to provide you with an overview of the C5 Corvette.

Chapter 1 provides a brief developmental history of the car and its production goals. Its first One Lap of America racing event is discussed, as is buyers' response to the new car. The chapter also overviews the C5-R racing success in the United States and Europe.

Chapter 2 discusses how to buy a Corvette and provides you with a detailed model guide, including production numbers. This chapter also outlines the power upgrades made during the C5 production. Finally, routine maintenance tips are discussed to keep your C5 in tiptop running condition.

Chapter 3 provides you with an overview of your C5's suspension. We also discuss selecting springs, shocks, and sway bars for the type of driving you will be doing. This includes making the right selection for using your car for the street, drag strip, autocross, or road-racing events.

Chapter 4 covers the various factory wheels and tires offered during production. Aftermarket wheels are also discussed, as well as choosing tires to fit your driving needs.

Chapter 5 covers brake pads and installing an aftermarket braking system to your C5. In general, this chapter discusses factory and non-factory braking systems.

Chapter 6 talks about your Corvette's driveline, including axles, rear end, transmission, clutch, and pressure plate.

Chapter 7 discusses some popular basic engine bolt-ons. This includes air intake systems, exhaust, throttle-body replacement, headers, and other bolt-on items.

Chapter 8 gets into more serious engine modifications, including adding a supercharger, turbo, or even changing your block. We also touch on head-and-cam packages.

Chapter 9 provides some background on drag racing your Corvette. This includes the type of C5 we recommend, driving tips, tires, and transmission choice.

Chapter 10 explores the world of autocrossing. These weekend events are held on big parking lots and are low-speed and very safe family events. However, the big dogs run in the Solo II division, where speeds are higher and driving is more aggressive.

Chapter 11 talks about taking your Corvette to a road-racing circuit and learning how to improve your driving skills, along with your car's handling. The chapter also discusses the Sports Car Club of America (SCCA) amateur racing events and selecting the right car to be competitive.

This book is designed to give you an overview of the car you want to buy or already own. It covers the car's development and the different models available. It also discusses simple or bold modifications you might want to make to your Corvette that suit your taste and budget. Hopefully this book gives you a greater understanding about the fabulous C5.

CHAPTER 1

INTRODUCTION TO THE C5

Development History of the Fifth-Generation Corvette

The fifth-generation Corvette was a "clean sheet" design. This term is used for cars produced that do not share components with the previous generation models. John Cafaro was 34 years old in 1988 when he was named production studio chief at GM. Cafaro had the task of designing the fifth-generation Corvette.

At the time, Dave McLellan was the chief engineer for Corvette. He and his engineering team worked closely with Cafaro on the new design. Cafaro and his design team knew they had a big task ahead of them. Customer expectations were going to be high, so the new design had to be a home run. The new car also had to be easier to build, with fewer components than its predecessor. Finally, this Corvette had to have a very low coefficient of drag to reduce fuel consumption and improve performance. With all of these challenges facing them, the design team knew they had to start with a fresh design.

Dave McLellan became Corvette's second chief engineer when Zora Duntov retired in 1975.

He was chief engineer when the C4 was introduced in 1984, after a one-year delay due to quality-control problems. The car was a huge hit in 1984, but poor quality plagued the new car and sales never matched those 1984 figures. By the late 1980s, the C4 design was getting old. New government regulations required that all new 1997 cars pass more demanding side-impact tests. The fifth-generation Corvette was designed to meet the new crash standards. Introduction was scheduled for August 1992. The design team worked full speed to meet their deadlines until a series of financial setbacks hit GM. Fortunately, support for a new Corvette inside GM was overwhelming. In September 1996, the Bowling Green Assembly Plant began producing the new fifth-generation Corvette.

John Cafaro (shown with wife Beth) was only 34 years old when he was given the assignment to design the fifth-generation Corvette.

Zora Duntov retired as Corvette's Chief Engineer in 1975. Many have called Zora the "Father of Corvette." Zora's passion for racing and his engineering ability helped transform the Corvette's performance image.

CHAPTER 1

Why 1997 Production Was Limited

As I mentioned earlier, the C4 had huge quality problems. Only one 1983 still exists and it rests in the National Corvette Museum. David Hill, who replaced Dave McLellan in 1993 as Corvette's third chief engineer, was committed to avoiding the C4 mistakes. Hill targeted 1997 production to be around 9,000 instead of the usual 30,000 units. In fact, Hill came very close to his target when a total of 9,752 Corvettes were built by the end of the 1997 model year.

Dave Hill became Corvette's third chief engineer in 1993. He helped bring the C5 into production after former engineer Dave McLellan retired.

Bowling Green Assembly Plant

The Bowling Green Corvette assembly plant opened in the spring of 1981 after the original St. Louis plant closed. The Bowling Green plant is located between Nashville, Tennessee, and Louisville, Kentucky. When C4 production ended on June 20, 1996, construction crews began dismantling the line right behind the last C4 as it was being built. In a few short months, Corvette Assembly Plant Manager Wil Cooksey approved the plant ready for C5 production. Corvette plant workers begin building the C5 in late August. By October 1, 1996, the first saleable C5 was ready for shipment.

Buyers' Early Response

Response from the motoring press and public to the new Corvette was overwhelming. Customers clamored to purchase the new C5 and dealers were swamped with orders they could not fill. This was because of Hill's conservative production schedule. Hill stood firm, insisted on high quality, and did not increase production. In retrospect, he was right. The 1997 C5 was introduced with a new crash-tested hydroformed frame, an LS-1 engine, and a rear-mounted transmission. This provided near-equal weight distribution (51.4/48.6) with the automatic transmission. Early production cars were only available with automatics. Wheel size was 17 x 8.5 front, and 18 x 9.5 rear, with Goodyear Extended Mobility run-flat tires (EMT) mounted on a state-of-the-art suspension. Hydro Form was a new technology introduced in Corvette. Long tubes of metal were plugged on both ends and placed in a jig. The tubes were filled with water under high pressure, which bent the metal to form the new frame. This one-piece construction was much stronger than welded frames. When the windshield frame, rear halo, and the removable roof panel were mounted to the frame, the passengers were very well protected. To save weight, the new car had no spare tire or jack. Top speed with the automatic was 172 miles per hour (mph). The MN6 6-speed versions of the car became available in March 1997. Only 1,077 Z51 performance suspension options were built in 1997. Out of that total, only 649 were built with the MN9 6-speed transmission option.

The C5 Registry

Dan Adovasio and Jake Drennon are friends who are passionate about Corvettes. Both were blown away by the C5, and this enthusiasm made them want to spread the word about this Corvette. They started a C5 Registry on Labor Day 1997, with 13 members. The Registry has grown to over 7,000 members worldwide. Their enthusiasm for the new Corvette caught the eye of Chief Engineer David Hill, and Hill was a

Jake Drennon (right) and Dan Adovasio are founders of the C5/C6 Corvette Registry. They were both photographed at the 2001 Parade des Pilotes the night before the 24 Hours of Le Mans.

INTRODUCTION TO THE C5

big supporter of their efforts until his retirement. In 1999, when the C5-Rs struggled against the Vipers, the Registry supported their efforts and brought large groups to cheer the team on at each race. This did not go unnoticed by David Hill, Gary Claudio, and Pratt & Miller. When the team announced their intention to race at Le Mans in 2000, Jake and Dan scheduled a trip to Le Mans for their members. The 24 couples spent two weeks touring the country in their Corvettes, including attending the Le Mans race. The trip was so well received that the Registry repeated the trip in 2001 and 2005.

The Registry has an active web site, www.C5-Registry.com, which is very helpful to C5 owners. The site has news, information, service bulletins, and other useful facts about the C5. The group also publishes a quarterly magazine that is filled with current information about the Corvette lifestyle. There are many Corvette Clubs and Internet sites that you can join. However, I have found the Registry to be an informative and fun group.

C5-R Corvette Racing Program

Early Efforts

In the early 1990s, Chevrolet decided to form a factory-Corvette racing effort to showcase the performance potential of the fifth-generation Corvette. This was the first time that a Corvette was raced by the factory since 1957. The ultimate goal was to build a production-based Corvette capable of winning international grand touring races. Daimler-Chrysler's Viper, Corvette's main competition, was headquartered in France. GM wanted an all-American team and crew for their fabled Corvette. The task was given to Doug Fehan, Corvette Racing's Program Manager.

Doug is a motor-racing genius. He has worked successfully in the motorsports industry for many years. His racing knowledge and experience were exactly what GM needed. Doug was able to contract Pratt & Miller Engineering to build two production-based Corvette C5 racecars. Chicago businessman Jim Miller and racecar fabricator Gary Pratt established Pratt & Miller in 1989. Doug picked them because of their extensive engineering design and fabrication skills. Work began on the new Corvette #001 racer, called the C5-R. A total of three cars were built, two

This Pratt & Miller aerodynamic model of the C5-R helped convince GM management to support a Corvette Racing Program.

The Registry made three trips to Le Mans. Each year the members were allowed to take hot laps around the famous 8.45-mile race circuit. Here they are driving under the famous Dunlop Bridge. The first 24 Hours of Le Mans race was held here in 1923.

Jim Miller (left) and Gary Pratt are longtime friends and partners in Pratt & Miller.

racecars and one street version. The two race versions were secretly tested in 1997 and 1998. The third car was needed to gain approval from the Automobile Club de l'Quest, or ACO. The ACO requires a "low-volume" street version to be built and available for inspection. The car must be very similar to the Le Mans race entry.

This street version met the ACO requirements, and the race version of the car was approved to race. The new 6-liter (360-cubic-inch) car's first appearance was at the 1999 24 Hours of Daytona. The #3 car ran as high as fourth overall and first in GT, until a late-hour oil leak pushed the C5-R down in the standings. It still finished third in class. Throughout the 1999 season, the Goodwrench-sponsored C5-R kept improving. It captured several pole positions and finished second or third behind the factory

First C5 Competition Test: One Lap of America

On Thursday, May 29, 1997, I got to sit in a new C5. It was a black, 6-speed, Z51 with black wheels, and was the 987th C5 built. Chuck Mallett and Jim Minneker would be driving a silver Z51 6-speed C5. Both cars came from Cauley Chevrolet, one of Chuck and Lance Mallett's One Lap sponsors.

These C5s were among the first Z51 6-speeds built at Bowling Green. Mallett worked around the clock getting the cars ready for the One Lap. Preparation on the silver car included adding a complete roll cage, fire system, Penske adjustable shocks; modifying the suspension; and adding racing seats, headers, and a SuperTrapp exhaust.

Goodyear ZR 17-inch S tires were mounted on wider, Enkei aftermarket 17-inch wheels. The car assigned to me was equipped with 17-inch Michelin tires, Enkei wheels, and a modified suspension, but no roll cage. My first impressions of the fifth-generation were positive. Compared to the C4, this car was roomy and very balanced.

The One Lap started at the Watkins Glen racetrack, but heavy rains cancelled the event. The teams were sent to their next stop in Brooklyn, Michigan. The competition debut of the C5 was about to begin.

We arrived at MIS at 5:20 AM, and Minneker finished fourth on a very wet track. Handling, not power, was the key to his good finish. Two cars appeared to be Mallett's chief competition, a 1995 Lingenfelter Trans Am and a Mosler Raptor. The mid-engined Raptor weighed 2,200 lbs and carried a 610-hp Lingenfelter Chevy small-block. The Trans Am was gutted, had Lexan front and rear windows, and pushed about 640 hp. The C5, on the other hand, was very well balanced and what it lacked in power, it gained in handling, comfort, and braking. After Michigan, we headed to St. Louis, Missouri, to Gateway Park, for a 467-mile run. Minneker again finished fourth; the car just did not have the speed that it needed to take first.

After Gateway Park, we headed west to Denver, Colorado, 883 miles away. Mallett and Minneker had to compete in two events while in Denver; the first was north of the city at a little track called Mountain View Raceway. The next event was at Second Creek Raceway, south of the city. Both tracks were tight, twisty, and narrow. Minneker finished seventh at Mountain View and fifth at Second Creek. Our next stop, Las Vegas, was 756 miles to the west.

We arrived at the Speedway on Tuesday morning at 6:30 AM. Minneker finished fourth and third. Our next race was at Hallett Speedway, 1,264 miles to the east of Las Vegas. The road through Arizona was long and straight, with no traffic. It was a good place to check out our C5's top speed. Our car settled at 181 mph and Chuck was able to slowly pull away from us with his extra 30 hp. After driving for 3,000 miles, the black C5 never skipped a beat and still was able to reward us with 28-mpg fuel mileage.

When we arrived in Hallett, the first group was flagged off at 5:45 AM on the 1.8-mile, 10-turn road course. The morning was damp and foggy, and Minneker had trouble hooking the C5 up at the standing start. We could tell that the clutch was slipping, but Jim managed to finish sixth overall. We were concerned about the clutch as we headed to Memphis, Tennessee, 452 miles away. Minneker called Corvette Engineering and received instructions on how to adjust the clutch. After the adjustments were completed, we resumed our trip and the clutch seemed fine.

INTRODUCTION TO THE C5

Vipers. Nevertheless, victory eluded Corvette during its first year of racing.

The cars returned to the 2000 24 Hours of Daytona with new 7-liter (427-cubic-inch) engines. The cars sported a new yellow and white paint scheme, and Pratt & Miller's veteran Canadian driver, Ron Fellows, put the #3 entry on the GTS pole. The Corvette finished second overall, thirty seconds behind the overall winning Viper. The C5-Rs experienced a lot of trouble at Sebring and did not finish high in the standings. The team visited Le Mans for the first time in 2000. At 4 pm, June 18, 2000, the two factory C5-R Corvettes thundered across the finish line in tenth and eleventh place. In addition, the #64 Corvette took a third place in the very competitive GTS class. This was the last time that the original cars were raced. A new car was constructed and appeared at the team's next race in Mosport. The car had a modified chassis and wider

We arrived at Memphis Motorsports Park in time for a 1/4-mile bracket drag-race event. Jim dialed in a 13.40 ET and finished first overall! Apparently, the fix from Corvette Engineering worked. Our next stop was Putnam Park, Indiana, 446 miles to the north of Memphis. Minneker was very familiar with the course and ended up second quickest overall. The new C5 was really showing its stuff and was sitting second overall in the event, just a few points behind the Mosler. Mallett packed the C5 and we headed east to Lancaster, Pennsylvania, 563 miles to the east. Lancaster had three events scheduled: two drag races and one oval event. The drags were rained out and the cars ran on a slippery 1/4-mile dirt oval. Minneker finished twelfth, two spots ahead of the Mosler.

Our last race was Watkins Glen. Minneker finished third, which placed the new C5 second overall, 55 points behind the Mosler. It was a dramatic first-competition debut for the new Corvette. Minneker gathered valuable information on the C5's durability in a very short time. I found out later that the racecar was fitted with a transmission cooler that was being developed as an option for amateur road racers. More importantly, this car was fitted with the 2001 Z06 385-hp LS-6 engine. The race validated to the press and potential buyers the strength of the new engine and driveline package.

Please visit www.cartechbooks.com for the extended version of Walt's One Lap story.

Four cars are started in one-minute intervals. Starting position is dependent on their overall position.

CHAPTER 1

This rare photo, dated March 8, 1994, shows when construction of the first C5-R was underway in the Pratt & Miller shop.

Pratt & Miller was required to build a street version of the C5-R to get approval to race at Le Mans. This car is identical to the racecar except it does not have a rear wing. Notice the two rectangular luggage box openings in the rear bumper. Two small suitcases must fit into these compartments for the car to qualify as a GT entry.

Mr. Goodwrench sponsored the two C5-Rs in 1999, which is why they were painted silver and black. The cars failed to win a race in their first season.

A new season and a new paint scheme. The #001 chassis won the GTO pole position at the 2000 24 Hours of Daytona. The #3 finished second overall, 30 seconds behind the winning GTO Viper.

Chassis #4 is shown under construction at the Pratt & Miller shop in Wixom, Michigan. This car was driven by the late Dale Earnhardt and Dale Earnhardt Jr., at the 2001 24 Hours of Daytona.

bodywork to accommodate larger wheels and tires. The new car also sported a new paint scheme that team members called the "whale" look. The new car finished 0.353 of a second behind the winning Viper.

First Victory

The 2000 season had four races left: Texas, Atlanta, Laguna Seca, and Las Vegas. The team was itching for a victory. Texas was experiencing a blistering heat wave. Nighttime temperatures were 108 degrees! Fellows qualified second, 0.193 of a second behind the pole-winning Viper. The Corvette hounded the Viper in the early stages of the race, and, mid way,

The C5-R's first win over Viper came in Texas, mid way through the 2000 season, in this car.

Dale Earnhardt (right) and co-driver Andy Pilgrim kid around before the start of the 2001 24 Hours of Daytona.

took the lead and kept it to the checkered flag. It was pandemonium in victory circle. Corvette finally beat the Vipers after one and half years of racing against the dreaded snake. Corvette captured another thrilling victory at the 10-hour Petite Le Mans race in Atlanta. Andy Pilgrim, a longtime Corvette competitor, co-drove this race with Kelly Collins and Franck Freon. Andy took the lead when he performed a thrilling pass on the Viper on the next-to-last lap of the race. Andy held the lead to the checkered flag for Corvette's second win of the season.

Championships

Corvette Racing started the 2001 season with a big surprise. Dale Earnhardt and Dale Earnhardt Jr., were hired to drive a C5-R at the 24 Hours of Daytona, with Andy Pilgrim and Kelly Collins. The publicity the team gained from these two famous drivers joining Corvette Racing was enormous. The race was filled with drama. It rained for most of the 24 Hours, and many cars retired from the race. For the first time in Corvette's history, two C5-Rs streaked across the finish line first and third overall. Ron Fellows, Johnny O'Connell, and Franck

It rained for 18 hours at the 2001 Le Mans 24 Hour race. The #63 C5-R finished eighth overall and first in the GTS class. The Audi R8 that is following was the overall race winner.

Kelly Collins (left), Andy Pilgrim, Doug Fehan, and Franck Freon celebrate their class victory at the Petite Le Mans and winning the 2001 Manufacturer's championship.

Freon drove the winning car, and the Earnhardts finished third with Pilgrim and Collins. Sadly, two weeks later, Dale Sr., lost his life at the Daytona 500. The team was shattered by the loss, but they continued their winning ways and captured the 2001 ALMS manufacturers' championship for Corvette. The team also finished first and second at Le Mans in the GTS class, and one car (the #63 car) finished eighth overall. The C5-Rs won their class at Le Mans again in 2002 and 2004. Now, four of these veteran racers are being successfully campaigned by private teams in Europe. The C5-R race program had a huge impact on the performance image of the C5 and continues to wave the banner for the fabulous fifth-generation Corvette. Corvette is now viewed as one of the premiere performance sports cars, and much of that credit goes to GM Racing and Pratt & Miller.

Callaway Competition

Reeves Callaway is an extraordinary car enthusiast. He became an early pioneer, adding turbochargers to cars in the early 1980s. In 1986, he partnered with Corvette to build twin-turbo Corvettes. Customers at Chevrolet dealerships ordered the Callaway turbos. Corvettes were shipped from Bowling Green to Callaway's Old Lyme, Connecticut, facility. The cars were modified and delivered to dealerships for customer delivery. Callaway Cars continued modifying Corvettes until the end of C4 production in 1996. In 1994 Callaway formed Callaway Competition in Leingarten, Germany. This part of their organization built limited-production, LM Corvettes that competed successfully at the Le Mans 24 Hour endurance race. This was done under the direction of Ernst Woehr. In 1998 Callaway introduced a totally revised C5 Corvette called the C-12. This limited-edition Corvette super-car sold for well over $200,000. Callaway Competition built several C-12R competition coupes, and one raced at Le Mans in 2001. The car won the GT Pole position and led its class for 13 hours, until an overheating problem put it out of the race. The C-12 continues to be a highly sought-out, C5-based wonder-car.

Reeves Callaway, shown riding in a C12 with his wife Sue at Le Mans, is the owner of Callaway Cars, Inc., in Old Lyme, Connecticut.

Callaway Competition built this C12-R racecar to compete in the 2001 24 Hours of Le Mans. The racer, based on a C5, won the GT pole and led its category for 13 hours.

This 2004 ex-Pratt & Miller C5-R was sold to GLPK Carsport in Holland. It competed in the 2005 FIA GT1 series and won two races. Here it is shown on its way to winning one of its races in Imola, Italy.

This C12 convertible shows the craftsmanship used when Callaway builds a car. This car is a head turner wherever it goes.

CHAPTER 2

BUYING A C5 THAT IS RIGHT FOR YOU

1997–2004 Model Analysis

When the fifth-generation Corvette was introduced in 1997, it quickly became apparent that it was no ordinary new-model change. Redesigned from the ground up, the new car had to overcome a lot of criticism from Corvette enthusiasts. When we say redesign, we are not kidding. The LS1 engine was completely new architecture and shared no common parts with the LT1 small-block 350 that traced its roots back to 1955. At the heart of every 1997 Corvette beats a brand-new, LS1 small-block, 5.7-liter, V-8 engine. Engineers retained the small-block's 5.7-liter displacement, traditional pushrod design, and 440-bore centers, but that's where the similarity ends. The new aluminum small-block V-8 is the first of its kind for Corvette. The block's "deep skirt" design helps reduce engine noise and vibration. Other improvements include a simplified valvetrain, unique "extended sump" oil pan, redesigned pistons, composite intake manifold, revised ignition system, and dual-wall, stainless-steel exhaust manifold. The LS1 is GM's first gasoline engine with Electronic Throttle Control (ETC), which results in more precise throttle

The 2004 Commemorative Edition Z06 was the end of the line for C5s. This model carried special badges to celebrate two GT1 class victories at the 24 Hours of Le Mans.

HIGH-PERFORMANCE C5 CORVETTE BUILDER'S GUIDE

response through all RPM ranges. The LS1 produces 345 hp and 350 ft-lbs torque—more than either engine offered on Corvette in 1996.

The frame, suspension, and body were also brand new. However, the biggest controversy was the new rear-mounted transmission. Many Corvette naysayers were convinced that this was a bad design and not reliable. As we learned in Chapter 1, during its One Lap of America competition debut, the new C5 driveline was bulletproof. Over the course of its eight-year production, subtle improvements were made to the original C5 design. It has become one of the most reliable Corvettes ever built. This is why the fifth-generation has become so attractive to used-car buyers.

How To Buy

Buying a car is a very emotional and individual experience. In the past, you usually had four options: word of mouth, newspaper ads, used car lots, or auto auctions. These are still good choices, but now a fifth option—the Internet—has been added to the mix. Word of mouth is still my favorite. If you learn about a Corvette for sale through a friend, this provides you with peace of mind and confidence in the seller's credibility. Newspaper ads usually advertise cars in your local area. This enables you to visit the owner's home and observe how they take care of their car. Is it stored inside? Is it parked in a safe spot? Is the owner neat and do they take care of their things? If they do, it's probably a safe bet they have treated the Corvette the same way. You can usually get a better deal from owners, since they do not have to cover car lot expenses such as payroll and inventory financing. However, be sure to have the car checked by a reliable Corvette mechanic before you close the deal. The quality of used-car lots varies, so

Dealerships are good places to shop for a used Corvette. Model selection is usually high and salespeople are knowledgeable about the product.

The Corvette convertible returned to production in 1998 and was an instant hit with buyers.

The hardtop was introduced in 1999 and was converted to the Z06 in 2001. The Z06 was popular with performance-minded Corvette buyers.

BUYING A C5 THAT IS RIGHT FOR YOU

The coupe was the first C5 body style introduced in 1997. Its sleek, sloping, back window helped its aerodynamics, and it has impressive luggage capacity.

What Are Your Needs?

This is one of your most important purchasing decisions. Has a Corvette always been your dream car? Or have you owned several Corvettes during your lifetime? Do you have a family? Do you have a second car to transport the family? It is a good idea to reflect on how buying a Corvette affects your daily lifestyle. After all, it is a two-seat sports car with limited carrying capacity. It is designed to be stylish, fast, and provide great comfort and handling, but it has limited utilitarian uses.

How Are You Going To Use Your Purchase?

First, you must decide how you are going to use your Corvette. If it is going to be a daily commuter, you might opt for an automatic. If you are going to road race or autocross you might prefer a 6-speed. How you are going to use the car must be settled prior to your search. Next, you need to determine how much you can spend. This dictates the year, color, options, and mileage on the car you purchase.

be careful where you shop. Dealerships have a reputation to uphold, especially if it is a Chevrolet store. They usually get their used cars from trade-ins or auto auctions specializing in Corvettes. Many times, they offer dealer warranties or the balance of the car's factory warranty. The down side is that the price is usually much higher than buying from a private seller. Dealers make a large profit on used cars because they buy trade-ins at wholesale prices and sell them as close to retail as possible.

Another buying option is to go to Corvette specialty stores. They know the product and usually offer good financing, plus they have a large inventory to select from. Often these stores also offer limited warranties on cars they sell. Non-specialty, local used-car lots are usually tougher places to find a good, clean, used Corvette. The Internet is a great place to get pricing information, but, much like online dating, it is very easy for the car to seem better than it really is. My advice is to never buy a car without seeing it and having it mechanically checked out. Let the buyer beware! Auctions are usually closed to the public, but some of you might have access to a friend with a broker's license. They may be willing, for a small fee, to allow you to buy a car from them. The best advice is to accompany them to an auction and carefully look over any Corvette you want to buy. Auction sales are usually "as is," and you do not want to be stuck buying a rebuilt wreck or a car with a bad mechanical history.

The Bowling Green Assembly plant is a state-of-the-art production facility that produced high-quality C5s like this silver export coupe.

CHAPTER 2

If you are looking to modify your Corvette purchase, you might want to consider buying a car that has already been modified, like this orange coupe.

Three versions of the fifth-generation Corvette are available. Each has its own distinct personality and use. The convertible is stylish, especially with the top down, but depending on where you live, you might not be able to drive topless very often. The hardtop, introduced in 1999, is the lightest and most solid C5 that was built. GM converted the hardtop into the Z06 in 2001, because it was the best platform for a performance version. The hardtop has a convertible-sized trunk and the top cannot be removed. If you want a performance car, this is our top choice, but if you want a Sunday cruiser, we would pass. Finally, you can choose the coupe. This version has a large, rear-window hatch that gives access to the entire rear of the car. The coupe offers the most storage space in the C5 lineup. Additionally, the middle roof panel is removable for topless driving. And, for the very few of you who care, the smooth shape of the coupe's roof provides 11 mph higher top speed.

Dealer or Private Owner?

As we mentioned above, we prefer buying a used Corvette from an owner. It is much easier to determine its pedigree and learn about any issues the current owner has with the car. Dealers use professional detailers who are very adept at covering blem-

Service Manager Bill Pilicka (left), Service Technician James Ritchey, and Assistant Service Manager John Wysocki work at Maher Chevrolet. Bill runs a Corvette-friendly service department and is a longtime Corvette owner.

Before buying a used Corvette, I highly recommend having the car inspected by a qualified Corvette specialty shop.

18 HIGH-PERFORMANCE C5 CORVETTE BUILDER'S GUIDE

BUYING A C5 THAT IS RIGHT FOR YOU

Aftermarket Corvette suppliers like Mid-America Motorworks, West Coast Corvettes, and Corvette Central are good places to buy parts for your car. VETTE is one of several specialty Corvette magazines on the market that are worth subscribing to.

This 50th Anniversary Indy pace-car convertible sits next to a 1953 Corvette. These 50th Anniversary cars continue to hold their value on the used-car market.

ishes on pre-sale vehicles. However, the positive side is that dealers usually offer good financing and warranty products that fit your budget and peace of mind. It just depends on how adventurous you are when you purchase a car.

Buying a Modified or Stock Corvette?

When Corvettes leave the Bowling Green Assembly Plant, they meet all of GM's production car standards. They are produced on a rolling assembly line and their construction methods are duplicated from car to car. This is why GM was willing to provide factory warranties with each car. If you are buying a Corvette to use as a daily

The 1999 and 2000 fixed-roof coupes are great cars to modify.

Before buying, be sure to test all of the options on a car—like this Heads Up Display (HUD)—to confirm that they are in good working condition.

CHAPTER 2

driver or to cruise long distances on vacations, we recommend buying an unmodified car. Most Chevrolet dealers can repair unmodified Corvettes. This provides you with a lot of options if you have a problem on a road trip. However, we do not consider a car modified if it includes a different air intake, cat-back exhaust system, or upgraded wheels and tires. A dealer usually overlooks these modifications, unless a modified intake system allows water to enter into the engine. A modified car includes non-factory brakes, engine modifications, superchargers, turbochargers, or nitrous oxide systems. If you are planning on using your new purchase for track events, a modified car might be just what you are looking for, especially if you were planning on adding any of these items yourself.

Test the multi-function instrument panel to make sure everything works.

If the car you are interested in buying has HUD, check the windshield to make sure it has its original "HUD" marked on the windshield.

Buying a Car With Warranty

What to Look For

The majority of fifth-generation Corvettes were sold with a 3-year, 36,000-mile factory warranty. For an extra cost, owners were able to extend this coverage to 5 years or 100,000 miles. As we mentioned above, dealers are quick not to cover modified cars. We recommend shopping for a car that has the largest amount of remaining

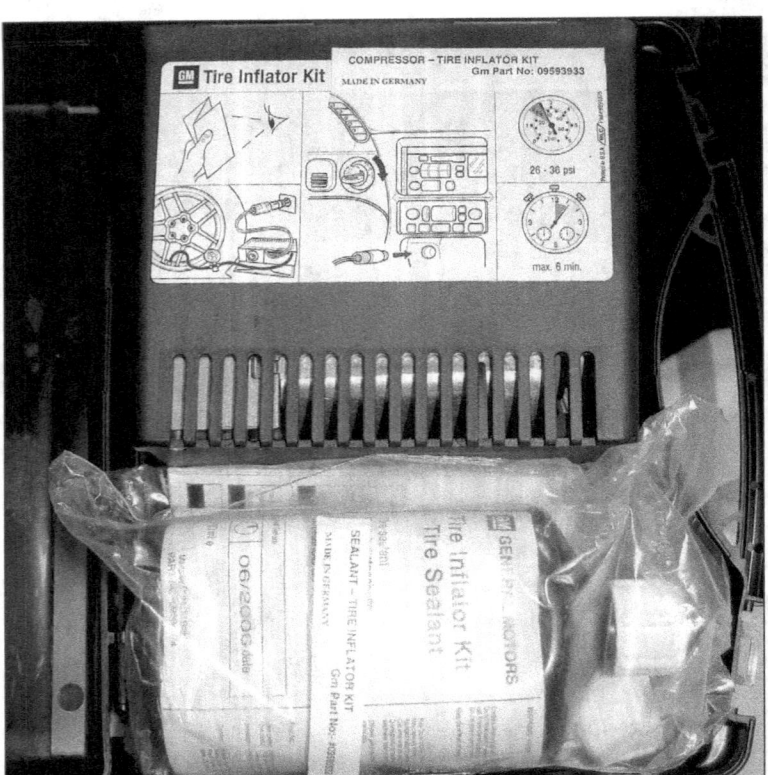

2001–2004 Z06s came equipped with this flat-tire repair kit. The kit includes an air pump and tire sealant chemicals that are used to stop tire leaks.

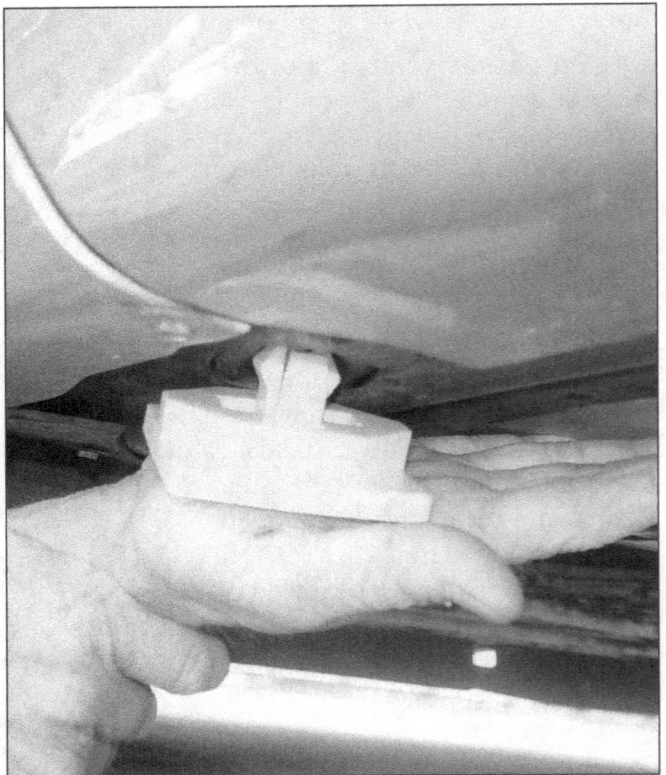

Frame pads are an inexpensive way of preventing damage to your C5's rocker panels when jacking up the car. They fit into four slots in the frame.

warranty if you want to have a worry-free Corvette driving experience. Be prepared to pay more money for a car with this coverage, but to a lot of owners, it is well worth the expense. When buying a car with a warranty, have the dealer check the computer records and determine what repairs this car experienced. Manufacturers keep a detailed record of each car by the vehicle identification number (VIN). If the car you are interested in buying has been plagued by warranty claims, avoid it. Shop around and find a dealer who has a service department run by a manager who is Corvette-friendly and has a good reputation. It makes owning your Corvette much more enjoyable.

Buying a Car Without Warranty

What to Look For

The majority of fifth-generation Corvettes are not covered by their original warranties anymore. It is really up to you to carefully inspect and evaluate any Corvette you are thinking about purchasing. A good, reliable Corvette repair shop is a huge ally to you during your buying project. We recommend taking any car you are considering buying to a good Corvette shop for an expert evaluation. Even if you have to pay for the inspection, it is money well spent. You can also establish prices for replacement parts such as seats, carpeting, etc., in a variety of aftermarket Corvette parts catalogs. Some of our favorites are Mid-America Motorworks, West Coast Corvettes, Zip Products, and Corvette Central. Even if the car is out of warranty, many dealers give you a warranty history on your potential purchase. The more the car has been modified, the less useful this information is to you. Three fifth-generation Corvette specialty models require a larger purchasing budget. They are the 1998 Pace Car convertible, the 2003 50th Anniversary, and the 2004 Commemorative Z06. Convertible and Z06 models usually carry the highest retail prices, followed by the coupes. The least expensive Corvettes are the 1999 and 2000 fixed-roof coupes.

Color plays a big role in the price of a Corvette. The more popular colors raise the value of the car. Red and black are the most popular Corvette colors. Next is silver, followed by yellow and blue. If your car is a daily commuter, you might want to consider automatic air conditioning, heads-up display, dual-power seats, and a rear 6-disc CD changer. The base suspension offers the softest ride, while the Z51 handling package is the stiffest. Selective ride control allows you to adjust your ride as you drive, but is expensive to repair. When you spot a car that interests you, first check the panel seams for gaps.

Look closely at the paint. Does it match from panel to panel, especially the front and rear body caps? Open up the rear hatch/trunk, hood, doors, and fuel door; look for overspray or paint ridges, indicating that the car has been repainted. Look for worn seat bolsters and floor mats to determine how the car was used. Remember to try every door handle, trunk, and window switch. Check all of the dashboard indicators and turn the lights on and off. Inspect the dash lights in a darkened area to make sure all the indicator bulbs work correctly. Operate all of the accessories such as the radio, CD player, remote mirrors, memory/electric seats, heads-up display, cruise control, horn, and the air-conditioning system. If the car is equipped with an

This One Lap car is only one of 1,077 Z51 cars built in 1997.

electric antenna, check it for proper operation. Walk around the car while someone turns on the lights and presses the brakes. Operate the turn and hazard lights. If you can get the car on a lift, check for oil leaks from the engine, transmission, rear end, and axles. Open the hood and check the oil level and color. A dark color indicates the car needs an oil change. Check the belts for cracking or age wear. Pay attention to any odd smells like burned oil or anti-freeze. Also check the brake and radiator fluid levels. Again, look for leaks. Carefully check the tires. First of all, make sure a non-Z06 car is equipped with Extended Mobility Tire (EMT), or run-flat tires. No C5 was equipped with a jack. Non-EMT replacement tires are much cheaper, but a flat can leave you high and dry. Check for tread depth. New tires usually have 10-11/32 of tread depth. A tire with only 3/32 of tread depth remaining needs replacing. New EMT tires can cost from $1,200 to $1,800 for a set of four. While you are inspecting the tires, look for uneven wear patterns that indicate an alignment problem. If the car is a Z06, make sure it has a flat tire kit with a pump. No Z06 was fitted with EMT tires from the factory. Instead, they were equipped with this tire kit. If the car is equipped with heads-up display, check the lower right side of the windshield and make sure it says "Solar HUD."

If the windshield has been replaced with the much-less-expensive non-HUD unit, it is difficult to read the HUD. Check the brake rotors by looking through the wheels and see if the rotors are grooved, cracked, or discolored. Drive the car and notice how the brake pedal feels. Does the pedal pulse? If it does, the rotors need to be turned or replaced. Look at the wheels and make sure they are free from curb damage and scuffing. Look underneath the front and inspect for damage. These cars are very low and have a tendency to bottom out frequently in parking lots. Check under the quarter panels and look for body damage due to improper jacking. Companies like MTI Racing and Mid-America sell frame supports that avoid jacking damage. Check to see if the car you are buying is equipped with these accessories.

Model Guide and Horsepower Ratings

1997–2004 Coupe

The Coupe was the only version of the new fifth-generation Corvette available when it was introduced in 1997. It had the lowest coefficient of drag (0.29 Cd), which made it the sleekest version of the fifth-generation Corvette. The first coupes delivered to customers were equipped with automatic transmissions. The MN6 6-speed option required an additional $815 and did not become available until March 1997. A total of 2,809 1997 Corvettes were built with this option. The Z51 sports-handling package was offered for $350, and it also became available in March 1997. Only 1,077 cars were built with this performance package.

The coupe was the most popular version of the C5 that was built during its seven-year production run. A total of 114,844 were built, making this the most available model on the used-car market. Exterior styling remained the same, with the exception of new wheels being added in 2000 and chrome exhaust tips in 2001. The interiors went through a number of upgrades. The nicest interiors are found in the 2004 models. Horsepower and torque were bumped up in 2001 and remained the same till the end of production. Top speed is 172 mph.

1998–2004 Convertible

After a one-year absence, the convertible was re-introduced into the Corvette lineup in 1998. The new convertible was 114 lbs lighter than the 1996 C4 version and was just as rigid as its coupe version. The convertible required no additional frame-bracing, thanks to its very solid Hydro-formed frame rail system. The roadster had a Cd of 0.33, which was excellent for a convertible. This was lower than the 1984 Corvette coupe, which was tested at 0.34 Cd. The automatic reached 0 to 60 in 4.9 seconds and the quarter mile at 13.4 at 105.5 mph. The top speed of 167 mph was achieved with the top down. A total of 89,610 convertibles were produced, making it the second most popular C5 ordered by customers. The RPO Z4Z, purple and yellow 1998 Indy Pace car version of this car was built to pace the 1998

1997-2004 Coupe

Year	Model	Price	Units	%
1997	Base Corvette Sport Coupe 345 hp/350 ft-lbs Torque	$37,495	9,752	100%
1998	Base Corvette Sport Coupe 345 hp/350 ft-lbs Torque	$37,995	19,235	61.88%
1999	Base Corvette Sport Coupe 345 hp/350 ft-lbs Torque	$38,591	18,078	54%
2000	Base Corvette Sport Coupe 345 hp/350 ft-lbs Torque	$38,895	18,113	54%
2001	Base Corvette Sport Coupe Auto 350 hp/360 ft-lbs Torque MT 350 hp/375 ft-lbs Torque	$39,830	15,681	44%
2002	Base Corvette Sport Coupe Auto 350 hp/360 ft-lbs Torque MT 350 hp/375 ft-lbs Torque	$41,630	14,760	41%
2003	Base Corvette Sport Coupe Auto 350 hp/360 ft-lbs Torque MT 350 hp/375 ft-lbs Torque	$43,735	12,812	36%
2004	Base Corvette Sport Coupe Auto 350 hp/360 ft-lbs Torque MT 350 hp/375 ft-lbs Torque	$43,735	16,165	47%
Total Coupe Production			114,844	

Indy 500 race. Only 1,163 replicas were produced, and it has continued to maintain a high resale value. Generally, convertibles have also retained the highest C5 resale value.

1999–2000 Fixed-Roof Coupe

In mid 1997, rumors began circulating about Chevrolet building a low-priced Corvette. The thinking was that if sales of the C5 were low because of high pricing, a de-contented model might bring young buyers into the showroom. The concept was to offer a car with cloth seats, manual air conditioning, and a 6-speed manual transmission, priced below $30,000. This car is a racer's dream. Fitted with minimal equipment and a solid, fixed roof, the proposed car was light and strong. Insiders named the potential new Corvette, "The Bubba Car." As it turned out, the new Corvette was a hit with the public and demand for coupes and convertibles was out-pacing production. The low-priced Corvette idea was dropped, and most of the content (standard accessories) was put back into the new Fixed-Roof Coupe (FRC). The FRC was still the least expensive Corvette, but not by much. All of the FRCs were produced with 6-speed transmissions and the Z51 handling package. Assistant Corvette Chief Engineer John Heinricy began race-testing the new car in 1998.

When the FRC was introduced in 1999, John's work paid off. The new car was legal to compete in the SCCA's T-1 Showroom stock category. It soon began winning every race it entered. I had the opportunity to look at one of the original "Bubba" cars at a tuner's shop. GM sent it to the tuner to be modified for a new testing program. The tuner was installing special electronic equipment into the car. It had cloth seats, manual air conditioning, and an automatic transmission. Its VIN was 0003. The first FRCs were equipped with automatic transmissions and many served as pace cars.

A total of 89,610 convertibles were built from 1998 to 2004.

1998-2004 Convertible

Year	Model	Price	Units	%
1998	Base Corvette Sport Coupe 345 hp/350 ft-lbs Torque	$44,425	11,849	38.12%
1999	Base Corvette Sport Coupe 345 hp/350 ft-lbs Torque	$44,999	11,161	34%
2000	Base Corvette Sport Coupe 345 hp/350 ft-lbs Torque	$45,320	13,479	40%
2001	Base Corvette Sport Coupe Auto 350 hp/360 ft-lbs Torque MT 350 hp/375 ft-lbs Torque	$46,805	14,173	40%
2002	Base Corvette Sport Coupe Auto 350 hp/360 ft-lbs Torque MT 350 hp/375 ft-lbs Torque	$48,155	12,710	36%
2003	Base Corvette Sport Coupe Auto 350 hp/360 ft-lbs Torque MT 350 hp/375 ft-lbs Torque	$50,735	14,022	40%
2004	Base Corvette Sport Coupe Auto 350 hp/360 ft-lbs Torque MT 350 hp/375 ft-lbs Torque	$50,735	12,216	36%
Total Convertible Production			**89,610**	

1999-2000 Fixed-Roof Coupe

Year	Model	Price	Units	%
1999	Corvette Fixed-Roof Coupe 345 hp/350 ft-lbs Torque	$38,197	4,031	14%
2000	Corvette Fixed-Roof Coupe 345 hp/350 ft-lbs Torque	$38,555	2,090	6%
Total Fixed-Roof Coupe Production			**6,121**	

The most famous FRC paced the 1999 Le Mans 24 Hour race in France. The buying public never embraced the FRC and only a total of 6,121 cars were built. However, the FRC is very

Corvette engineer John Heinricy tested this 1999 FRC with ZR-1 wheels. The car was also equipped with prototype Sports Car Club of America (SCCA) T-1 handling components. SCCA approved this equipment based on John's testing and evaluation.

popular among tuners and racers. It is the least expensive car to buy and the lightest, strongest Corvette ever produced. This model offers a lot of value for the money. We prefer the 2000 model because it was filled with more standard equipment for the same low price over the 1999 version. Top speed is 168 mph.

1999–2001 Boxcars

In 1999, Corvette Engineering decided to produce a limited run of production cars that could be used for racing. This was in response to requests from various Corvette race teams. These teams wanted to race the new C5 in the Speedvision GT series. Their only option was to buy a new car, strip it of all of its street equipment, and build it into a racecar. Once approval was given, the cars were built at Bowling Green by special teams. The finished car included the frame, suspension, steering wheel, engine, brakes, transmission, and rear end. The cars were called C5-R, R for race. Twenty cars were built in 1999 and were sold for $20,000 each. They carried a VIN GMM0001 through 20, or General Motors Motorsports numbers1 through 20. Each car included FRC bodywork that was packed in boxes. Racers named the new Corvette "boxcar." Reese Cox was the first tuner to complete a boxcar and he raced it successfully in the Speedvision GT series in 1999 and 2000. Ten more cars were built in 2000 and sold for $19,500 each. These new cars did not include bodywork, but the anti-lock brake system was added to the cars before they were delivered. Twelve cars were produced in 2001 for the same price of $19,500 each, which ended a very unique chapter in the fifth-generation Corvette history. Many of these cars are still being raced successfully in the Speed GT Series. Some have had their bodies converted with C6 body panels.

2001–2004 Z06

Testing for a new performance version of the C5 began in 1997. Plans were to introduce the new Fixed Roof Coupe first and then use that body style for the upgraded Z06 package. The upgraded engine was used during the 1997 One Lap of America race.

This 1999 FRC served as a pace car at the 1999 24 Hours of Le Mans. It was one of only 37 FRCs built with an automatic transmission.

In 2000, anti-lock braking systems were added to the boxcars in lieu of body panels. In 1999, most of the body panels were broken in shipping, so they were deleted in the 2000 cars.

Because of poor sales for the fixed-roof coupe, that model was dropped in 2001 when the first Z06 was introduced. Unlike the fixed-roof coupe, Corvette enthusiasts ran to their dealerships to buy the new Corvette "hot rod." The 385 hp and 385 ft-lbs of torque 2001 Z06 accounted for 16% of 2001 Corvette sales. The engine featured red fuel rail covers marked LS6.

Early Z06s experienced high oil consumption due to faulty engine ring packs. Check any 2001 Z06 warranty claim record with a local dealer to make sure that the car does not have this problem. This was quickly corrected and the new LS6 engine became a very reliable unit. The new car featured upgraded suspension, close-ratio transmission, and larger wheels and tires. The car had special badging on the exterior and interior.

The instrument panel featured the Z06 emblem and a higher redline on the tach. The Z06 was also equipped with a new, lighter, titanium exhaust system that produced a very distinct growl. The 2001 models were not available with the heads-up display, but this became available in 2002. The engine was further refined for 2002 and now produced 405 hp and 400 ft-lbs of torque. During its four-year production, a total of 28,388 Z06s were purchased. Today, it is a

Only 20 "boxcars," like this one, were built in 1999. These cars were only sold to approved race teams. It was much cheaper and faster to convert them to racecars than to use a production car.

MTI Racing's owner Reese Cox built the first boxcar in 1999. Here, he is shown competing at a race in Daytona.

Boxcars are still being raced extensively in SCCA's SPEED GT series. Here, Lou Gigliotti, driving his boxcar with C6 bodywork, is having a tight race with a Porsche.

very popular used car for performance-minded enthusiasts. The cars are light, nimble, and very fast for a reasonable price.

Routine Maintenance

Tires

Except for the Z06 models, C5s left the Bowling Green Assembly plant equipped with P245/45ZR17s, front, and P275/40ZR18s, rear, EMT Goodyear tires.

They are designed to run up to 200 miles at 55 mph without any air. These tires were mounted on 17 x 8.5 front and 18 x 9.5 rear rims equipped with tire-pressure sensors. Two wheel styles were offered for non-Z06s during the C5's eight-year production: the original "Wagon Wheel" from 1997 to 1999 and the more popular thin, five-spoke wheels used from 2000 to 2004.

All Z06 Corvettes were equipped with Goodyear F1 Super-car, non-EMT tires. The front 265/40ZR17 tires were mounted on 10-spoke 9.5 x 17-rim tires. The rear 295/35ZR18 tires were mounted on 10.5 x 18 rims.

Engine

Two engine options were offered throughout the C5's eight-year production: the LS1 and LS6. The LS1 was installed in every Corvette except the Z06. From 1997 to 2000, it produced 345 hp/350 ft-lbs of torque. Starting in 2001, the LS1 engine received an LS6-style block and was upgraded to 350 hp/360 ft-lbs of torque for the automatic and 375 lb-ft of torque for the 6-speed. The LS6 was only available in the Z06 and was available in two horsepower ratings. The 2001 engine produced 385 hp/385 lb-ft of torque. From 2002 to 2004, the LS6 produced 405 hp/400 ft-lbs. This engine featured a stiffer engine block, new heads with bigger valves, and a new high-output intake manifold.

Interior

Interiors of all C5s remained pretty much the same throughout its production run. Subtle refinements were made, but the basic layout was unchanged. Two styles of seats were available: the standard seat and the upgraded sport seats both featured the name "Corvette" beneath the headrest.

2001-2004 Z06

Year	Model	Price	Units	%
2001	RPO Z06 Fixed Roof Coupe 385 hp/385 ft-lbs Torque	$48,005	5,773	16%
2002	RPO Z06 Fixed Roof Coupe 405 hp/400 ft-lbs Torque	$48,155	8,297	23%
2003	RPO Z06 Fixed Roof Coupe 405 hp/400 ft-lbs Torque	$50,735	8,635	24%
2004	RPO Z06 Fixed Roof Coupe 405 hp/400 ft-lbs Torque	$50,735	5,683	17%
Total Z06 Production			**28,388**	

Total Fifth-generation Production

Year	Model	Units
1997	Coupes	9,752
1998	Coupes/Convertibles	31064
1999	Coupes/Convertibles/Fixed-Roof Coupes	33270
2000	Coupes/Convertibles/Fixed-Roof Coupes	33682
2001	Coupes/Convertibles/Z06	35627
2002	Coupes/Convertibles/Z06	35767
2003	Coupes/Convertibles/Z06	35469
2004	Coupes/Convertibles/Z06	34064
Total Production		**248,695**

* Data provided by the Official C5 Registry, www.C5-Registry.com

The Z06 was introduced in 2001 with special badging, extra horsepower, and upgraded suspension. It was a hit with Corvette performance buyers

BUYING A C5 THAT IS RIGHT FOR YOU

Sport seats were also produced with an opening on the backrest where you could insert competition shoulder belts. The 2003 Commemorative editions featured one-color interiors, which became very popular.

Suspension

Throughout the fifth-generation's eight years of production, the cars were offered with a wide variety of suspension options. It is worthwhile to take a few minutes to review these options.

FE1: All 1997–2004 C5s were available with the base suspension FE1 package. Cars built with FE1 came equipped with lighter sway bars, springs, and general-performance shock absorbers. The FE1 package provides a comfortable ride, but when pushed to the limit, it does not perform as well as the optional suspension packages.

Optional suspension packages included:

F45: (Selective Real-Time-Damping Electronic Suspension). This system offers a technology that reads the road surface at each wheel and adjusts the shocks to achieve a stable and flat ride. The system provides three settings: Tour, Sport, and Performance. This was not available on the hardtops or on the Z06.

Goodyear EMT tires were standard on all Corvettes from 1997 to 2004, except the Z06.

The 2000–2004 thin-spoke-designed wheel was very popular. It was offered in silver, high polish, or 50th anniversary gold.

The "Wagon Wheel" design was very unpopular with Corvette buyers. Many turned to the aftermarket to replace these wheels with a better design.

The 10-spoke Z06 wheel came with non-run-flat Goodyear Supercar F1 tires. This wheel was available in silver or high-polish finish.

Z51: (Performance Handling Package). This option was designed for the driver who wanted the ultimate suspension system. It included larger sway bars, stiffer springs, larger

The LS1 was originally rated at 345 horsepower, but was increased to 350 horsepower in 2001. The LS1 continued to be the base Corvette engine through 2004.

The LS6 was introduced in 2001 with 385 horsepower in the Z06. It was increased to 405 in 2002 and remained at that rating through 2004.

HIGH-PERFORMANCE C5 CORVETTE BUILDER'S GUIDE

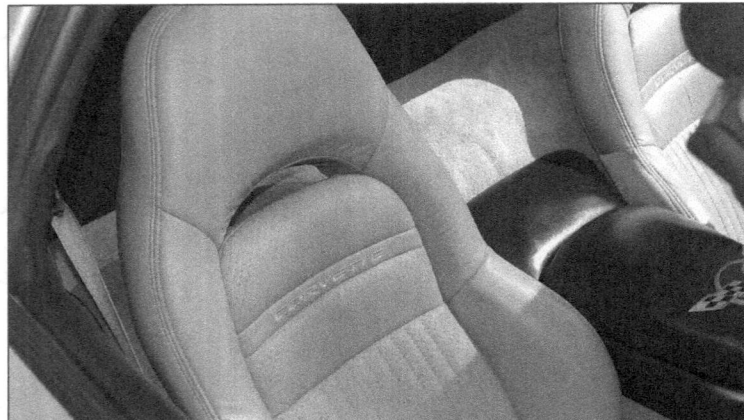
Sport seats had an opening under the headrests that allowed installation of six-point racing seat belts.

A new two-tone interior was made available in the 2004 commemorative edition of the Corvette.

shocks, G92 performance axle, and a power-steering cooler. This was tuned for road-racing and autocrossing events and proved very successful in competition. On the street, it still offers an acceptable ride and the ultimate in car control.

F55: Magnetic Selective Ride Control (MSRC) was first offered in 2003 and replaced the F45 option. This new system used magnetic-charged particles inside the shock assembly. The particles were activated by electronic signals from the control box to adjust ride stiffness.

FE4: (Z06 High Performance Suspension). The chassis tuning, known collectively as the "FE4, Z06 High Performance Suspension" was offered from 2001 to 2004 on all Z06 Corvettes. It begins with added front roll stiffness via a higher-rate, front stabilizer bar. Its diameter is 1.181 inches, up 0.055 inches from the 2000–2001 Z51 bar. In back, to add roll stiffness and reduce acceleration squat, a new rear spring has a rate that is 10 percent (%) higher than Z51. The rear jounce bumpers are half an inch shorter, which increases rear suspension travel a bit. The Z06 uses a small, rear-spring rate increase and more rear-suspension travel. This helps get the power down to the ground when exiting turns. FE4 comes standard with adjustable shocks that change the shock rate via three electronic settings. The most aggressive is the competition setting. Overall, the Z06 was the best-handling C5 offered from the factory.

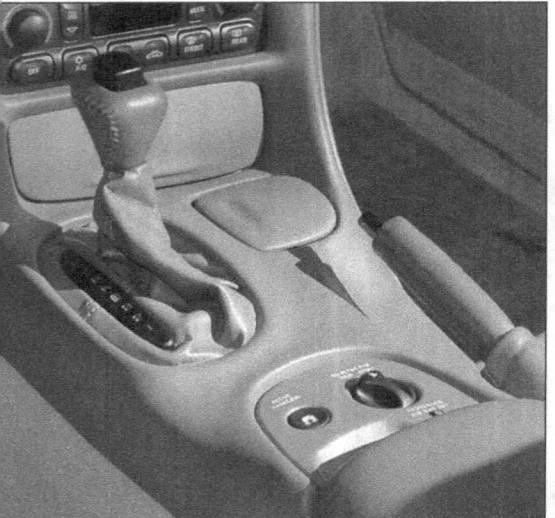
The F-45 suspension package has three settings: Tour, Sport, and Performance. These settings are changed using a switch on the console.

The revised Z06 suspension allows drivers to perform high-spirited maneuvers on the racetrack and still keep the car under control.

BUYING A C5 THAT IS RIGHT FOR YOU

C5 Corvette Suspension Options

Option	Description	GM Part Number	Production Line Code
Z51	Power-Steering Cooler	26057898	
Z51	Front Spring	22178729	AY
Z51	Rear Spring-Coupe/Convertible	22146646	AU
Z51	Rear Spring-Hardtop	22179020	RJF
Z51	Rear Shock Absorbers	10416669	TBC
Z51	Front Shock Absorbers	10279661	TGB
Z51	Rear Sway Bar	10283945	XB
Z51	Rear Sway Bar Bushing	10401553	White Colored Mark
Z51	Front Sway Bar	10234745	White Paint Circle
Z51	Front Sway Bar Bushings	10280526	White Colored Mark
Z51	Factory Production Code is RPO FE3		

FE3 (Z51) Changes and Additions For 2000 Model Year

Option	Description	GM Part Number	Production Line Code
Z51	Rear Sway Bar (Bar size 23.6 x 3.5)	10424743	
Z51	Rear Bushings (2) (Called Insulators)	10424744	
Z51	Rear Clamp (2)	10426591	
Z51	Rear Sway Bar End Links (4)	10423035	
Z51	Rear Spring (6-Speed Trans.)	22179020	
Z51	Rear Spring (Automatic Trans.)	22146646	
Z51	Rear Shock Absorbers	10416669	
Z51	Front Sway Bar (Bar size 28.6 x 4.5)	10424741	
Z51	Front Bushings (2) (Called Insulators)	10424742	
Z51	Front Clamp (2)	10254830	
Z51	Front Sway Bar End Links (4)	10424745	(See Note)
Z51	Front Shock Absorbers	10279661	
Z51	Front Spring	22178729	
FE1	Rear Base Springs	22146323	AT
FE1	Front Base Springs	22178728	AX
FE1	Front Shocks (Base)	10279660	A
FE1	Rear Shocks (Base)	10416668	TBB
FE1	Front Sway Bar (Base)	10227075	Orange Paint Circle
FE1	Sway Bar Bushings	10280525	Orange Colored Mark
FE1	Rear Sway Bar (Base)	10283944	XA
FE1	Rea rSway Bar Bushings (Base)	10401552	Orange Colored Mark
F45	Front Spring	22178748	AZ
F45	Left Rear Adjustable Shock	22199889 *	A49
F45	Left Rear Adjustable Shock Effective 3/29/99	22186431	G3B
F45	Right Rear Adjustable Shock	22139890 *	A40
F45	Right Rear Adjustable Shock Effective 3/29/99	22186430	G3A
F45	Left Front Adjustable Shock	22186429	D29
F45	Right Front Adjustable Shock	22186428	D28
ALL	Stabilizer Bracket (Holds sway bar to cradle)	10423035	
ALL	Clamps Front (around rubber bushings)	10284830	
ALL	Clamps Rear (around rubber bushings)	10283947	

*Effective the week of March 29, 1999:

- The Rear Shocks of the F45 Suspension were issued a new part number.

- The shock manufacturer for all FE and Z51 shocks is Fichtel & Flo – Florence, KY

- The F45 shocks are manufactured by GM's electronic division, Delphi, at another location

- Front Stabilizer Bar (mm) – Base and F45 suspension 23 x 3.8 mm. The Z51 Bar is 25.4x4 mm

- Rear Stabilizer Bar (mm) – Base and F45 suspension 19.1 x 2 mm. The Z51 Bar is 21.7x3 mm

Note: The Z51 cars have metal end-links in the front and plastic end-links in the rear. All non-Z51 cars have plastic end-links both front and rear.

Note: When reviewing your RPO codes on your C5's RPO code sticker, you may notice that when Z51 is selected, the RPO code of FE3 (Heavy Duty Suspension) is also there. FE3 is the RPO code the factory production line employees use when building the C5 with the Z51 package. At the factory, all FE3 components are color coded with either white tags or a white-colored crayon mark.

Note: Production Data courtesy of the C5 Registry, www.C5-Registry.com

CHAPTER 3

SUSPENSION UPGRADES

If you like to take weekend drives in the country, a Corvette convertible is hard to beat.

Corvettes are also fun to take to a weekend track event. Put on a helmet and go have fun.

Like building a good foundation of a house, the first place to start when you modify your C5 is the suspension. The very first thing you need to do is determine how you are going to use your Corvette. The way you drive your car determines what kind of suspension modifications are best suited for you. For example, if you plan on taking long weekend trips to the country, you want a smooth-riding car that is fast and comfortable. If this car is only to be used as a drag car, you want to get maximum weight transfer over the rear wheels. Finally, if you plan on attending track events or road races with your C5, then you need to concentrate on balance and neutral handling. As mentioned in Chapter 2, C5 Corvettes were available with five suspension options during their eight-year production. Two were performance oriented (Z51 and FE-4) cars designed for autocrossing and weekend road-racing track events.

Fifth-generation Corvette suspensions were built with four major components: shocks, sway bars, springs, and an aluminum control-arm suspension system. All Corvettes have been fitted with aluminum upper and lower-control arms and suspension uprights since 1984. The materials are lightweight and durable. The suspension uprights are interchangeable in the front and rear because they are the same design, but the front and rear control arms

SUSPENSION UPGRADES

Ride height is adjusted by turning screws located on each side of the front spring. The spring rests on the front lower control arm.

Since 1984, Corvettes have been built with state-of-the-art, aluminum front- and rear-suspension parts.

are different. The control arms are referred to as an unequal-length design. That means the upper and lower arms are different lengths. This design is found on all fifth-generation Corvettes. Corvettes are well known for their outstanding handling, and this unequal-length control arm design is one of the reasons. Composite transverse leaf springs were first fitted to Corvettes in the rear of all 1981 models. Lightweight and inexpensive to build, these springs eliminate the coil steel springs usually found in most car suspensions. Another advantage of composite springs is that the suspension height can be adjusted by turning the ride-height screws. These screws are located at the corners of each front and rear spring. Front composite springs were introduced to Corvette in 1984. All Corvettes built since 1984 have composite front and rear springs.

Corvette springs are made of composite plastic and are attached transversely to the left and right suspension parts. Spring rates are available from 350 lbs to 1,300 lbs, depending on your driving requirements.

While all C5 composite springs look the same, their differences are found in their spring rates. In other words, how stiff is each spring? Base suspension cars have the lightest spring rates, and the 2004 Commemorative Edition Z06 has the stiffest spring rates. All Z06 models were equipped with a 10-percent stiffer spring than the Z51 handling

CHAPTER 3

When the Z06 was introduced in 2001, it provided owners with a good combination of street and track handling.

Z06 Corvettes are equipped with these aluminum sway-bar end links. Some Corvettes have plastic end links, which should be replaced with the Z06 units. The end link attaches the sway bar to the lower control arm.

GM suspension engineer Mike Neal and his team validated the Z06 suspension by running numerous endurance tests on racetracks around the country.

package. This added roll stiffness and reduced rear squat under hard acceleration. The stiffer the spring, the more firm the ride. Again, you need to decide what kind of driving you want to do with your C5 to make the best spring-rate decision. Shock absorbers control the amount of up and down movement the suspension makes over bumps and dips in the road. Shock absorbers also help the tires maintain contact with road during hard cornering. The F45 and F55 suspension options are fitted with electronically adjustable shock absorbers. The FE4 fitted on all Z06 models had the stiffest shocks offered on production C5s. The Z51 sports-handling package available on all non-Z06 Corvettes used shocks built by Sachs. Z06s also used shocks built by Sachs. Shock valving was changed in the Z06 in three areas. Low-velocity suspension movement was increased at all four corners. GM suspension engineer Mike Neal said, "adding low velocity damping slows body roll, firms the ride a bit, and improves the front suspension's response in transient maneuvers, such as quick lane changes or autocross chicanes."

Sway bars are attached to the frame and supported by rubber bushings. Each end of the bar is attached to the front and rear lower control arms via a plastic or aluminum link. Aluminum links were introduced in the 2002 model year for the FE4 and Z51 suspension options. The thicker the bar, the less lean your Corvette exhibits in a hard corner. The stiffest sway bars were offered on the Z06 high-performance packages from 2001 to 2004. In 2001, a higher-rate, front sway bar was introduced on the Z06. The new bar was increased to 1.181 inches, up 0.055 inch from the 2000–2001 Z51 bar. Wheel alignment specifications were changed for the 2001 Z06 because of the new Goodyear F1 Supercar non-run-flat tires. Camber of -0.75 degree was a huge increase over other C5s. This setting is used at all four wheels. These Goodyear tires work best with a static negative camber. According to GM suspension engineer Mike Neal, "The more pliable sidewall of the F1 Super Car tire allows that much negative camber without an adverse effect on tire mileage."

SUSPENSION UPGRADES

The non-run-flat Goodyear F1 tire was standard on all 2001–2004 Z06s.

The Z06 has a much-improved active-handling system, which gives the driver a wider range of control.

The 2001 Z06 had one final upgrade that we need to discuss. It was a more advanced Active Handling system. Designated AH2, it was a significant improvement in a system that was already good. The key changes made affected sideslip angle and rear-brake stability control, and improved coordination with traction control. The system was also fitted with a competitive mode. The improved sideslip angle control means the system can sense if a driver is too slow to react or is overreacting in a corner that exceeds the cars limits. The Active Handling system applies the right amount of differential braking to maintain the car's balance. The AH2 is better coordinated with traction control, which uses either rear-brake intervention and engine torque limiting to control rear-wheel spin. Compared to AH1, the revised Active Handling's use of traction control is skewed more towards rear brakes than engine controls. The result is less engine "sags" and better engine response after a traction control incident.

Selecting Springs, Shocks, and Sway Bars

Street: In my opinion, C5 Corvettes equipped with the F45 or F55 suspension options offer the best ride compromise. Both suspension options give the driver three suspension settings on the console. A simple flick of the switch from Tour, Sport, or Performance allows the driver to change the stiffness rate of all four shock absorbers. The F55 option became available in 2003 and is called "Chassis Continuously Variable Real Time Damping" (CCVRTD) suspension, or MagneRide. MagneRide shock absorbers utilize magnetorheological (MR) fluid inside the shock assembly. This fluid is a synthetic liquid with carbon iron particles (97% to 99% iron) that provide electromagnetic properties. The shock's dampening changes when these particles are subjected to a direct-current magnetic field strength. The MagneRide controller is a dual-processor unit capable of making 1,000 adjustments per second in all four shocks. The controller receives wheel movements via position sensors and the wheel movement data; the controller determines body motions (pitch, roll, and lift). Non-MagneRide Corvettes (1997–2002) equipped with F45 can be upgraded to F55 option. You can add GM Performance part number (PN)12499507, the C5 Corvette MagneRide Shock Upgrade kit. This upgrade kit uses the existing F45 wheel position sensors, driver select switch, and main suspension system wiring harness.

Drags: The classic drag-racing photo shows a car starting its race with its nose high in the air and the rear tires firmly planted on the ground. Front-engine, rear-wheel-drive cars tend to have more weight on the front wheels, so the trick is weight transfer.

CHAPTER 3

Weight transfer is the key to good rear-wheel traction. Notice how both of these cars' front ends raise under hard acceleration.

Corvette owners who drag their cars usually mount their battery in the back. Hardcore drag racers install narrow front tires on 5-inch-wide rims. Typical tire sizes are 5.25 x 16 on the front and 11.50 x 16 cheater slicks on the rear. Racers also use lightweight front brake rotors and calipers to reduce unsprung weight on the front wheels. Front and rear springs are usually from the FE1 base suspension package that allows the nose of the car to rise in the air and transfer weight to the rear wheels. Modified automatic transmissions are a favorite Corvette drag-racing tool. The C5 hatchback is also popular with Corvette drag racers. The large rear hatch window puts a lot of weight over the rear wheels. Engine choices start with street stock LS1 or LS6 engines all the way to twin-turbo, 1,000+ horsepower, 427+ cubic-inch engines. Elapsed times and trap speeds at the finish line are falling every day, so go to your local drags and find out what people are turning in their Corvettes.

Autocross: Autocrossing started in the early 1950s and has grown to a very popular weekend sport. The SCCA sanctions the Pro Solo and Solo autocrossing series each year. Local SCCA clubs across the country hold autocross events in their areas. Autocrossing is usually a pretty safe sport. Traffic cones are set up in a large parking lot or airport runway. The cars that negotiate the course the fastest win their class. Each driver is assessed a time penalty for every cone they knock down. The trick is to drive quickly and smoothly and not take out any cones. Car preparation varies: street-class rules are very limited in what you can modify on your Corvette. Street Prepared classes allow limited modifications to your engine and suspension. Drivers of all classes are required to wear helmets. The 2001–2004 Z06 is the car of choice in the Stock category. The cars are nimble and have enough power to do well on longer courses. In Street Prepared, the 1999–2000 FRC and 2001–2004 Z06s are very popular. The FRC is much less expensive to purchase and most of the suspension and engine parts are going to be changed in Street Prepared. The Z06 does have a closer ratio gearbox, which is an advantage on shorter courses. Autocrossing

The SCCA autocross nationals are held each year in Topeka, Kansas. Corvettes are very competent autocross competitors.

SUSPENSION UPGRADES

Z06s are very popular in the SS autocross category. Notice the tire warmers being used on the yellow Z06.

Multi-time National Pro Solo champion Danny Popp blasts his way to another A-Street Prepared victory in his Z06. He won his class at this event by 4.078 seconds and missed setting the fastest time of the day by 0.3 second!

really teaches drivers car-control in a safe environment. The sport accepts both young and older men and women. It is a good way to exercise your Corvette on the weekend, and I recommend starting with the SCCA website for more information on track events and regulations.

Road Racing: There are several ways to road race your Corvette. You can race your Corvette in local track days or Car & Driver's One Lap of America. In addition, you can compete in SCCA's amateur racing series or race in the SCCA SPEED GT World Challenge series. Track days are held at various race circuits around the country. The organizers charge a daily fee, give your car a safety inspection, and determine your driving skill. Depending on your skill level, they either let a qualified driver ride with you or let you drive alone. If your car and engine are modified, the safest place to see what your car can do is on a closed racetrack. Some Corvette tuner shops offer track-day support services, for a fee, for which they prepare, store, transport, and maintain your car at the track. MTI Racing in Marietta, Georgia, is one example of a tuner that provides this service. MTI Racing attends track days around the South each year. They bring a support trailer and mechanics to help their customers maximize their track time. Their trailer is equipped with brake pads, rotors, tires, oil, fluids, and parts to keep you car running during the weekend. MTI Racing also offers driving instructions to help clients maximize the performance of their Corvettes and improve their driving skills.

The Car & Driver One Lap of America is usually held in mid May to early June. *Car & Driver* magazine sponsors the event. Much like autocrossing, Corvettes can run in the street-class or modified category. A C5 won the event overall in 2003, and Corvettes are usually sprinkled among the top finishers. As outlined in Chapter 1, this is a grueling event that takes a lot of physical stamina and superb driving skills. The event

Phil McClure finished third in the 2004 SPEED GT drivers' championship, driving this 2001 C5 boxcar.

CHAPTER 3

Track events are a good way to safely experience your C5's handling limits. Here, two C5s sweep through a fast right-hand corner at over 100 mph.

MTI Racing provides their customers with a complete trackside service package. Here they are changing front brake pads on a customer's Z06.

Autocrosser Danny Popp drove this modified 500-hp, 1999 FRC aggressively during the 2005 One Lap of America. Danny and co-driver Jerry Onyx finished third overall.

usually visits 10 to 12 racetracks located around the country in six days. A fast, comfortable, reliable car usually does well. Check out the rules and schedule at *Car & Driver*'s website.

Again, the SCCA offers a wide variety of amateur racing classes for Corvette drivers. The showroom stock category, called T-1, is the least expensive. The C5 is an excellent choice to race in the T-1 category. The best C5s for this are the 1999–2000 FRC and the 2001–2004 Z06. The SCCA allows competitors to install the factory GM Performance Parts T-1 package, which includes better shocks, larger sway bars, heavier springs, and a transmission cooler. However, once you have committed to this kind of racing, your car is not usually streetable. In order to save weight, some interior accessories are stripped from the car. Complete roll cages make it difficult for passengers to use the right seat. Mandatory fuel cells have to be installed for safety, and other safety items must be added for track and driver safety. Like the autocross series, each SCCA region holds races, and the drivers who accumulate the highest three points per category are invited to the annual runoffs. GM engineer John Heinricy drove a 1999 FRC to several T-1 National championships. He has won a total of five National Championships driving Phoenix Racing C5 Corvettes.

The SPEED GT racing series is an all-out racing series sanctioned by the SCCA. Each event is 50 minutes in length and is televised on the SPEED channel in a one-hour show. The SPEED GT Corvettes are all-out racing cars. All of their interiors have

SUSPENSION UPGRADES

Chris Ingle has had good success in SCCA local and national SCCA races driving this 2001 T-1 Z06.

The interior of John Heinricy's T-1 showroom-stock-winning 1999 FRC shows why these T-1 cars are not very streetable.

John Heinricy has placed many Phoenix Racing Corvettes in the winner's circle. This GM engineer is a master road-racing driver.

SPEED GT driver Leighton Reese re-bodied his 2000 C5 boxcar with C6 body panels in 2005 and is among the top runners in this competitive series.

been stripped and filled with regulation roll cages. Most of the Corvettes running in this series are re-bodied C5s. Specifically, they are the boxcars built by GM from 1999 to 2001. The regulators have allowed the Corvette competitors to install the newer C6 Z06 body panels onto the old chassis. The new body is better aerodynamically and is more appealing to the race fans. But underneath beats the heart of my favorite Corvette, the C5.

Installing Front and Rear Composite Springs

Now that we have covered the various ways to race your Corvette, let's use a real-world example of how to install a new set of composite springs into your C5. We visited MTI Racing in Marietta, Georgia, to watch them install new composite springs in a C5. This particular C5 had recently been upgraded with a 550-hp, LS2 engine package. The stock Z51 suspension system worked well with the original 345-hp LS1 engine. However, with the new LS2 installed, MTI's owner, Reese Cox, thought this car needed improved handling. During a test drive, Reese noticed the front end rising dramatically under hard acceleration. The nose also dipped under hard braking. Reese didn't feel the car's suspension was up to the task of handling such an increase in power. Reese, a former road racer, knew that the owner was

Vette Brakes and Products produces C5 aftermarket composite springs. MTI Technician Chris Iverson is getting ready to install one of their springs into a customer's car.

MTI Technician Mason Harris removes a C5's stock front composite spring.

going to use this car for street use and track events. The owner needed a compromise in handling and ride. Reese decided to install Vette Brakes & Products (VBP) Extreme front and rear composite springs. Reese told me that top Corvette teams use 1,200- to 1,300-lb spring rates in the front of their cars! However, he recommended installing a VBP 850-lb front and a 750-lb rear spring in this car.

MTI Racing installed VBP PN97320 Extreme 850-lb front and VBP PN97344 Extreme rear 750-lb springs. The MTI team attacked the spring installation like the pros they are. The first thing they did was park the car on a flat surface and measure and record the ride height at each corner of the car. Removing the front spring was more involved and took the most time. The front spring rests on top of the lower control arms and is mounted above the engine cradle. The rear is bolted underneath the lower control arms. The front spring needs to be pulled through the engine cradle for removal.

The rear spring is just unbolted and drops straight down away from the car. Having the car on a lift and having all the right tools made this a quick conversion. MTI started the project by removing the C5's front brake calipers. To do this, they used a 15-mm box wrench to remove the upper and lower caliper bolts that hold the unit to the suspension upright. Once removed, the caliper was stored on the upper control arm. Next, they placed a floor jack under the front suspension for support when they removed the upper control arm bolts. Before they removed the upper control arm bolts, they removed the 10-mm brake-line bolt located directly below the upper control arm. This prevents bending the line when the upper control arm is loosened.

Next, they removed the four 15-mm upper control arm bolts. Once this was completed, they removed the two 13-mm lower shock absorber retaining bolts. Next, they loosened the 18-mm tie rod end bolt and gently tapped it with a hammer to break the knuckle free from the joint. Next, they placed a floor jack under the car's lower control arm to lower the unit. MTI used PB spray lubricant to help remove the screw in the front spring height adjuster. This has to be removed before taking the spring out of the car. They removed the four 13-mm spring shackle bolts attached to the front engine cradle. The old factory Z51 spring was removed. The new VBP 850-lb front spring was ready for installation. They reversed the removal procedure to install the new spring. They torqued the bolts per the Corvette Shop manual specifications.

Moving to the rear spring, MTI placed an 18-mm socket on the lower rear spring adjuster bolt and a 21-mm wrench on the upper adjuster nut. Then they loosened the rear spring adjuster. Before they could completely remove the nut, they placed a jack under the spring and removed the O-ring retainer on top of the adjuster. Next, they removed the nut and lowered the jack to remove all of the tension from the spring. Then they placed the jack stand under the middle of the rear spring and removed the four 13-mm spring shackle bolts.

SUSPENSION UPGRADES

The front upper control arms are secured to the frame with four 15-mm bolts.

This shows a rear spring being removed. After it's secured with a jack, four 13-mm shackle bolts, which hold the spring in place, are removed. Remember spring tension must be relieved first. Always follow the Corvette shop manual when performing this task.

The new VBP spring was ready for installation. They reversed the spring removal procedure to install the new VBP rear spring. The bolts were torqued per the Corvette shop manual specifications. They reinstalled the wheels and checked to make sure the car sat even at all four corners. They used the screw-type adjusters to bring the car to the previously measured ride height.

Once the car was back on the ground, it was time for a test drive. We were surprised at how well the car rode. In spite of the much higher spring rate, the Corvette absorbed bumps without any major jarring or thumping. Reese took the car out for a test drive and agreed with my assessment. Under hard braking, front dive was minimal and the nose remained flat even when it was under hard acceleration. We think the car is now very capable of utilizing its new power more effectively.

Installing Coil-over Front and Rear Springs

Coil-over springs are designed to replace the factory transverse composite leaf springs. Road-race drivers believe that these springs provide more suspension adjustments when setting up a car to race at a new track. These springs are not inexpensive, but do have their place in the right competition settings.

This rear coil-over spring and shock are adjusted by turning the lower adjusting nut up or down.

This is how a front coil-over spring installation looks when completed. The transverse composite spring is not used for this application.

HIGH-PERFORMANCE C5 CORVETTE BUILDER'S GUIDE

The system is pretty simple. A coil spring is placed over the shock. The spring sits in a cradle, which bolts to the frame at the top of the suspension and is secured to the lower A-arm with bolts. The cradle has a large adjusting nut that is turned to increase or reduce the individual spring rate. To install the first step is to follow the composite front and rear spring removal process. Follow the installation instructions and torque specifications provided by the coil-over spring manufacturer.

Installing Shocks

The bottoms of the front shocks are secured to the lower control arm with two 13-mm bolts.

I recommend staying with the original shocks installed at the factory unless you are going to be doing high-performance driving. Each suspension option was designed around the shock that was installed for that particular car. However, if you decide to change the shocks, it is a straightforward job. You need a jack, safety stands, and a good toolbox to complete the change. The front factory shocks are held in place with two 13-mm bolts that are secured to the lower control arm. The top of the shock is held in place with one 15-mm bolt. The rod of the shock goes through a hole in the top shock tower frame. The 15-mm bolt on top of the shock secures a washer and a rubber bushing. The radiator overflow tank and windshield washer tank must be removed to gain access to these bolts. Snap-on makes a special, double-D wrench that must be inserted into the top of the shock tower rod. This allows you to loosen the 15-mm bolt while the double-D keeps the rod from turning. Some people secure this rod with vise grips, but often it destroys the threads on the shock.

The rear shocks are secured with one large 15/16 bolt at the bottom and two 13-mm bolts on the top that are attached to the frame. In both jobs, wheel removal is a must in order to have enough working room for the project. The most aggressive factory shock for the C5 was installed on the 2004 commemorative edition Z06. These shocks are a good value for the money. They

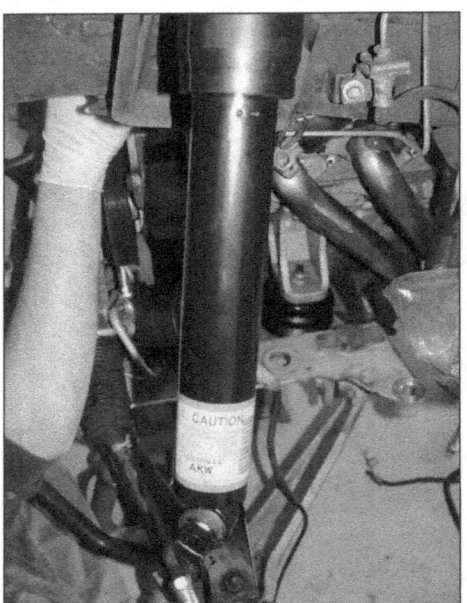

Adding these 2004 Z06 shocks to an older C5 is an inexpensive way to dramatically improve your car's handling. The ride is harsher, but the handling is impressive.

work very well on an older Z06, FRC, or cars equipped with Z51 suspensions. The front shocks are GM PN10339944 and the rear is PN10339945. These shocks provide good car control, and dollar for dollar they are hard to beat.

Aftermarket

Remember, when installing high-performance shocks, be sure to review your driving requirements. Aftermarket shocks are available as a replacement for the factory shocks, or you can find extreme-high-performance units that give you maximum adjustability. Some gas shocks have lines attached to them. These lines are hooked to a braided line that ends at an auxiliary cylinder. The cylinder has an adjustment screw to allow you to finely tune your ride. Coil-over shocks can also be adjusted for ride firmness. The adjustable coil springs and adjustable shocks on a coil-over suspension provide an endless number of adjustments.

Coil-over springs and remote reservoir shocks provide racecar-like handling at a premium cost.

SUSPENSION UPGRADES

Sway Bars

The stock C5 with the Z51 handling option is a very stable platform, with 345-hp under the hood. But if you start pushing over 550 hp at the crank, your suspension performance suddenly becomes critical. Fortunately, MTI Racing's owner Reese Cox has spent a lot of time at racetracks driving Corvettes. We decided to tap his experience and learn how to improve a modified C5's braking and handling. He suggested replacing factory Z51 factory sway bars with ADDCO's tubular 35-mm front/25-mm rear sway bars.

He told us cars steer more precisely through corners with these bars. Because they are tubular they are also lighter. They also make the car more stable at higher speeds and provide excellent emergency maneuvering. To change C5 sway bars, the first step is to remove the sway bar end links with an 18-mm wrench and a number 6 Allan wrench. Next, use a 13-mm wrench or socket to remove the four bolts that hold the bar to the frame. MTI Racing Technician Chris Iverster installs the new ADDCO 35-mm front tubular bar onto the test C5. A 13-mm socket is used to install the four sway bar bushing brackets to the frame. Tighten these bolts to 43 ft-lbs of torque. MTI installed solid Z06 end links that replaced the stock plastic end links. Tighten the links to 55 ft-lbs of torque and remove the four 18-mm upper and lower rear sway bar bolts. The two 18-mm end-link bolts are also removed. The bar can now be removed from the car. The new ADDCO rear tubular bar can be installed. The lower sway bar bolts are tightened to 71 ft-lbs of torque. The upper bolts are tightened to 49 ft-lbs of torque. The end links are tightened to 52 ft-lbs of torque. The car is now ready for a test drive. The bigger bars did not have an adverse effect on the car's ride. However, turning into corners was very crisp and instant. We did not experience any body lean, no matter how hard we pressed the car in a corner. This is a very worthwhile upgrade over the optional Z51 factory sway bars. The finished car felt very precise, and a flick of the wheel provided instant response to the driver. We feel confident knowing that the car's handling is now more precise with the addition of these sway bars.

Lowering the C5 Corvette

C5s can be lowered about 1 inch in the rear and 3/4 inches in the front with the stock bolts if you have the Z51 suspension. If your car is equipped with the base suspension (FE1) or the Continuously Variable Real Time Damping (F45) suspension, lowering the car makes it ride stiffer. You can use the spring jackscrews to lower the car as much as they allow. Then road-test it, and if you don't like the ride, simply crank up the adjustment. This does not damage the shocks because the F45 system "sees" the decrease in ride height. Keep in mind that F45 cars have base springs. Softly sprung cars may have more of a problem with lowering than Z51s. You can lower the FE1 and F45 about 1/2 inch in the front and rear safely. Adjusting both front and rear bolts to

Aftermarket sway bars like these Callaway units greatly improve the Corvette's ability to turn into a corner quicker. The 35-mm front and 25-mm rear bars are a common upgrade.

After a new front spring is installed, the ride height is adjusted by turning these spring adjuster bolts up or down.

their maximum gives you approximately 3/4 inch in the front and 1 inch in the rear. While this does not sound like much, it makes the car look and feel a lot lower. This puts the air dam 2 inches off the road after the procedure. You might consider either cutting off the lower 1 inch of the air dam or raising the car about 1/2 inch so it won't scrape so much. Before lowering your car, measure the height of the front and rear wheel wells from the ground through the center of the wheel. It should be somewhere around 27-3/8 inches in front and 28-5/8 inches in the rear. Write down these numbers.

Lowering the Rear

With the car parked on a level surface and the front wheels blocked, jack the rear of the car and support with two jack stands. It is actually easier to do the lowering if the wheels are removed, especially when it is time to measure the bolt height to ensure that the car is level (you might want to remove the wheels now also). At each end of the transverse leaf spring, locate a long bolt, with the threaded end pointed upward.

You should see about 1 inch to 1-1/2 inches of exposed thread on the bolt (this is on the top of the leaf spring). Using an 18-mm socket and ratchet on the bottom of the bolt, tighten (clockwise) until only two or three threads are exposed on the top part of the bolt. Use an 18-mm wrench to hold the top nut in place as you turn the bolt. Leave two or three threads exposed before it contacts the nut. The nut has a small "C" clip on it so it won't back out. It takes about 5 minutes per side to lower the rear about 1 inch. It is a good idea to measure the exposed threads on each side to ensure they are the same.

MTI Technician Mason Harris adjusts the rear suspension ride height with this rear spring bolt.

Lowering the Front

The car definitely has to be raised in the front. With the car safely raised, on jack stands, and with the front wheels removed, find the end of the transverse leaf spring next to the shock. Locate the 10-mm end of the ride height adjustment bolt. It has a retainer clip. With some suspensions (like the F45) it is easier to get at the top of the bolt if the lower shock absorber bolts (13 mm) are removed so the shock can be moved out of the way. Using a 10-mm socket on the top of the stud, turn counter-clockwise (like unscrewing—even though you are not, you are just on the opposite end of the bolt so it looks that way) until tight. Back off the bolt about a 1/8 to 1/4 turn to ensure it does not freeze in place in case you want to raise the car at some future date. Reattach the lower shock mounts, put the wheels back on, and remove the jack stands.

At this point, the car may not appear to have been lowered very much. Take it for a drive around the block and allow things to settle. Then, with the car parked in the same spot, re-measure the height of the wheel wells as above. The difference between the two measurements is the amount the car was lowered. Make sure that both sides of the front and rear are the same measurements. Adjust as necessary. Drive the car for a week or so, then have the alignment checked by a good shop. Align as necessary. If the car feels like the suspension is riding on the rebound bumpers, you may be too low. The best fix is to raise the car by about 1/4 inch and test-drive it again.

After a spring change, the car should be driven and its ride height re-measured on a flat surface.

CHAPTER 4

WHEELS AND TIRES

This "Wagon Wheel" design was installed on all 1997–1999 Corvettes built for the U.S. market. This wheel design was not very popular with C5 buyers.

The Goodyear EMT run-flat tire was standard equipment on all 1997–2004 Corvettes, except the Z06.

Gold magnesium wheels were fitted to 1997–1999 export Corvettes. The design was popular with owners, but they were easily damaged and expensive to replace.

Selecting the Right Rim

Fifth-generation Corvettes were offered with four different wheel designs. The original "Wagon Wheel" design came standard on all cars built between 1997 and 1999. They were sized at 17 x 8.5 inches front and 18 x 9.5 rear. These wheels were designed to accommodate the EMT or "run flat" Goodyear tires. The tires were sized at P245/45ZR17 front, and P275/40ZR18 rear and were standard equipment on all new C5 Corvettes.

The EMTs were required because this was the first Corvette offered that was not equipped with a spare tire, jack, and lug wrench. The Goodyear EMTs were designed to run 200 miles with no air at 55 mph. The Wagon Wheel rims were painted yellow (option code PA6) in 1998 and fitted to all Indy pace car replica convertibles. All export cars were fitted with different offset, five-spoke, gold-colored magnesium rims from 1997 to 1999. Magnesium wheels were also offered as an option for cars built for the USA between 1998 and 2001. There are *different part numbers* for domestic versus export wheels. This means that six different part numbers are used for 1997 to 1999 wheels.

In 2000, a new standard wheel was fitted to all new domestic and export Corvettes. A limited supply of magnesium wheels was still available and offered at discounted prices until supplies were exhausted in 2001. The new wheel was a much more pleasing five-spoke design, and it was available in painted silver or a high-polish

HIGH-PERFORMANCE C5 CORVETTE BUILDER'S GUIDE

finish. These wheels were popular with buyers and continued to be fitted to the standard Corvette until production stopped in 2004. In 2001, the new Z06 offered a wider, ten-spoke wheel. The wheels were fitted with a non-run flat, F1 Super-car, Goodyear high-performance tire. The wheel was finished in matte silver or a high-polish finish. This Z06 wheel was the only one available for this body style from 2001 to 2004. The rims were 17 x 9.5 inches wide in the front and 18 x 10.5 inches in the rear.

This thin five-spoke rim was introduced in 2000 and remained in production until 2004.

The five-spoke rim was also available with a highly polished finish. This seems to be the wheel of choice for many C5 owners.

The 10-spoke Z06 rims became available in 2001 and were fitted to all 2001–2004 Z06 Corvettes.

They were fitted with 265/40ZR17 front and 295/35ZR18 rear.

One other factory Corvette wheel became popular with owners who autocross and road race their C5s. During extensive development testing of the Fixed Roof Coupe (FRC), Corvette engineer John Heinricy made an interesting discovery. If FRCs were fitted with 1996 Corvette A-Mold Grand Sport wheels, the car was consistently faster on a road course. John worked with the SCCA to make these wheels legal in the Showroom Stock T-1 racing category. Not only do these wheels work well on the racetrack, they look great on the street. They are a low-cost way to make your C5 look a little different. I recommend using the 17 x 9.5-inch wheel in front and the 17 x 11-inch wheel in the rear. As an additional bonus, these wheels are among the lightest factory wheels ever offered for a Corvette. Another popular factory GM wheel upgrade is fitting standard C6 wheels to a C5. Many C6 owners are fitting their cars with aftermarket wheels, and the C6 wheels are becoming available. Check swap meets, the Internet, and your local newspaper to find a set of these wheels. They come in 18-inch-front and 19-inch-rear sizes. The 2006-and-later Z06 wheel does not fit a C5: the wheels stick outside of the bodywork and can damage your body panels. I do not recommend fitting these wheels to a stock C5.

Installing and Testing GM Wheels and Tires on a C5

Danny Kellermeyer is a retired GM engineer, and he owns a barnyard full of C5 racecars. Two of his racers started life as 1999 and 2000 "boxcars." John Heinricy drove one of

---

Domestic Standard Aluminum 5-Spoke RPO QD4

Front - 17" x 8.5" - PN9592413
Rear - 18" x 9.5" - PN9592414

Export Standard Aluminum 5-Spoke RPO QF3 *

Front - 17" x 8.5" - PN9592613
Rear - 18" x 9.5" - PN9592615

* The exports have a different offset measurement at the mounting point so as to bring the wheel and tire in-board under the fender well approximately 1/2 inch. Each export wheel has a black line drawn around the circumference between the beads. This black line can only be seen when the tire is removed from the wheel. Very few export cars were equipped with these wheels.

Domestic / Export Magnesium 5-Spoke RPO N73 **

Front - 17" x 8.5" - PN9592638
Rear - 18" x 9.5" - PN9592640

** These wheels have always had the offset to meet export requirements; however, they were not very popular because they were expensive ($4,000 per set) and un-repairable if they were damaged.

WHEELS AND TIRES

This 1999 FRC was used by GM engineer John Heinricy and others to validate the SCCA T-1 showroom stock race package.

This 2000 FRC is fitted with 1996 black Grand Sport rims and Goodyear non-run-flat Goodyear F1 tires.

these boxcars to victory at the 1999 season finale Speedvision GT race. Danny uses Grand Sport wheels on his C5 racecars. We were curious why he uses these wheels on his C5 racers.

We called Danny at his shop and here is what he said: "John Heinricy did a lot of work testing the car with Grand Sport wheels. He assembled a GM Performance Parts T-1 package for the FRC to make it competitive in SCCA's showroom stock class. During the testing, John turned faster lap times with the 17-inch front/rear Grand Sport wheels compared to the factory 17-inch front/18-inch rear wheels. John was so impressed with the results, that he worked to get SCCA approval. The SCCA approved his request to run these wheels in the T-1 showroom stock category. What made this approval interesting was that these wheels were not available on the standard production car." Danny continues, "I figured if it worked for John it would work for me and we have won a lot of races with this setup."

I decided to try this combination on a C5 street car to see if I could match Heinricy's results. I mounted two 9.5 x 17-inch rims on the front and two 11 x 17-inch rims on the rear of a 2000, FRC. I also decided to mount similar tires offered by Goodyear on the 2001–2004 Z06. After all, the Z06 was the high-water mark for C5 Corvette performance. I found a set of 2001 to 2004-style Z06 Eagle Super-car tires in 17-inch sizes. Specifically, P275/40ZR17 front and P315/35ZR17 rear tires were mounted on the project car.

I selected a tire store that uses the latest Hunter mounting, balancing, and alignment equipment. I was pleased with the final results. The tires were mounted on their rims blemish-free and were smooth at all

Stock C6 wheels are a popular addition to C5 Corvettes.

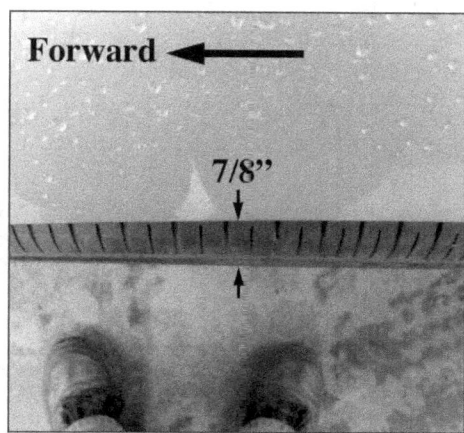
Factory C6 Z06 wheels extend outside the body of a C5. This causes damage to the paint over time.

HIGH-PERFORMANCE C5 CORVETTE BUILDER'S GUIDE

CHAPTER 4

Retired GM engineer Danny Kellermeyer uses Grand Sport wheels on his winning, 1999 boxcar racecar.

This 2000 boxcar owned by Kerbeck Chevrolet is what Danny Kellermeyer's car looked like before it was converted into a racecar.

Danny has won many championships with his pristine 1999 C5 Boxcar.

This 1999 T-1 FRC is fitted with yellow Grand Sport wheels.

speeds. Stick-on weights were used to avoid the ugly outside weight look on the wheels. John Taube, a retired Goodyear engineer, gave me the recommended alignment settings for top performance. I set the camber at one degree negative to help make the car turn into corners more precisely. On the road, I was immediately impressed with the ride and the lack of tire noise. Compared to the original equipment (OE) EMT tires we took off, these Goodyears were very quiet. The alignment change did make a dramatic improvement in the way the car attacked a corner. Very little wheel input was required to set the car up for a quick turn. We hit several heavy rainstorms and wet-weather traction was excellent. However, with wider tires it is always a good idea to slow down and look for the gray spots on the highway to avoid aquaplaning.

The last part of this wheel/tire experiment was to determine how well this combo performed on a racetrack. I contacted the former FIA GT1 driving champion and the 2000 factory C5-R race driver Justin Bell to participate in my test. He agreed to compare this wheel/tire package to a standard Z06 at Moroso Park in West Palm Beach, Florida. I was delighted to have such a talented driver compare our test car to a Z06. I arranged to have a stock 2002 Z06 at the test for a comparison.

After a tire-pressure check [32 pounds per square inch (psi) in the front and 33 psi in the rear], Justin took the car to his wet skid pad. His reaction?

"This car has a lot of grip for a non Z06. The tires are very predictable when they break loose, and it was easy for me to regain control in a slide. Overall, I was quite impressed."

So far so good. Our next stop was the 10-turn, 2.5-mile road course at Moroso Park Raceway. Justin

WHEELS AND TIRES

The 315/35ZR-17 Goodyear Eagle tires on 11-inch rims are stuffed under the back of this 2000 FRC.

Justin Bell was able to match lap times of his Z06 school cars with this 2000 FRC, with the Grand Sport wheels and Goodyear tires.

decided to take the Z06 out for three hot laps and then jump into our project car for a direct comparison. Track and weather conditions were the same, so he was able to give us some candid feedback. When he was finished driving the Z06 he took my project car out for some hot laps. I mounted a G-meter in the cabin to note our braking and cornering forces. I saw 1.1 G under hard braking and 0.98 G in several tight corners. This car was equipped with VBP's cryo-slotted rotors and Hawk HP Plus brake pads. Justin ran the first lap with the active handling on and the next two laps with it switched off. His times improved dramatically with the system in the off position. Lap times matched the Z06 on the last lap.

After we came into the pits, Justin told us, "Well, first of all, I know the Z06 very well, so I know exactly how it should handle. I ran the car with the active suspension set in the competition mode. But the interesting thing I noticed immediately on the project car is that the tires are wider, lower, have huge grip, and the brakes are very impressive. These factors increase the corner entry speed to a fair degree, meaning the mid-corner speed also is increased. The net result of this is that your one-setting, active-handling system is permanently activated. In my opinion, this is because the parameters in which it was designed have been exceeded. I could feel the grip of the car, but I couldn't use it. By deactivating the system, I could then appreciate the tires on this car. It allowed me to roll the car into the corner with a lot more speed off the brakes. It allowed me to maintain on-throttle, mid-corner speed, and it really allowed me to come out of the corner with a lot more stability than I am used to in a standard C5. So, I enjoyed the tire—it felt a lot more like a Z06 than other C5s that I have driven. I don't recommend driving with the system off in everyday driving, but in track events like an autocross the car is faster with the system off. So for the person who wants more out of their C5, I highly recommend adding these wheels and tires."

There you have it from experts, the 17-inch-wheel combo is a winner on a stock C5.

Tire Pressure Sensors

Tire pressure sensors are standard equipment on C5s. They are an

Good tire equipment is required when mounting these large tires on expensive rims.

excellent safety feature, especially since the spare tire and jack have been eliminated from Corvettes since 1997. When I added the Grand Sport wheels, I decided to leave the original sensors on the original wheels. I ordered a new set of sensors from GM, and they fit perfectly.

If you want to keep your sensors on your original wheels like I did, order the following part numbers for 1997–2000: Sensor PN10438853, Retaining Nut PN10268439, O-ring Washer PN10268438. These part numbers are the same for all four wheels. In 2001–2004, GM went to an FM bandwidth sensor, with the following part numbers: Sensor PN2571358,

Justin Bell is a former FIA GT champion and an ex-Pratt & Miller C5R Corvette driver.

Be sure to select the right tire pressure sensors to install on your car. There are two types—one for 1997–2000 Corvettes and another for 2001–2004 Corvettes.

Retaining Nut PN25708165. Note: the O-ring comes with the sensor on the 2001–2004 units.

Once the sensors were installed, I discovered that they didn't work. So I visited John Wysocki at Maher Chevrolet and he showed me how to reprogram the sensors. John demonstrated the process by pressing the option button on the dash until you get the "English Language" message. When that message appears, hold the button. With your other hand, press the reset button twice and hold it until you get the tire training message on the dash, and then release the buttons. The next step is to get out of the car and hold a magnet over the LF valvestem until the horn sounds once. Repeat the process (LF, RF, RR, LR) for all four tires. Like magic, John had our tire sensors working. The reprogramming took about five minutes, thanks to John and Maher Chevrolet.

Installing and Testing Aftermarket Wheels and Tires on a C5

One of the big advancements in the C6 Z06 is its new wheel-tire package. The car is fitted with 18 x 9.5-inch front and 19 x 12-inch rear wheels. Goodyear was selected to be the OE tire supplier. Their answer to being selected was a completely redesigned EMT Eagle F1 Super-car tire. The Z06 is fitted with 275/35R-18 front and 325/30R-19 rear tires. I have spent a lot of time watching standard C6s being dismantled. I have been amazed at how similar the C6 chassis is to the C5. I wondered if this Z06 wheel and tire combo would work on a C5. I called Goodyear and spoke with tire engineer Mike Skurich about our C5 project idea. Mike was optimistic about us using this setup on a C5. He reminded me that these tires were developed for the C6, but their C5 performance should be very similar. We asked if he could provide me with some background on the development of this tire; he agreed. He

Racecar driver Justin Bell was quite surprised at how well this C5 performed on its new rims and tires.

This is how the tire pressure sensors fit onto the Factory Reproduction rims.

WHEELS AND TIRES

GM chassis engineer Mike Neal and Goodyear used this 2003 Z06 as a chassis and tire test vehicle for the C6 Z06 tire. Pratt & Miller fit this car with a C6 Z06 aluminum chassis for this testing program.

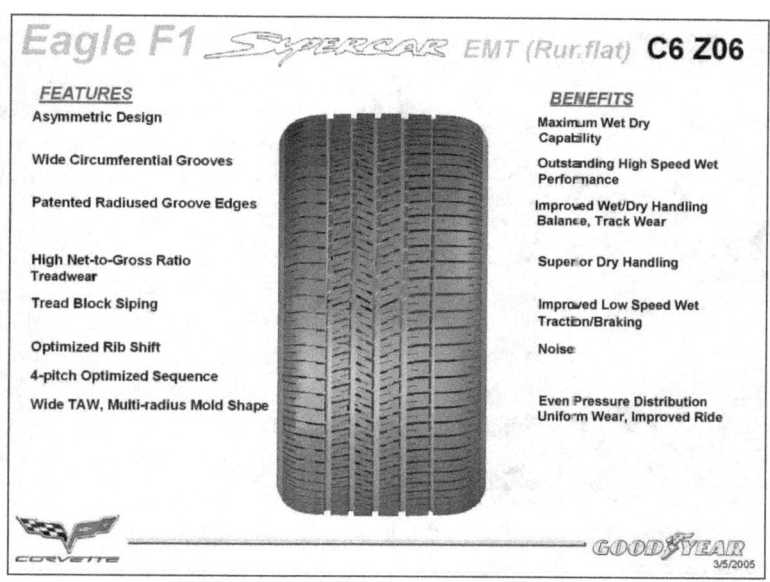

Goodyear provided this chart, which describes the characteristics of the new Z06 EMT Eagle F1 tire.

The C6 Z06 wheel design is very popular with Corvette owners.

began working closely with the Z06 Corvette Chassis development team headed by GM's Mike Neal in 2001. He also worked with Dave Hill's engineering team.

Goodyear learned a lot from their original EMT tire that was standard equipment on the 1997 C5. Specifically, they learned how to reduce tire noise and improve the ride. The mold geometry and profile had a huge impact on improving performance. This tire has less material, which reduces heat, sidewall thickness, and weight. The Eagle F1 tire has an asymmetric mold shape that really helps performance. Its tread depth was reduced from 10/32 to 8/32, which results in less tire heat. Rim flange protectors grip the rim when it is deflated, but also help sidewall stiffness for improved handling. GM reduced the run flat criteria from 200 to 100 miles (how long you can drive before repair at 55 mph), and this opened up new design opportunities for Goodyear. The Eagle F1 features a six-rib design versus the five-rib design found on the C5 Z06 tire. This provides a uniform void for water dispersion and more even tire pressure distribution. Even tire pressure helps footprint contact with the ground. Mike finished the discussion by telling me that the best suspension setting for these tires is -1.0 degrees camber, front and rear, and 30 lbs of tire pressure, front and rear, as recommended by Chevrolet. I decided to order a set of these new tires.

My next challenge was to find suitable wheels for my new tires. The stock GM 2006 and newer Z06 wheels protrude too far out of the C5 fender wells for my taste. A company called Factory Reproductions offers Z06-style wheels in a variety of sizes that fit C5s. I contacted Mid America Motorworks, an authorized dealer for Factory Reproductions. Their helpful staff recommended installing 18 x 9.5-inch front and 11 x 19-inch rear rims, because they are compatible with the new Goodyear tires. Factory Reproduction wheels are made from 356 aluminum. They use the counter-pressure casting method for maximum strength in each wheel. Each casting is CNC machine finished, pressure tested, and inspected for lateral run-out. The 18 x 9.5-inch fronts have a 57-mm offset and the

The Factory Reproduction wheel is designed to fit C5 Corvettes. This rear wheel measures 19 x 11 inches.

19 x 11-inch rears have a 64-mm offset. I ordered a set per Mid America's recommendation. The wheels are PN 624-023 front and 624-025 rear.

The wheels and tires quickly arrived and needed to be properly installed. I again turned to Maher Chevrolet to mount my new wheels and tires. Service Manager Bill Palicka agreed to let me photograph the installation. Service Technician James Ritchey at Maher mounted all four 2006 Z06 tires (275/35ZR18 front and 325/30ZR19 rear) on the Factory Reproduction wheels. James removed my 2000 wheel sensors from my existing rims. James reminded me that it is important to use the correct sensors for your car or they do not work. Two types of C5 tire sensors are available: one for 1997/2000, and the other for 2001/2004. John also told us that 1997/2000 sensors require tire sensor grommet PN25754190 if you install them on C6 wheels. This assures proper rim seal. James installed the sensors and mounted my Eagle tires. He then water tested each tire for leaks. I installed four chrome Z06 wheel caps, PN9597006, that made the wheels look like original equipment. Each wheel was carefully balanced, and James used adhesive weights for a perfect balance. Next, the wheels were mounted on the car, and James checked for clearance. The 11-inch rims are designed for tire size up to 295/30ZR-19 tires. However, we installed 325/30ZR-19 tires, which reduces inner tire well clearance. I cut the inside of the removable plastic liner to provide more clearance for the rear tires and reinstalled the liner.

Next, the car was taken to the tire alignment rack. After the alignment was completed, I was ready for a test drive. I experienced no tire vibration, even at higher speeds. Maher did a great balance and alignment job on this project. I enjoy the looks the C5 gets with the new wheels and meaty Eagle F1 Goodyear tires. The tires handle great in the wet, and talk about cornering grip! I am amazed at how these tires stick to the pavement during hard cornering. Even though the factory Z06 wheels do not fit, these aftermarket Factory Reproduction wheels fit and look very original.

This is what the front and rear C6 Z06 tires look like when mounted on the Factory Reproduction rims.

Maher Chevrolet's technician, James Ritchey, mounts a 325/30ZR-19 tire on a Factory Reproduction 11-inch rim.

The three red arrows indicate where the removable plastic inner liner was cut to provide tire clearance for the 325/30ZR-19 rear tires.

WHEELS AND TIRES

The car was put on the alignment rack before it was driven to ensure that the suspension was correctly set. I strongly recommend doing this on a routine basis.

Puncture Repairs for Speed-Rated Tires

The sound of hissing air is one of the worst things a driver can hear. If you own a late-model Corvette with speed-rated tires, this sound could be your worst nightmare. Starting in 1997, Corvettes were delivered with run-flat tires. To save weight, they were not equipped with tire-removal equipment. If you have replaced your original tires with non-run-flat ZR tires, a hissing sound could leave you stranded on the side of the road. I want to walk you through some do's and don'ts if you get a puncture in one of your tires. This part of the story came about when I picked up a drywall screw that pierced my tire and caused a slow leak.

I took the car to a tire service to get the tire repaired and came away with a new understanding about fixing these high-dollar tires. Speed-rated tires may be repaired only once, and the puncture must be in the tread area within the outside grooves of the tire. No repairs are allowed beyond the outside grooves or in the sidewall area of the tire. If the tire is damaged in those areas, it must be replaced. The repair must seal the tire from loss of air and prevent moisture from damaging the carcass of the tire. I watched as the tire technician marked the damaged area with chalk. They removed the screw and tire from the rim.

Next, they placed the damaged tire on a tire spreader and used a high-speed wire brush to buff the damaged area on the inside of the tire. Next, they used a 7/32-inch carbide cutter to clean out the puncture, and they cleaned it from the inside of the puncture. Then they used chemical vulcanizing cement on the repair plug, pushed it through the puncture, and trimmed off the plugs' excess. Next, they coated the buffed area with chemical vulcanizing cement and let the cement dry.

Finally, they installed a radial tire patch over the buffed area. The technician used a stitching wheel to seal the patch. He started from the center of the patch and worked to the ends to eliminate any air bubbles. The final repair step was to cut off the end of the plug 1/8 inch from the surface of the tire. They remounted, balanced the tire, and checked it for leaks with soap and water. The repaired tire was reinstalled on the car.

I was fortunate that this puncture happened near my home. I am going to install a portable jack from a C4, tire wrench, portable air pump, and puncture-repair kit for this car. In the meantime, keep a close eye on your expensive tires and remember, these tires are rated for speeds over 149 mph. To ensure your safety, please follow the repair procedures of the original tire manufacturer. We hope you never hear a hissing sound!

Final Thoughts

You have many options if you want to change the wheels and tires on your C5 Corvette. Wheels are a very personal choice, and many aftermarket companies produce them for your car. My personal preference is sticking with original-equipment-

The new wheels and tires give this 2000 FRC a very modern and aggressive look.

This can be your worst nightmare—a flat tire!

This tire picked up a large screw on the outer edges of the tire. This made it un-repairable.

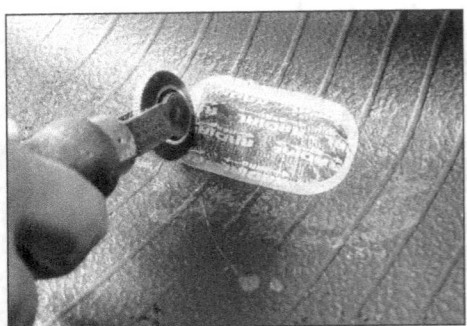

Even though this tire was un-repairable, we used the damaged tire to demonstrate how patches are secured during a repair.

style wheels and tires. It makes the car retain a factory appearance while giving it a unique look. In this chapter, I discussed different options that you can explore, and my Factory Reproduction and Goodyear approach is only one of many you have to choose from.

So, my advice is to keep looking at cars with different wheels and tires, determine the look you like, talk with the owner, and be prepared to spend some money to give your C5 your own unique look. The aftermarket offers a wide variety of wheel styles and sizes. It all boils down to personal preference. I always recommend that if you find wheels you are interested in, talk to the owner. Find out if they encountered any fitment issues when they installed their aftermarket wheels. Some aftermarket tuners like Mallett Cars, Lingenfelter, and MTI Racing offer C5 rear-wheel tub kits that allow you to install larger wheels. These kits are expensive, but if you want large wheels to fit inside your fenders, this is probably your only option. Tire choices are also very personal. Many different brands of high-performance tires are available for your Corvette. Goodyear, Pirelli, Bridgestone, Michelin, Kumo, Toyo, BF Goodrich, etc. are some of the many tire manufacturers making Corvette tires. High-performance Corvette tires are extremely expensive, and their wear characteristics vary. Before you shop for new tires, review your driving habits before selecting the tire that fits your driving style.

Some of these tires have impressive handling when new, but because of their soft rubber they wear out completely in less than 15,000 miles. Other tires might not handle as well, but their harder compound rubber extends their tread life up to 30,000 miles (depending on your driving style). So spend time deciding on your driving requirements when purchasing your new tires. After all, making the right tire choice enables you to maximize your Corvette's performance capabilities.

Many aftermarket wheels and tires are on the market for Corvette. This 18-inch Michelin tire is mounted on a very popular aftermarket rim.

Cruising with a good set of tires brings a driver peace of mind on a long trip.

CHAPTER 5

BRAKES

Shortly after the birth of Corvette in 1953, a Russian immigrant named Zora Arkus-Duntov joined Corvette. Zora was exactly what Corvette needed—he was very European, a trained engineer, and passionate about sports cars. He was quickly promoted to Chief Engineer and set to work on transforming the 1953 Motorama Corvette show car into a legitimate sports car. He had his work cut out for him. The first Corvette was a boulevard cruiser, not a sports car. It came equipped with a 6-cylinder engine, removable windows, and an automatic transmission.

The first thing Zora and his team worked on improving was the Corvette's drivetrain. In 1955, a 190-hp, 265-cubic-inch, small-block V-8 was offered. The improved power immediately showed another weakness in the car—brakes. The drum brakes were inadequate for the car's performance. The top sports cars of the day came from Europe, and many, like Jaguar, were fitted with Girling disc brakes. Zora knew disc brakes were the answer to Corvette's braking problems. However, the low Corvette sales volume prevented the bean counters from approving this much-needed braking solution. Undaunted, Zora and his engineers

Zora Duntov quickly started transforming the original six-cylinder, automatic-transmission 1953 Corvette into a respectable sports car.

kept modifying Corvette's drum-brake system to reduce fade. They added vents, fans, and different brake linings in hopes of making the brakes more fade resistant. Corvette race drivers learned to drive their racers quickly without the use of brakes. Instead of braking into corners, drivers used their engine's torque to slow the car down. It worked, but the cars lost a lot of time to their competitors in the corners. Only the superior power of the small-block engine kept Corvette ahead of the competition.

In 1963, a new competitor was introduced that quickly ended Corvette's dominance in production racing. The competitor was named Cobra. This British/American hybrid was the brainstorm of Carroll Shelby, who was also an ex-racer and the 1959 winner of Le Mans. The Cobra was 1,000 lbs lighter than the Corvette and was equipped with disc brakes. It was no contest; the Cobras

HIGH-PERFORMANCE C5 CORVETTE BUILDER'S GUIDE

CHAPTER 5

Duntov's answer to the Cobra was this 2,000-lb, 500-horsepower Grand Sport. Only five of these wonder cars were built, and in today's collectors market they are priceless.

left Corvettes in the dust. Zora knew he had to reduce Corvette's weight, increase its power, and add disc brakes. His answer was to build a lightweight Corvette called the Grand Sport.

At 2,000 lbs, with a 500-hp engine and disc brakes, Zora knew this car was a Cobra beater. However, the corporate minions decided racing was not good for GM's family image and placed a ban on all types of racing in the summer of 1963. GM ordered the Grand Sports and all of their development hardware crushed. Zora was devastated and enraged at this executive decision. He almost lost his job when, instead of crushing the Grand Sports, he sold three cars to oil magnate John Mecum. The sale was made under the condition that Mecum stay mum about the purchase. Mecum's crew arrived at the research and development center in the middle of the night. They loaded the three Grand Sports on a closed trailer and took them to Texas. In November, three Grand Sports appeared on the docks in the Bahamas along with "vacationing" Corvette engineers.

Shelby was enraged when the Grand Sports trounced the Cobras in the prestigious Governors Trophy races. Shelby was not the only one upset. GM managers called Zora into their office, and, to this day, it is a mystery why he did not lose his job. However, the point was made to Corvette fans—they knew their favorite car could be a winner against Cobra if the executives left Zora alone.

Undaunted, Zora continued working on making the production Corvette competitive. In 1965, the car was finally equipped with 4-piston disc brakes and a 425-hp, 396-cubic-inch big-block. Zora's next trick was introducing the L-88 engine and many "off-road" options for the L-88 package. Finally, Corvette began to routinely beat Cobras on the racetracks.

In 1984, Corvette replaced the beefy 4-piston disc-brake system on the new C4 with a 1-piston lightweight brake system. While the new Corvette was lighter than its predecessor, racers quickly complained about the new car's inadequate brakes. It took Corvette four years to give their buyers a fix; this was because the solution was part of the secret ZR-1 development program. Prototype ZR-1 brakes were given to showroom stock Corvette race teams in 1986. After two years of extensive racing, Corvette engineers felt these brakes were ready for production.

Roger Penske acquired the very first L-88 powered Corvette coupe in late 1965. The L-88 did not become available to the public until 1967. This prototype is awaiting the start of the 1966 12 Hours of Sebring, where it went on to win its class.

BRAKES

Corvettes won every SCCA showroom stock race from 1985 to 1987. Because of their dominance, they were banned and made to run in their own Corvette Challenge series. GM built all of the 1988 and 1989 Challenge cars; the series ended in 1989.

Hawk makes a wide variety of aftermarket brake pads that fit stock C5 brake calipers. Their horsepower Plus pads provide very aggressive stopping power, but are noisy and dusty and not recommended for street applications.

In 1988, the ZR-1 brakes were included in the Z51 option on the standard Corvette. The new option included 2-piston front calipers and 13-inch front rotors. The option was popular, and these calipers became standard equipment in 1989 and remained until 1996. The only difference was that some C4s were equipped with 12-inch rotors, while others had the 13-inch rotors.

C5 Brakes

When the C5 was introduced in 1997, it retained the same basic, 2-piston front and 1-piston rear-brake design used on the C4. Here are the C5 brake specifications:

C5 brake specifications

Type: Power-assisted disc with anti-lock brake system (ABS), front and rear
Front: 12.6 x 1.26 in (325 x 32 mm)
Rear: 11.8 x 1.0-in (305 x 6 mm)
Swept Area: Front: 263 in^2 (1,696 cm^2) ; Rear: 158 in^2 (1,018 cm^2)

The front calipers were strengthened with vertical ribs. The car's lighter weight and improved brakes were a hit with racers. The only weaknesses they discovered were premature warping and cracked rotors under racing conditions. Owners began experiencing the same problem on the streets. Corvette strengthened the rotors, and the brake problems were solved for street driving. However, for those owners who use their car for track events, the stock brakes are still not strong enough for high-speed use. If your budget is limited, don't despair; a low-cost upgrade is available. You can replace your stock brake pads with more aggressive aftermarket pads. I have had good success with Hawk brake pads, but other aftermarket vendors also offer top-quality replacement pads for Corvettes.

I also recommend replacing your rotors with slotted and cryogenically treated units. One vendor

Lou Gigliotti (in his boxcar) tortures the stock C5 brakes on his way to winning the 1999 SpeedVision GT race at Laguna Seca, California.

HIGH-PERFORMANCE C5 CORVETTE BUILDER'S GUIDE

CHAPTER 5

Cryo-treated rotors are more durable than factory rotors, and are not affected by rapid heating and cooling cycles encountered on a racetrack. They also work very well in street applications.

that I am familiar with, VBP Inc., offers these rotors, which are treated by heating and cooling them multiple times. This process bonds the metal molecules together, which creates a much stronger rotor. This rotor can be heated under extreme braking conditions many times without warping. Many racers use these rotors and have reported very few failures and extended brake life. I put 20,000 miles of hard use on a set of these brakes and never experienced one problem.

Selecting and Installing New Brake Pads and Rotors

If your brake pedal is pulsing during a stop or you hear a squealing noise coming from your brakes, it's time to fix them. If you want to save some money, you can change your front and rear brake pads and rotors by yourself on a weekend. When you inspect your rotors and they are damaged, don't turn them— replace them. Turning your rotor takes metal off the surface, which allows them to heat and warp faster. New rotors are a good investment, and this change-out procedure works for both stock and aftermarket brakes.

Jacking the C5

Unlike previous Corvettes, the C5 was sold to the public without a jack. This was due to run-flat tires being installed at the factory. The quarter panels on C5s curve under the door, and the fiberglass covers the metal frame rails. Most C5 do-it-yourselfers raise their car with a hydraulic service or "floor" jack. I recommend placing aftermarket frame pads under your car before jacking it up. These frame pads can come as four individual parts, or you can purchase one long metal strip that is secured by five bolts to the frame of your car. This is the type I use on my car. The metal strip allows you to jack your car up in any location between the front and back of the strip. They are available from MTI Racing in Marietta, Georgia.

If you do not have access to a vertical car lift and must use floor jacks, here are some pointers. Do not use a floor jack to support the car while working underneath it. Hydraulic jacks can fail. If that happens while you are under the car, you may not live to enjoy your C5. Use the floor jack only to lift the car. Use jack stands to support it. The floor on which you are going to work must be reasonably level. If you want both ends off the ground, start with the front. If you do the rear first, you won't be able get the jack under the front.

The lower control arms mount to a pair of robust aluminum castings called suspension crossmembers or cradles. There are two—one in the front and one in the back. They are both secured to the frame by four bolts each and are the easiest jacking points when a floor jack is used. Each is a rectangle formed by two longitudinal rails and two cross-car rails. Do not, under any circumstances, use the front or rear leaf springs as jack points. To jack the front, drive the front wheels up on wood blocks that are at least 12 inches long, 3.5 inches wide, and 1.5 inches thick. Some floor jacks have a tall frame, and thicker blocks may be necessary. Because of C5's longer wheelbase, you can lift the front by just rolling the jack under the nose. Jack the

Tight racing like this is very hard on brakes during sports-car races.

56 HIGH-PERFORMANCE C5 CORVETTE BUILDER'S GUIDE

BRAKES

MTI Racing offers a permanent frame protection lifting solution with these aluminum frame pads.

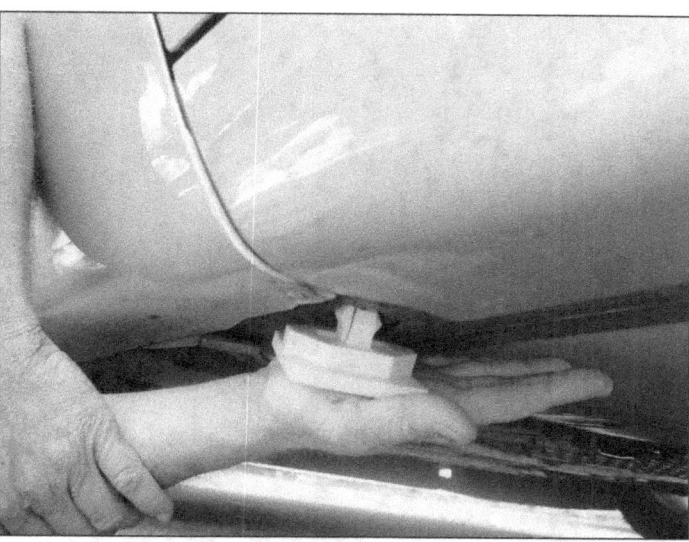

These frame pads come in a set of four and can be ordered through Corvette supply catalogs. They are easily removable and kept in the car when they are not needed.

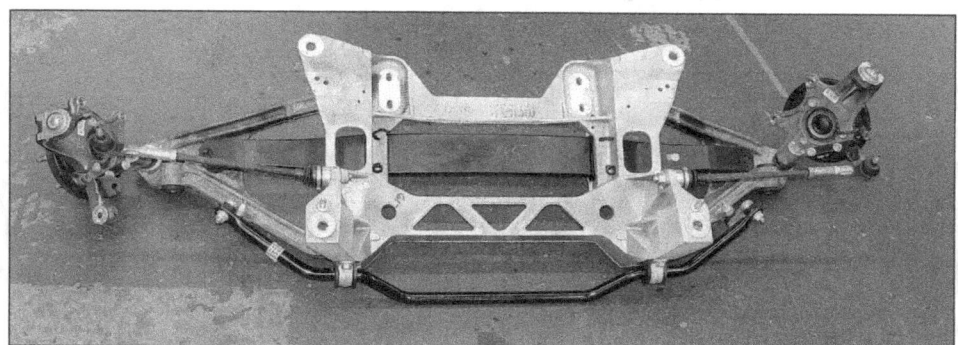

Corvettes have front and rear aluminum cradles. This rear cradle holds the composite spring, lower control arms, suspension uprights, and rear sway bar. Missing in this photo is the differential, which also bolts to this cradle. The cradle is secured to the frame with four bolts.

front with the front suspension crossmember. Each rail has two reinforcing ribs. To lift the car without damaging the crossmember, the jack's lifting pad must span those ribs. Most floor jacks are sized such that, coming in from the nose of the car, the front ribs are an easy reach. If you choose the rear pair of ribs, know that the LS1's expensive, cast-aluminum oil pan is very near and, in the darkness under the car, may be mistaken for the crossmember. Take care that you do not lift on the oil pan. In the back, jack the rear suspension by spanning its two reinforcing ribs with the jack pad.

Once you have either end of your C5 up on a floor jack, place your jack stands. The bottom of each hydro-formed, perimeter frame rail, near where it turns inboard to clear each wheel, contains a welded-in (1997 and early 1998) or riveted-on

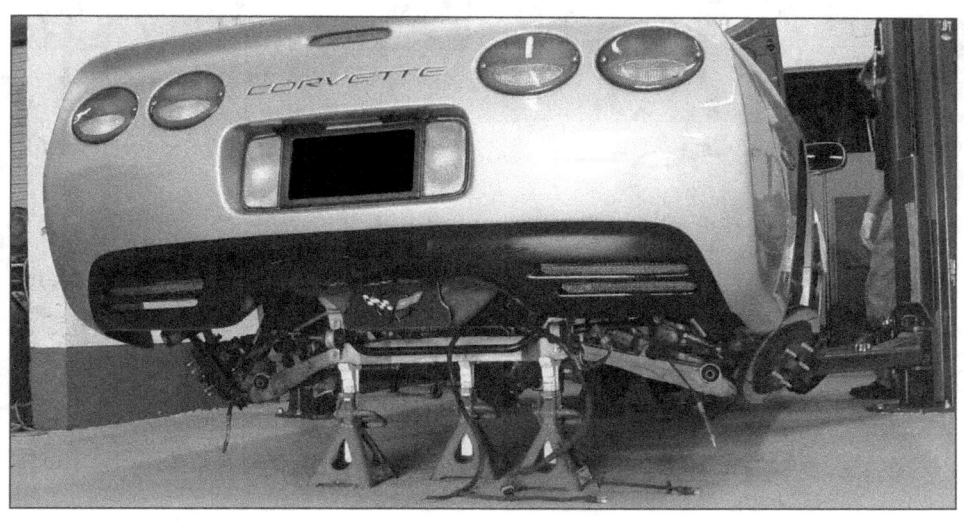

This photo shows the proper way to support the rear of a Corvette on its rear cradle, using safety stands.

If your brake fluid is dark and dirty, it is a good idea to remove it and bleed the system until all of the fluid is clear.

Technician Richard Loucks uses a turkey baster to remove some fluid from the master cylinder before changing brake pads.

After the car is securely in the air, Richard removes the wheels.

To change brake pads, the top 15-mm pin bolt must be removed and the bottom bolt should be loosened.

(later 1998s) circle of steel with a slot in it. These "shipping slot reinforcements" are used to hook the car onto the truck that brings it from Bowling Green. Stands should be placed such that those reinforcements rest on each stand's support pad. Do not allow the surrounding rocker panel material to get stuck between the jack stand and the frame. We think the above is the best way to put a C5 on stands; however, alternatives are listed in the service manual.

Once the car is jacked up, and safety stands are in place, open the hood and remove the master-cylinder brake reservoir cap. Check the condition of your brake fluid. If the color is dark brown or black, it is vital you flush the system and fill it with fresh fluid. See the bleeding procedure below to accomplish this task. If your brake fluid is clear or light colored, take a food baster, remove about an inch from the reservoir, and empty the fluid into a sealable container.

Once the caliper is swung back and the pistons have been returned into their sleeves, the new pads can be installed.

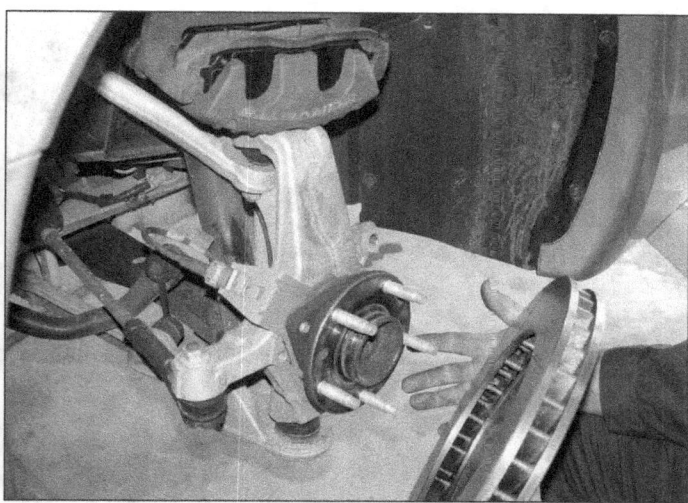
If you are changing rotors, the caliper must be completely removed, as shown, before the rotor can be changed.

Leave the cap off for now and don't spill any brake fluid onto your paint—it is very caustic and damages your paint. Be sure to cover your fenders completely when performing this task. If you have stock wheels, remove the plastic vanity caps that cover the lug nuts. Next, use a 19-mm wrench to remove the four standard lugs and the anti-theft socket to remove the locking lug nut. Remove the wheel from the car.

Two methods are available for moving the two brake pistons back into the caliper. This is necessary in order to install new brake pads. As your pad material wears off, the pistons move out of the caliper. New pads require you to move the pistons all the way back into the caliper. The first method you can use is to place two large screwdrivers on the pads and force the pistons back into their slots. The other method, which I prefer, is to remove the caliper from the rotor and use a large C-clamp to accomplish the same thing. This is why you remove fluid from the master-cylinder reservoir. As you push the pistons back into place, the brake fluid returns to the reservoir. The front caliper is held in place with two 15-mm pin bolts. Use a 15-mm box wrench or socket to remove the upper caliper bolt and loosen the lower bolt that holds the caliper to the suspension upright. They are located behind the brake caliper. Once the top bolt is removed and the bottom bolt is loose, wiggle the caliper back and rotate it off the rotor. If the rotor is being replaced, remove the caliper completely from the rotor and suspend it away from the rotor.

If you are changing the rotor, grab the rotor at the 3- and 9-o'clock location and gently rock it back and forth to work it off the front wheel bearing. If the rotor has never been removed before, you might encounter a locking metal washer. Pry this off to allow rotor removal. Now that the caliper is suspended, place your C-clamp on the brake pad that is resting on the two pistons. Turn the C-clamp until the pistons are flush with the caliper.

Keep checking the master cylinder to make sure brake fluid is not seeping out of the reservoir. As you remove the old pads, pay close attention to how they are secured. I like to replace one pad at a time to make sure that I get the right pad in its proper position. New brake pads usually come with anti-squeak grease. Be sure to apply this to the back of each pad before installation. After your new pads are successfully installed, mount your new rotor onto the wheel-bearing spindle and reinstall your caliper.

Reverse the removal procedure. Torque the pin bolts to 23 ft-lbs to secure. Repeat this process to the other front wheel and continue to check your brake fluid level. When you have completed both wheels and the car is back on the ground, you are ready for the next step. Fill the master cylinder and reinstall the cap, start the car, and pump the brake pedal several times until the pedal is back to normal. Slowly move the car back and forth until you are confident you have a good pedal. Now road-test the car and bed your new pads. New brake pads are shipped with a thin coating to protect

CHAPTER 5

C-clamps are used to push the brake pistons back into the caliper as shown. This method can be used with the caliper on or off the car.

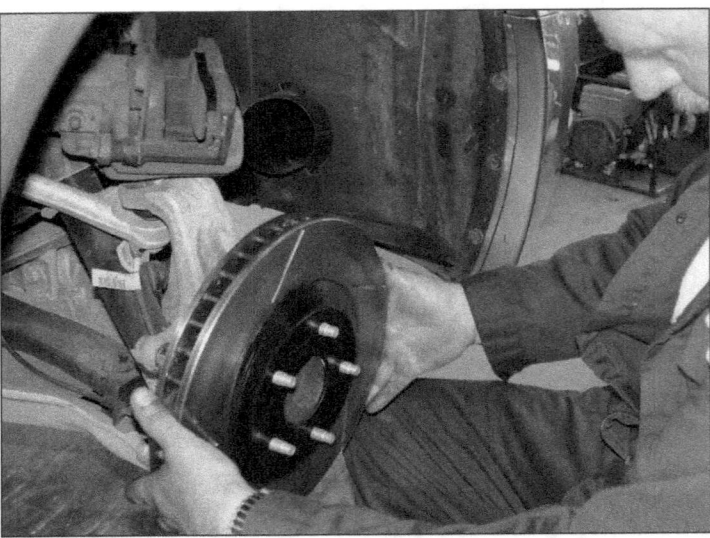

Once the new pads are in place, Richard installs a new front rotor and reverses the caliper removal process.

the pad material. Bedding burns off the coating and helps the pads adhere to the rotor. This is an often-overlooked procedure, but critical to good brake wear. On a back road with no traffic, accelerate to 60 mph and brake the car hard to 10 mph. Repeat this eight times in rapid order and then drive the car to cool the brakes. Repeat this process one more time, and your brakes should be completely bedded when you are finished.

Now let's move to the rear brakes on your C5. The rear brakes do not usually wear as quickly as the fronts due to the weight bias of the engine being located in the front of the car. However, they do wear out, and it is a good thing to inspect and repair as necessary. The parking brake assembly is located in the rear wheel hub assembly. The rear brake rotor has a built-in mini brake drum that contacts the brake pads when the handle is pulled. Before starting this project, do **not** put your parking brake on. Leave it in the off position for this project. If you engage the parking brake, you will never get the rotor off the wheel bearing. Repeat the same wheel-removal process on the rear that was used on the front. Repeat removing a small amount of brake fluid from the master-cylinder reservoir. After the rear wheel is jacked up and stabilized with a safety stand, it is time to begin. If you are only changing pads, remove the top-caliper 15-mm pin bolt and loosen the bottom 15-mm bolt. Rotate the caliper downward to replace the pads. To replace the rear brake rotors, remove the two 21-mm bolts that secure the caliper to the suspension upright.

Once you have removed these two bolts, wiggle the caliper to remove it from the rotor. Bend a coat hanger wire into a double S-hook and hang the caliper above the suspension. Use your C-clamp to push the single brake piston back into the caliper. Cover your new pads with the supplied anti-squeak compound. After removing the old pads, install your new pads. If you are changing the rotor, grab the rotor at 3 o'clock and 9 o'clock and gently rock it back and forth to work it off the rear wheel bearing.

The rear brake has one piston and a built-in brake drum on the rotor. The brake drum is for the parking brake.

Try not to disturb any of the parking brake mechanisms. If the parking brake is full of dust, you can clean it with a can of brake cleaner. Install your new brake rotor and reverse the removal process. Always check your Corvette shop manual for the correct torque specifications for your year car. When you are finished, follow the same testing and bedding procedure that I outlined for you for the front brakes.

To change pads, follow the same procedure that was used on the front brakes.

Carefully wiggle the rotor to remove it from the rear wheel bearing and parking brake assembly.

Installing Aftermarket Calipers and Rotors

As we have discussed before, the fifth-generation Corvettes left Bowling Green, Kentucky, with excellent original-equipment brakes. They were capable of stopping the car in 115 feet from 60 mph. The factory four-wheel disc-brake system was designed for Corvettes producing 300 rear-wheel horsepower (rwhp)

If you are changing rear rotors, the two 21-mm bolts that hold the caliper to the suspension must be removed.

and 336 rwhp (Z06). But, if you pack your C5 with gobs of horsepower and torque, you should seriously consider turning to the aftermarket for new brakes.

Stock factory brakes were not designed for this kind of performance. My C5 fits into this category. Its LS1 engine has been replaced with a stroked LS2 that is producing close to 500 rwhp. The car accelerates very quickly and a good set of brakes is vital to my survival. When Reese Cox, owner of MTI Racing, suggested that I install a set of aftermarket brakes on my ride, I agreed. Many companies offer high-performance brake kits such as Wilwood, Brembo, Baer, AP, Stainless Steel, etc. However, MTI Racing uses Wilwood Disc Brakes on their 630-rwhp, C5 development car, with excellent results. They also have installed these brakes on a number of their customers' track-day cars. These track-day Corvettes are driven very hard by their owners at a variety of road-course tracks in Georgia, Florida, and Alabama.

Reese recommended installing Wilwood's black, Superlite, 6-piston Big Brake Front Kit (PN140-8031). On the rear, he recommended installing the Superlite, 4-piston, Pro Series Kit for OE Parking Brake applications (PN140-8032). Both kits are shipped with Wilwood's BP-10 Smart brake pads. In addition, Reese suggested we install Wilwood's Stainless Flexline front and rear brake hose kits. The front lines carry PN 220-8176 and the rear PN 220-8177. Both brake kits bolt on to C5s without any modifications to the car. I was sold, and arranged to have the new brakes shipped to MTI Racing.

As soon as our brakes arrived, MTI began installing my new system. I downloaded a complete set of instructions from Wilwood's website: www.wilwood.com. I found the kits' part number and printed instructions for the front and rear brakes. Each set of instructions was five pages long, and they were clear, concise, and informative. This helped me document MTI's installation process. It was obvious that the MTI Technicians had done this job many times. In spite being sloweddown by waiting for photos to be shot, the job was completed in less than three

CHAPTER 5

This twin-turbo Lingenfelter Corvette is fitted with Baer six-piston front calipers and high-performance brake rotors.

Wilwood makes an excellent, six-piston, front caliper that bolts directly onto a C5. These brakes provide an owner with a fade-free, high-performance driving experience.

Track days are fun for owners, but they take their toll on cars. Having a trackside support group like MTI Racing provides owners with a worry-free day at the track.

hours. The front and rear Superlite brake kits came complete with rotors, hats, attaching hardware, calipers, and brake pads.

The optional stainless-steel brake lines that I ordered are not part of this kit, but fit perfectly. The first step in installing these brakes was to remove the factory brake calipers and rotors. They started by removing the front brake calipers. Next, an MTI technician assembled the Wilwood brake hat onto a front slotted brake rotor. Each 13-inch rotor requires (12) 1/4-20, 12-point, stainless-steel bolts to secure the hat to the rotor.

Each bolt was coated with Loctite prior to installation. Next, each bolt was torqued 85 in-lbs, to secure the hat to the rotor. Wilwood recommends safety-wiring each bolt with 0.032-inch-diameter stainless-steel wire. The Wilwood Superlite 6 front-brake caliper is equipped with one large and two small brake pistons.

This design provides even wear over the entire pad surface. Calipers are available in red or black. For this installation I chose Wilwood's aggressive E Pad, because the car was going to be tested on the Road Atlanta road course. These pads are made for high-speed track work, not everyday street use. Wilwood makes an excellent BP-10 Smart Pad designed for street driving and light track use. Rotor installation is made easy by following the arrows located on each rotor.

This is a very handy job aid. The front caliper brackets bolts were inserted into the factory caliper bolt holes. During installation, Red Loctite 271 was applied to the two 21-mm factory bolts, which were then torqued to 65 ft-lbs. Next, the new 13-inch slotted rotor was installed onto the wheel bearing. Then, MTI Racing mounted the 6-piston caliper and verified its alignment to the rotor. Shims were provided to ensure that the caliper was centered on the rotor. Once the caliper alignment was correct, the 6-piston caliper was secured with two 11-mm nuts and torqued to 47 ft-lbs. The same procedure was used to secure the rear, 4-piston, Superlite rear caliper, with some minor exceptions. When removing the rear rotor, be careful to not disturb the parking brake mechanism. This is also a good time to clean the parking brake assembly with brake cleaner. The torque specifications remain the same as for the

BRAKES

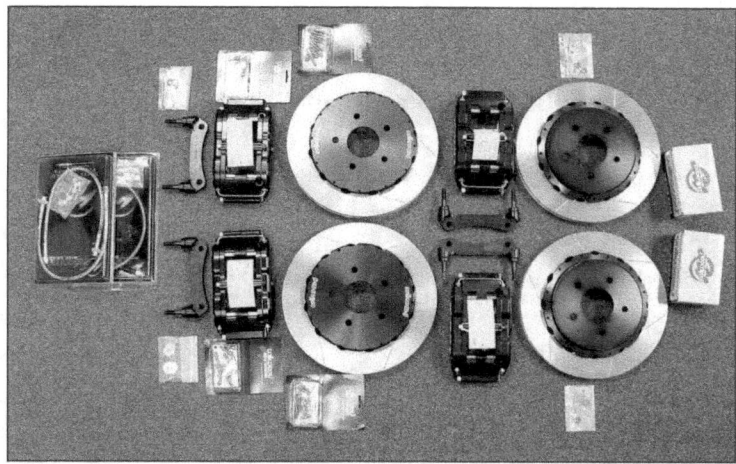

Wilwood provides all of the necessary parts in its kits, to allow competent mechanics a fast, trouble-free C5 brake installation.

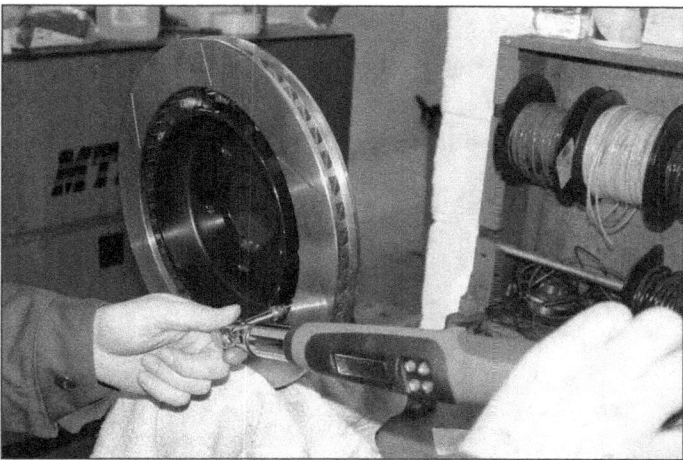

Wilwood rotors are shipped unassembled. Here, an MTI Racing technician torques the bolts on a rear rotor.

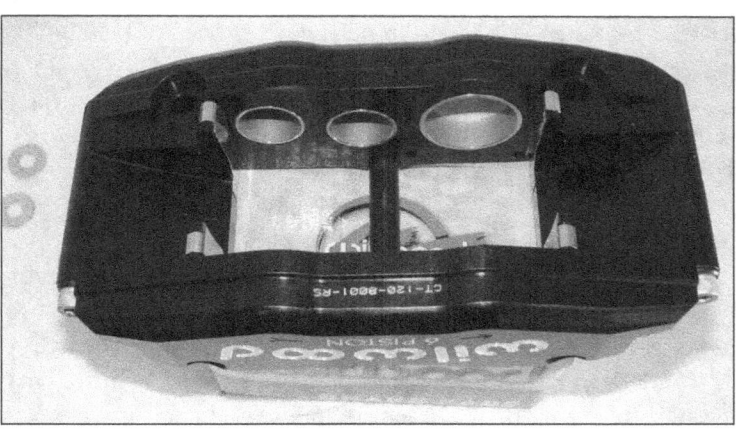

Here is another view of the Wilwood Superlite front six-piston caliper.

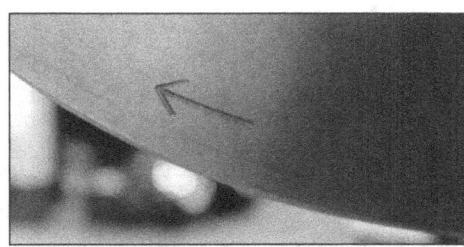

Each Wilwood rotor is marked with a direction arrow for proper installation.

front calipers. Next, MTI installed Wilwood's stainless-steel braided flexline hoses, which are highly recommended for this application.

Bleeding the Brake System

After replacing any part of the braking system, it is important to remove any accumulated air that might have entered one of the openings by using a process called "bleeding." Brake fluid in the C5 is conventional, glycol-based Delco Supreme 11 and meets the DOT3 specification. Do not use silicone-based DOT5 brake fluids. They are not compatible with the car's ABS and can pose a safety hazard. Because no change interval is specified for brake fluid, many aggressive drivers never think about that; however, for highest brake performance, brake fluid should be changed every two years. Those running their C5s hard in road-race or time-trial events may want to change brake fluid more frequently and may even test the fluid using a device such as the Mac Tools BFT900, which compares moisture content of a known-fresh sample to what is in the master cylinder. If the fluid fails the test, it should be changed. Road racers may also want to upgrade to a higher-performance brake fluid such as Motul DOT 5.1 or Wilwood 570.

Like the factory-fill fluid, these are glycol based, but their 509-Fahrenheit (F) dry boiling point and 365-F wet boil exceed those of DOT3 and even DOT4 fluids by a significant margin. Additionally, the viscosity of these fluids is half that of DOT4 fluids and a third that of DOT3 products. The lower viscosity enhances ABS operation.

The proper way to bleed a system is to have an "inside person" sit in the car and push the brake pedal when commanded. A second person, the "outside person," uses a clear plastic host attached to a small bottle. The bottle has a magnet attached that is secured to the brake rotor during the bleeding sequence. The plastic line is pushed onto the top of the small caliper bleeder valve. The outside person starts at the right rear wheel and moves to the left rear, right front, and left front to complete the process. When the outside person is ready, he tells the inside person to push the pedal and hold it. When the outside person opens the bleeder valve on the caliper, fluid and air escape as the brake pedal goes to the floor. The inside person holds the pedal on the floor until the valve is tight.

The pedal is then pumped three or four times, until the pedal is firm again. This process is repeated at each wheel until no air is seen in the clear line. The master-cylinder fluid level is checked and filled when necessary as the outside person bleeds each caliper. MTI Racing used Wilwood 570 Racing Brake fluid to refill the reservoir during the bleeding process. Fluid changes are accomplished by bleeding each brake caliper such that clean fluid gets from the master cylinder to the caliper. Comprehensive brake-bleeding instructions are found in the service manual.

Road Test

After the brakes were properly bled, I took the car out on the road and followed Wilwood's pad-bedding instructions. I made eight hard stops from 60 to 10 mph and then drove the car on the interstate to cool the brakes. The process was repeated for eight stops and cooling the brakes again on the interstate. When finished, I had a hard, responsive brake pedal, and the power of the brakes was amazing! MTI Racing installed a set of Wilwood E Pads designed for racetrack applications. In spite of their intended purpose, these pads did not make any noise and have remained relatively dust free.

The car was taken to the Road Atlanta road course located in Flowery Branch, Georgia, to test the new brakes. Reese Cox put on his helmet and started hot-lapping the 12-turn course. Reese reported that the brakes inspired a lot of confidence, as he was lapping the hilly 2.54-mile Road Atlanta course. He reported that he had a firm pedal throughout the test and experienced no brake fade.

He noted that even after slowing from 150 mph on the back straightaway for a 30-mph corner, the brakes did not fade. I did some brake tests and averaged 96 feet when braking from 60 to 0 mph! You had better be holding on when you hit the brake pedal! I like the finished look of the calipers, and they show up very well behind my chrome Z06 wheels. Each caliper has plenty of wheel clearance. So, if you are adding more grunt to your engine, I recommend adding high-performance aftermarket brakes to your C5.

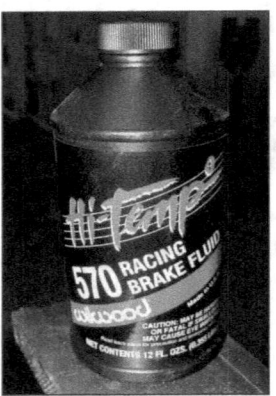

High-temperature brake fluid is a must when installing a high-performance braking system.

A magnetic brake-bleeding bottle is secured to the rotor during the brake-bleeding process.

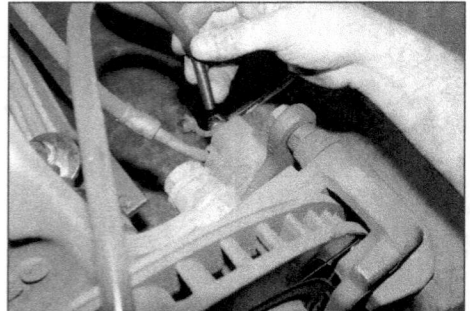

A clear hose is attached to each caliper bleeder screw so the technician can watch for air bubbles during the bleeding process.

When the driver pushes the brake pedal at 170 mph, he or she wants to be assured the car stops quickly and safely.

CHAPTER 6

DRIVELINE

Beginning in 1997, the C5 Corvette's 6-speed manual and automatic gearboxes were attached to the rear differential at the back of the car. Unlike traditional rear-wheel-drive cars that have the driveshaft behind the engine and transmission, the C5's is located between the engine and transmission. The main benefit of this configuration is so that engineers could design a near-perfect 51/49-weight distribution into the new car. Both fifth and sixth gears in the 6-speed are overdrives: 0.74:1 (fifth gear) and 0.50:1 (sixth gear), respectively.

This radical driveline design was a departure from all previous Corvette models. The new C5's transmission was located in front of the rear differential. The clutch and pressure plate remained mounted to the engine. A torque tube enclosed the driveshaft, which connected the flywheel, clutch, and pressure plate to the transmission. The driveshaft rotated on two large, fiber composite bushings attached to the front and rear of the torque tube.

The differential (1) is bolted to the rear cradle. The transmission (2) bolts to the differential and the torque tube.

The Tremec 6-speed transmission is a compact and rugged design.

HIGH-PERFORMANCE C5 CORVETTE BUILDER'S GUIDE

CHAPTER 6

The torque tube is shown attached to the transmission and differential.

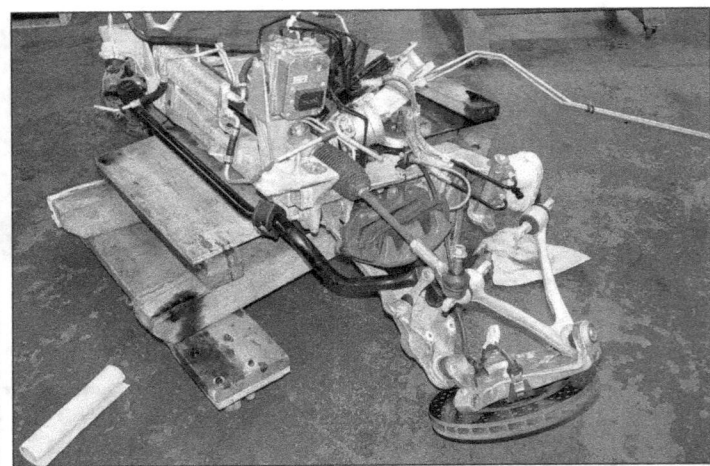

In the front of the car, the engine is bolted to this aluminum cradle. The cradle also hosts the front suspension, spring, anti-locking braking system (ABS), and a cooler.

The differential and transmission are shown bolted to the rear frame cradle.

MTI Racing has just completed removing the complete drivetrain out of the bottom of this 2000 C5.

The shifter linkage runs along the tube to the transmission. While this was a radical design departure for Corvette, the rear transmission concept has been used on other exotic sports cars, like Ferrari, for years. Another reason Corvette engineering shifted to this approach was to provide more interior room in the new car. With a front engine design, engineers always try balancing the car's weight to the ideal 50/50 distribution. Moving the transmission to the rear also enabled them to move the engine behind the front axle. The rear-mounted transmission and axle housing are bolted to a large aluminum cradle. This cradle is secured to the frame by four bolts. The rear suspension, spindles, lower control arms, brakes, sway bar, and springs are also mounted to this cradle. The engine is mounted to a large aluminum cradle at the front of the car. In addition, it has the suspension spindles, lower control arms, front sway bar, brakes, and anti-lock braking-system module attached. This cradle is held in place by four bolts that attach it to the frame. Lift the car into the air and, once the cradles are supported, then remove the eight bolts and the entire driveline from the car. Most shops prefer this method if they have to perform any major mechanical repairs to a C5.

DRIVELINE

Axles

The C5 has two rear axles connected to the rear uprights via a wheel bearing. The axles are splined on the inside and fit into the rear-end housing; they are held in place by clips. Both ends of the axles feature universal joints covered by rubber boots that protect them from weather-related damage. All of the engine's torque and horsepower are transmitted through these axles to the rear wheels. Sticky tires like drag radials really take their toll on these units. I strongly recommend changing these to stronger aftermarket units if you plan to continuously drag-race your 'Vette.

Rear axles are attached to wheel bearings on the rear suspension upright and splined into the differential. Rubber boots protect the universal joints from water and dirt.

If you are planning on doing a lot of drag racing, I recommend installing stronger aftermarket axles or frequently inspecting these parts for wear.

Driveshaft

The C5 driveshaft is encased inside an aluminum torque tube. The torque tube is attached to the engine bellhousing in the front and to the transmission case in the rear. The driveshaft is held in place by bearings inside the torque tube. In 2001, a stronger driveshaft was put into all C5s to cope with the higher performance of the Z06. The driveshaft was changed from a metal matrix composite to aluminum alloy 6061, and was increased in diameter from 55 mm to 63 mm. Driveshaft couplings also were upgraded on manual-equipped models for additional strength and durability.

The driveshaft is located inside this torque tube, which is bolted to the engine and transmission.

Rear End

The C5 rear end is mounted on the rear chassis cradle, and the automatic or manual transmissions are bolted to the front of the rear-end case. C5 Corvette automatics were equipped with a standard 2.73:1 axle ratio and an optional 3.15:1 ratio. All 6-speed cars came standard with a 3.42:1 ratio.

CHAPTER 6

Final drive
Automatic 2.73:1 (Std.) / 3.15:1 (opt)
6-speed 3.42:1
Application: Std. on coupe and convertible, optional on coupe, Std. on Z06 only.

Servicing

The rear-end axle side covers have a tendency to leak differential fluid, especially the one on the driver's side. If you are buying a C5, it is important to review the car's service history to see if this problem occurred and was fixed. I strongly recommend routinely checking this part of your differential, because loss of fluid could have expensive consequences. Each time you have your car's oil changed, make sure the technician checks the level and condition of your differential fluid.

Removing and Replacing

This job requires a proper lifting device, tools, and a Corvette service manual for your year vehicle. Follow the service manual step by step if you have never done this before. Removing, servicing, and replacing the rear axle assembly in a C5 require removing major mechanical components in the car. This job is much easier with two people. So here we go: start by removing the wheels, the exhaust system, and the rear brake calipers. You can leave the brakes attached to the suspension upright or remove the calipers from the rotors. If you take the calipers off the rotors, support them with a bent piece of wire connected to the frame.

Next, the upper control arm bolts on the rear suspension need to be removed from the frame (See top photo page 70). The shocks also need to be unbolted on the bottom of the lower control arm. The rear suspension cradle and the rear of the torque tube need to be supported with adjustable safety stands.

The four rear cradle bolts and all associated wiring need to be released. The rear of the torque tube needs to be unbolted from the transmission. Once everything is properly released, the rear cradle needs to be lowered via the safety stands. Once the cradle clears the four bolts, the entire unit is slid back away from the torque tube. Next, the transmission needs to be removed from the rear end.

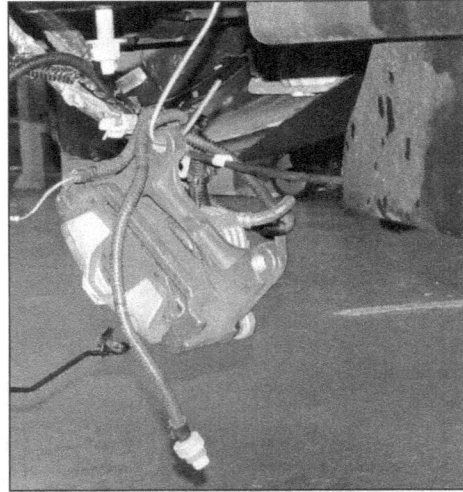
This rear brake caliper has been removed and secured with a bent piece of wire.

The side differential covers have a tendency to leak. The arrow indicates the area where the cover is attached to the differential case. The lower portion of this cover has been leaking, as evidenced by the dark stains.

MTI Racing technicians David Munder and Jesus Garcia remove this C5 differential from the rear frame cradle.

DRIVELINE

The differential, transmission, and torque tube have been removed as one unit from the rear frame cradle.

The rear end can now be serviced on the cradle or completely removed and serviced on a workbench. Just reverse the removal procedure to reinstall either unit. Again, this job is much easier if you have access to a vertical lift. It can be done on the ground with safety stands, but the preferred method is using a lift.

Transmissions

Three transmissions were offered for C5s from 1997 to 2004: the M-30 automatic (option code MNO), the MNO (6-speed), and the M-12 (Z06 only). The automatic is a 4-speed overdrive unit that came standard with the GU2 rear axle (2.73:1). This transmission was also available with the G92 performance axle (3.15:1). All 6-speed cars were equipped with the GU6 axle (3.42:1), including the Z06.

M-30 Automatic Transmission (4L60-E)

This transmission was introduced to the C5 in 1997. It continued to be the only automatic transmission available in the C5 to the end of production in 2004. It came standard with a 2.73:1 final drive ratio, and the 3.15:1 performance axle was optional. In later C5s, a lighter automatic transmission case was installed. By optimizing the design of the automatic transmission case, Corvette engineers were able to trim some material and reduce thickness in some areas. This resulted in a weight reduction of 3.3 lbs without sacrificing reliability. This transmission is modified by a number of aftermarket tuners for drag racing.

M-12 6-speed Manual

This transmission is unique to the Z06 and was introduced in 2001. It is the only transmission available for the Z06. It has more aggressive gearing (see the above chart) to increase torque multiplication in most forward gears, allowing for more rapid acceleration and more usable torque at higher speeds. A transmission temperature

Gear Ratios			
	4-Spd auto	6-Spd	M-12 6-Spd
1st Gear	3.06:1	2.66:1	2.97:1
2nd Gear	1.63:1	1.78:1	2.07:1
3rd Gear	1.00:1	1.30:1	1.43:1
4th Gear	0.70:1	1.00:1	1.00:1
5th Gear	–	0.74:1	0.84:1
6th Gear	–	0.50:1	0.56:1
Reverse	2.29:1	2.90:1	3.28:1

The M-30 4-speed automatic transmission has proven to be a reliable design. When these units are modified, they are excellent for drag racing.

sensor was added to protect the M-12 from higher thermal stresses. The sensor warns the driver via the Driver Information Center with a "TRANS OVER TEMP" light if thermal loads become excessive, meaning that the transmission could be damaged if not allowed to cool down.

Synchronizers

Carbon blocker rings have been installed on all manual-transmission forward gears to provide for smoother shifts and additional robustness.

Servicing

The transmission fluid levels should be checked at every oil change. Oil changes are also a good time to inspect your transmission for any leaks that could damage your car or transmission. Consult your owner's manual to determine the manufacturer's recommended fluid changing schedule.

Removing and Replacing a Six-Speed or Automatic Transmission

This job requires a proper lifting device, tools, and a Corvette service manual for your year vehicle. Follow the service manual step by step if you have never done this before. Removing, servicing, and replacing the 6-speed or automatic transmission in a C5 require removing major mechanical components in the car. This job is much easier with two people. Start by removing the wheels and the exhaust system. Next, the upper control arm bolts on the rear suspension need to be removed from the frame. The shocks also need to be unbolted on the bottom.

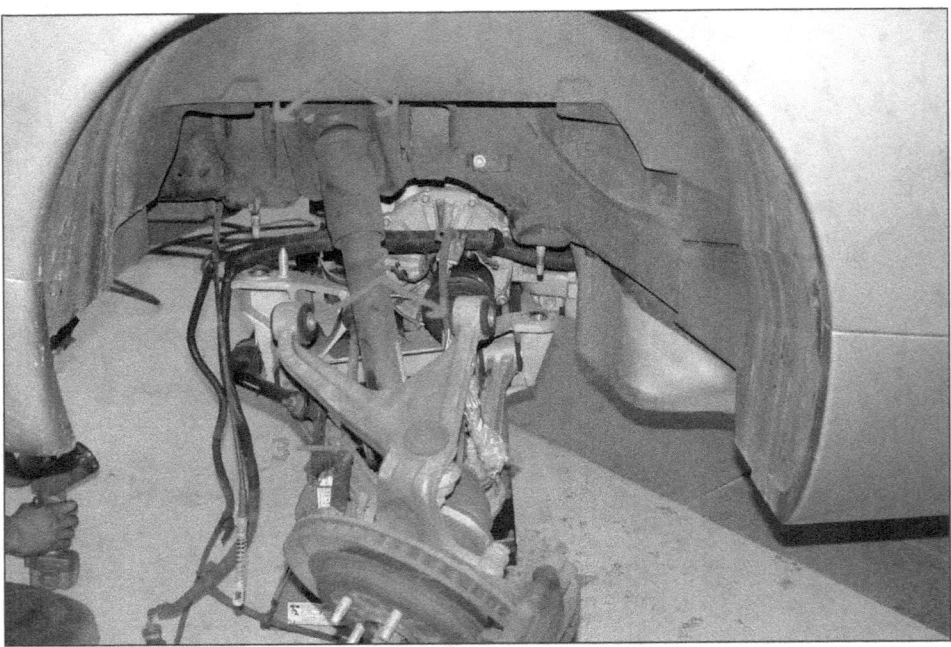

To remove the differential and transmission, you must remove two bolts (1) from the upper control arms (2) and the lower shock bolt (3). Notice where the two frame studs are located that secure the cradle to the frame.

The rear suspension cradle and the rear of the torque tube need supporting with adjustable safety stands. The four rear-cradle bolts and all associated wiring must be released. The rear of the torque tube needs to be unbolted from the transmission. Once everything is properly released, the rear cradle needs to be lowered via the safety stands. Once the cradle clears the four bolts, the entire unit is slid back away from the torque tube. Once this part of the driveline is clear, it can be lowered and moved out for servicing. Just reverse the removal procedure to reinstall either unit. Again, this job is much easier if you have access to a vertical lift. It can be done on the ground with safety stands, but the preferred method is using a lift.

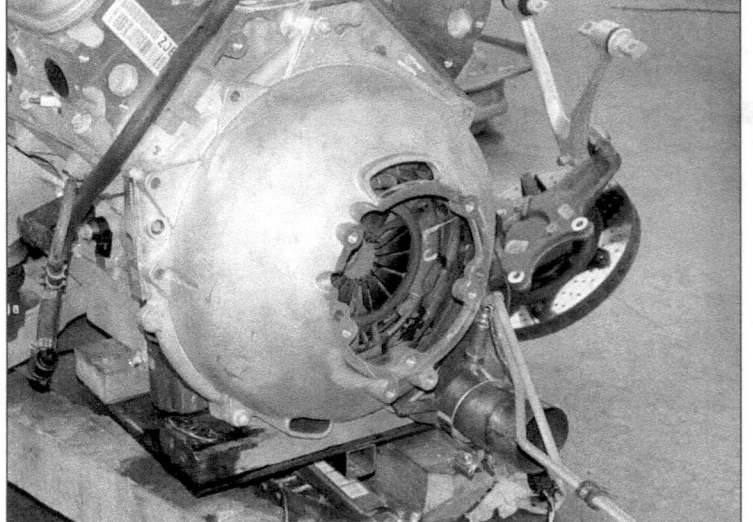

The torque tube is attached to the bell-housing behind the engine. The clutch and pressure plate are located inside the bell-housing.

Clutch and Pressure Plate

All Corvettes with the 6-speed manual transmission (optional on coupes and convertibles, standard on Z06), feature a revised clutch with greater clamping power to accommodate increased engine torque. This new clutch design also provides for lower pedal effort, making manual-equipped Corvettes easier to drive. The pressure plate and clutch mechanism are operated with the clutch pedal that is assisted by a hydraulic piston to lighten the pedal pressure. The pressure plate is multi fingered and the pressure plate, flywheel, and clutch weigh about 60 lbs.

Lightweight flywheels, pressure plates, and clutches are available from the aftermarket. These units usually weigh 24 to 28 lbs. Because this unit is bolted directly onto the engine crankshaft, reducing this weight really improves engine performance. However, the lighter clutches and flywheels make it more difficult to drive a 6-speed car. Less flywheel mass means the car stalls more easily unless you keep the RPM at higher levels under starting conditions.

Servicing

The clutch really does not require any routine servicing, except making sure the clutch master cylinder is filled to its correct level. Many people think brake fluid is used in Corvette hydraulic clutch systems. In the late 1980s, as a solution to squeaky clutch master cylinders, GM developed a specific clutch fluid (PN 12345347) and it is specified for the C5.

Removing and Replacing

This job requires a proper lifting device, tools, and a Corvette service manual for your year vehicle. What I am providing in this explanation is just an overview on what is required to complete this job. Follow the service manual step by step if you have never done this before. Removing and replacing the clutch in a C5 requires removing major mechanical components in the car. This job is much easier with two people. Start by removing the wheels, rear brake calipers (if you do

This lightweight Fidanza flywheel is made of aluminum and greatly reduces the weight on the crankshaft of an LS engine.

The factory flywheel, pressure plate, and clutch weigh a total of 62 lbs. However, this heavy design provides smooth starts and good reliability.

Once the pressure plate and clutch are removed, remove the bellhousing, which allows you to inspect or replace the flywheel.

CHAPTER 6

This modified LS engine is getting a Fidanza flywheel, SPEC pressure plate, and clutch added during its rebuild.

not want to bleed the brakes), and the exhaust system. Next, the upper control arm bolts on the rear suspension need to be removed from the frame. The shocks also need to be unbolted on the top. The rear suspension cradle and the front of the torque tube need supporting with adjustable safety stands. The rear of the engine must also be supported with a safety stand to keep the engine in place when the torque tube is removed. The four rear-cradle bolts and all associated wiring need to be released. The front of the torque tube needs to be unbolted from the bellhousing. Once everything is properly released, the rear cradle needs to be lowered via the safety stands. When the cradle clears the four bolts, the entire unit is slid back away from the engine. Once this part of the driveline is clear, it is lowered and moved out of the way. Next, remove the lower bellhousing dust cover. This gives you access to the clutch assembly. The pressure plate and clutch can now be removed from the flywheel by unbolting the pressure plate. Once the pressure plate and clutch are removed, you can now inspect the flywheel. If it is warped or scarred from abuse, replace it. If it is in good condition, clean the surface and reuse it. If you want to use an aftermarket flywheel, this is the time to install one of these units.

Selecting Correct Clutch for Your Requirements

If you are just replacing the factory clutch and pressure plate, you are ready for reassembly. Just reverse the removal procedure and torque all of the bolts per the factory shop manual. Count on at least eight hours for this job. If you are going to install a lightweight aftermarket unit, first you must remove the factory flywheel. Because this is a pretty involved job, I strongly suggest you do some research on the type of clutch you are going to require. Because of their high, unsprung weight, the factory Z06 clutch unit offers you good reliability

This SPEC 2 clutch is lighter than the factory GM unit, but produces more starting torque at the flywheel.

with high performance. If you are only slightly modifying your engine, and you are going to use your car for everyday driving, I recommend installing one of these units. Their mass allows smooth starts and they very rarely chatter. This makes driving in bumper-to-bumper traffic much easier. However, if you are going to perform major engine work, like upgrading the head, cam, and block, you need to upgrade your clutch. As I have suggested before, talk with Corvette owners who have made this change or visit some Internet Corvette chat rooms before purchasing one of these clutch assemblies. Once you have your new clutch in hand, just reverse the removal procedure.

Radiator Service

Engine cooling is critical to the longevity of your LS1 or LS6 engine. A few common-sense maintenance

Dex-Cool was installed in every C5 at the Bowling Green Assembly Plant. When re-filling your radiator, use a GM-approved Dex-Cool product.

DRIVELINE

During your routine cooling checks, it is acceptable to add some distilled water to top off your system.

Several companies, like Royal Purple, make a wetting agent coolant additive to improve your engine's cooling. Check with your dealer before you add these products to make sure they are approved for your car.

checks are sure to keep you car running in tip-top condition. Coolant put into LS1s at Bowling Green is a mix of 45% tap water and 55% ACDelco, Dex-Cool, a unique ethylene-glycol antifreeze with a non-silicate, anticorrosive chemical package. Dex-Cool was jointly developed by GM and Texaco and became factory-fill in most GM cars for the 1996 model year and newer. It is available at dealerships and auto parts stores under a variety of brand names. Just be sure to look for the GM-approved logo on the label. Its non-silicate formula is longer lasting and better for durability of cooling system parts than silicate-based anticorrosive packages in old-style antifreezes. Dex-Cool has an orange-pink color and has proven to be very reliable in Corvettes. If small additions of coolant are necessary, distilled water will suffice. If a large addition of coolant is required, first find the leak. Then add a 50/50 mix of distilled water and Dex-Cool. We suggest distilled water because tap water in some areas may be more acidic or have more alkaline than in Bowling Green.

C5's coolant change interval is five years or 150,000 miles, whichever comes first. As good as Dex-Cool is, that interval seems long. Thus, I suggest changing coolant in LS engines at three years/90,000 miles. If you are changing coolant, mix Dex-Cool and distilled water at approximately a 50/50 proportion. Avoid antifreeze products other than Dex-Cool, unless antifreeze with a silicate anticorrosive package is unavoidable. However, as soon as Dex-Cool is available, drain the coolant, flush the system with water, and refill with the Dex-Cool/water mix.

A good cooling system performance upgrade is the addition of Red Line Oil's SuperCool. It consists of a chemical surfactant or "wetting agent" that improves heat transfer from engine parts to the coolant, along with a non-silicate, anticorrosive package. Adding SuperCool in the manufacturer-recommended proportion results in the coolant stabilizing at a lower temperature,

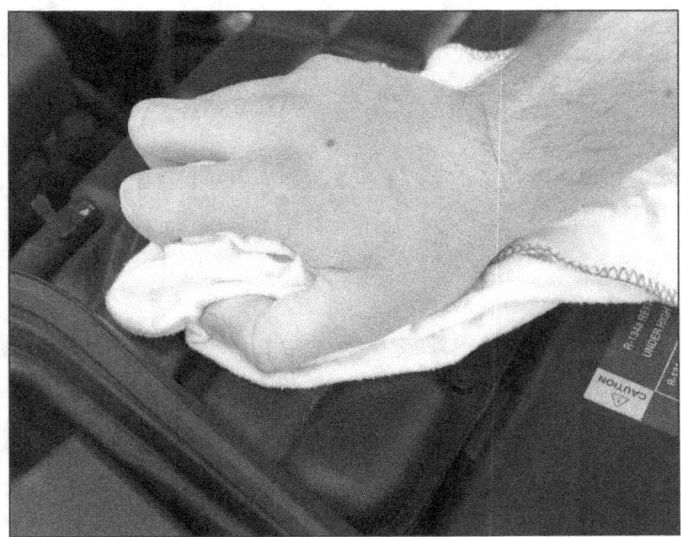

If your engine is hot and you want to check the coolant, use a large rag or towel, place it over the coolant cap, and slowly turn it one 1/4 turn. Do not remove the cap until all of the hissing has stopped. If the engine is overheated, do not remove the cap until the engine is completely cooled.

CHAPTER 6

C5 engine temperature is monitored with a gauge on the dashboard or by pressing the gauge button on the console to get a digital readout.

once the thermostat is open. Other additives are unnecessary and do not use the "sealing pellets" that were recommended in past model years. They restrict parts of the cooling system and, due to improved technology in engine parts that come in contact with coolant, are unnecessary.

Cooling system work may involve hot liquid. If the engine is at operating temperature, it's possible that coolant surge tank cap removal will cause an explosive boiling in the system. This could result in potential injury. The C5 tank cap is threaded to allow simple pressure relief. If the cooling system is hot, turn the cap 1/4 of a turn. When the hissing stops, turn the cap further until it comes off. If the engine is running hot, say, with a coolant temperature of 220 F and above, allow the engine to cool before removing the cap.

Changing coolant in an LS1 is a little more time consuming than it was with older Corvette engines, because the engine block coolant drains are not accessible when the engine is in the car. The left drain is hidden behind the engine mount bracket, and the right drain is behind the starter. Because of this, you can't fully drain the system; you only can flush it. This work may also involve working with hot engine parts or hot liquid. We suggest you use some automotive work gloves such as those sold by Mechanix Wear. We like them because they protect hands but still allow good feel.

The radiator drain is at the lower-right corner of the radiator. Open it and let it run until the flow stops, close the drain, and refill the system with water. Run the engine until the thermostat opens, shut off the engine, carefully release the pressure in the cooling system, and open the radiator drain again. Repeat this procedure until the coolant coming out of the radiator runs clear. You may need to do this tedious flushing trick several times to get the water to run clear. Once the flushing is done, close the drain and fill the system with 6.5 quarts

The radiator drain is located underneath the lower radiator hose on the right side of the radiator.

The coolant level in this tank should be kept 1/2 inch above the cold fill mark on the tank.

DRIVELINE

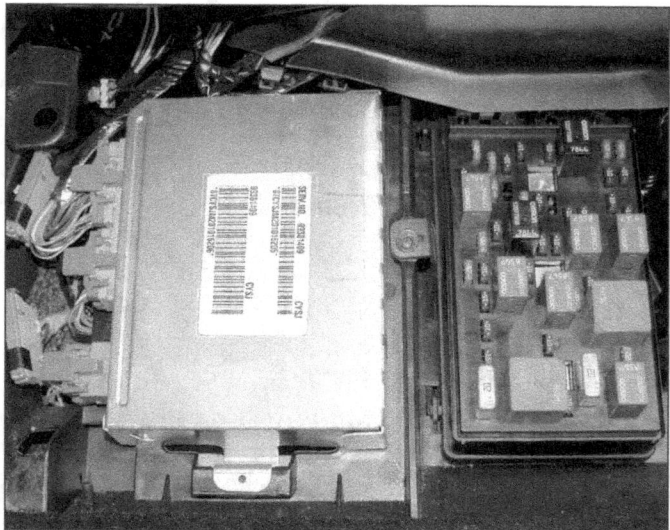

You can find additional circuit breakers by removing a panel on the right-hand side of the floor in the passenger compartment.

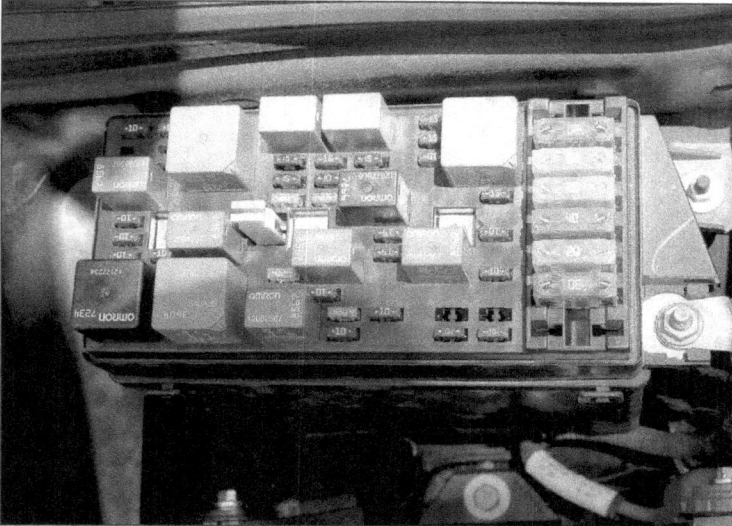

This circuit breaker box is located on the right-hand side of the engine compartment, next to the battery. A plastic screw cover has been removed for this photo.

of Dex-Cool (50%) and, optionally, a bottle of SuperCool additive (Check with your dealer before you do this). Add distilled water until it reaches the base of the surge tank neck. Start the engine and let it idle for a minute, then cycle engine speed from idle to 3,000 rpm and back, until coolant temperature reaches normal operating temperature. Remove the tank cap, observing the cautions discussed previously. The coolant level should be about 1/2 inch above the "cold full" mark on the tank. If it is not, top off with distilled water, replace the cap, start the engine, and repeat the above procedure.

Electrical

Most C5 fuses, circuit breakers, and relays are away from engine heat in a compartment behind the

Carefully inspect the battery for leakage. This has been a problem area for C5s. The Power Control Module (PCM) is located directly underneath the battery.

The ACDelco CS130D alternator is a durable and dependable unit.

HIGH-PERFORMANCE C5 CORVETTE BUILDER'S GUIDE

right front wheel next to the battery. The PCM is in yet another cavity under the battery, which is a problem with C5s. Because of engine heat, batteries sometimes leak and the battery acid damages the PCM, which sits right under the battery. When buying a C5, be sure to carefully inspect this problem-prone area. Removing the right wheel-well filler-panel exposes it. Additional fuses and circuit breakers, mainly interior and instrument panel cluster (IPC) items, are located under an easily removable panel at the front of the passenger-side foot well under the carpet.

The alternator on a C5 is the dependable ACDelco CS130D series unit. CS130Ds are quite durable, but should you ever have to replace one, the job is easy. The alternator is driven by the customary serpentine belt system, but the LS1 uses two belts—one for the HVAC (Heating, Ventilation, Air-Conditioning System) compressor and the other for the alternator and accessories. The air filter element is contained in an easy-to-open housing in front of the radiator. The factory element is an ACDelco A917C. It should be inspected every 10,000 miles and replaced, if necessary. A common performance upgrade is the oil-impregnated, gauze filter (PN 33-2111) from K&N Engineering. While the initial expense of the K&N may be higher, eventually it becomes a better value because all K&Ns are reusable. Inspect it every 10,000 miles. If it is at all dirty, simply remove it, clean it, re-oil it, and put it back in place.

Above: This photo shows the front of an LS engine without the radiator installed. You can see the two belts that operate the engine's accessories. Arrow #1 points to the HVAC belt and arrow #2 points to the serpentine belt. These should be checked and replaced if they show cracking.

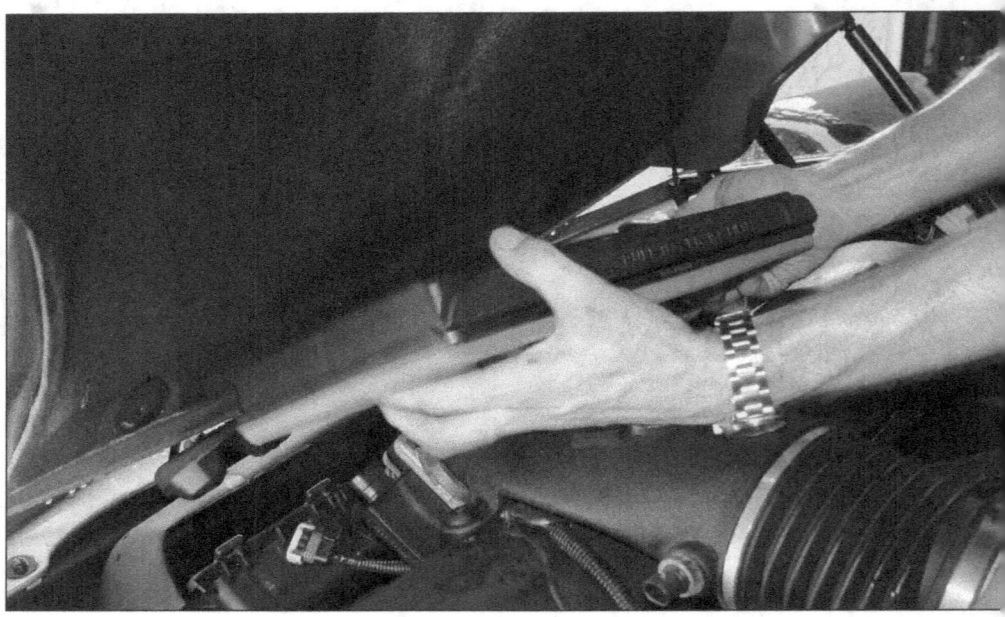

Right: If your C5 still has its factory air cleaner, check and replace your filter with an ACDelco A917C. If it has an aftermarket unit, check with the manufacturer to determine its required maintenance.

CHAPTER 7

BASIC ENGINE BOLT-ONS

Air Filters

Air filters, air filters! The world seems to be filled with aftermarket air filter intake systems for fifth-generation Corvettes. Which one really improves your car's performance? I am not here to evaluate every aftermarket Corvette air intake system offered. However, when I found one that worked while researching this book, I wanted to share the good news with you. C5s were all fitted with general-purpose, quiet, air intake systems when they left Bowling Green, Kentucky. This factory system flowed 1,120 cubic feet per minute (cfm). Corvette engineers were required to fit a system that made all Corvettes quiet enough to sell in all 50 states. The aftermarket industry quickly found out that adding more air (and noise) to LS1/LS6 engines produced a nice bump in horsepower.

I discovered that Callaway Cars offers an innovative air intake for a C5. I saw impressive horsepower gains when Callaway installed one of their Honker air intake systems on a stock C5. The C5 gained 16 hp and 10 ft-lbs of torque. The Honker directs cool air from outside the engine compartment. The air flows through a well-engineered base, filter, duct housing, and bellow assembly. The last part of this design moves the Mass Air-Flow Sensor (MAFS) close to the throttle body. This integrated design approach is what allows the Honker to achieve maximum efficiency. This system flows at 1,486 cfm, which converts to a big bump in performance. Intrigued, I wanted to see if we could reproduce Callaway's gains on my car.

I ordered a Callaway C5 Honker system for my C5. Callaway Cars sent me a Honker that fits 1997-2000 Corvettes. My system arrived in a well-packed box, with clear instructions and no missing parts. My C5 at the time of this install was equipped with an LS1 engine with an MTI Racing head-and-cam package. The engine also had long-tube headers, performance cats, and a performance aftermarket cat-back exhaust system. The engine produced 408 rwhp. The aftermarket filter system installed on this car was exposed and drew its air from inside the engine compartment. The Honker gets outside air from a hole that is cut in the radiator shroud. Thus, it should not make any difference in power if the hood is open or closed.

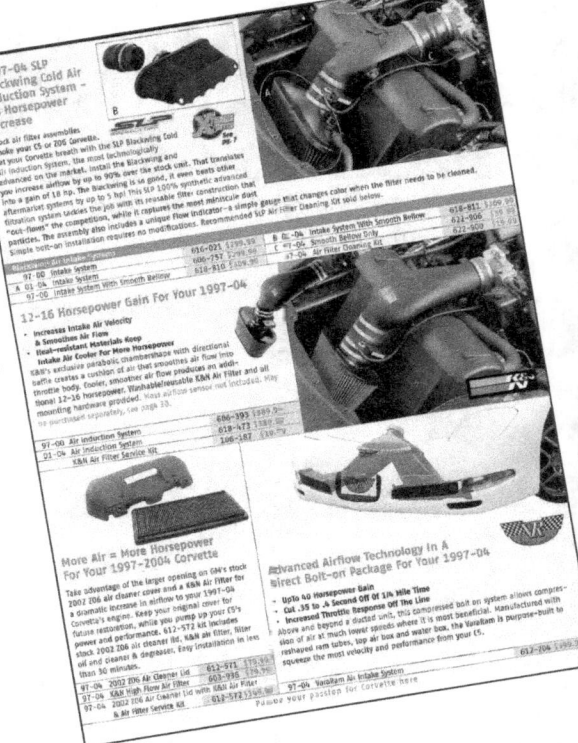

This Mid-America Motorworks catalog illustrates the horsepower claims that manufacturers make about their air intake systems. The intakes on this page promise a 16- to 40-horsepower increase if you add their product.

To prove the point, two dyno tests were performed with the old system. First, the car was tested with the hood open and again produced 408 rwhp. Next, the hood was closed

CHAPTER 7

The factory air intake system must meet requirements for noise and emissions in all 50 states.

Callaway produced a 16-horsepower and 10 ft-lbs of torque gain with this Honker air intake that was fitted on a stock LS6 engine.

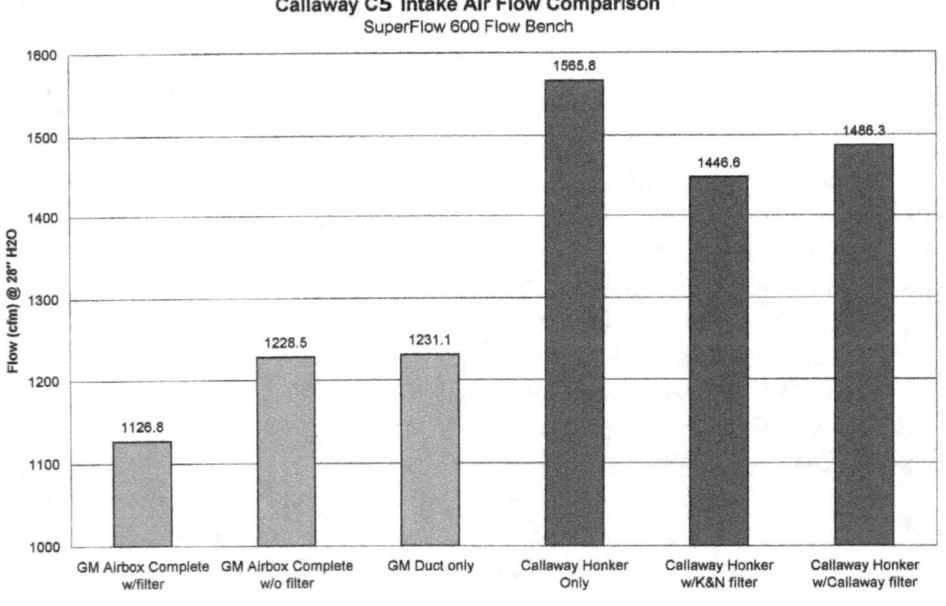

Callaway Cars Inc., in Old Lyme, Connecticut, is an engineering company that tests all products before they are released. This chart validates the airflow improvements of their Honker air intake system over the stock GM intake.

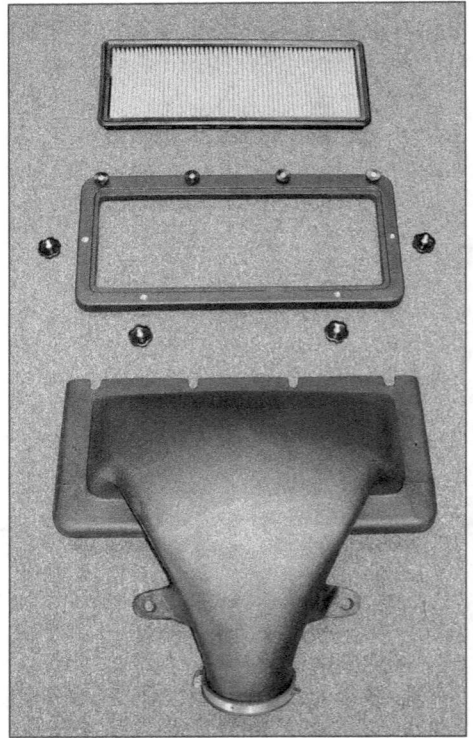

Cold air is drawn in through an opening in the radiator shroud and passes through a high-performance filter into the MAFS and throttle body

and retested. The LS1 now dropped to 399.9 hp or a loss of 8.1 hp! So far so good. With the base established, MTI Racing removed the old system and installed the Honker. Installation was straightforward and everything fit. Here are some of my installation observations. Callaway sent detailed instructions, clamps, filter, housing, and parts. The Honker includes a Callaway-designed "green" filter. The green filter is popular in

BASIC ENGINE BOLT-ONS

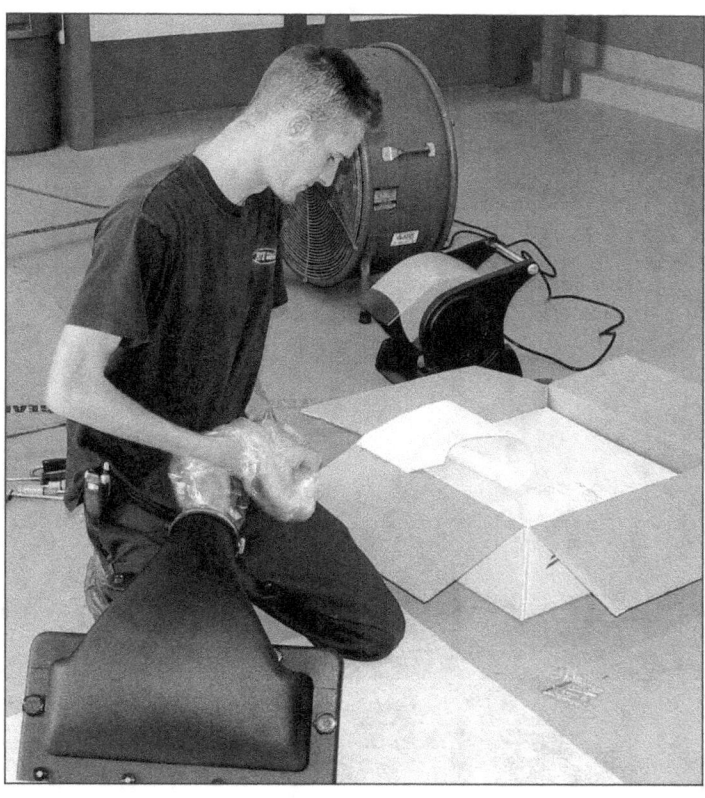

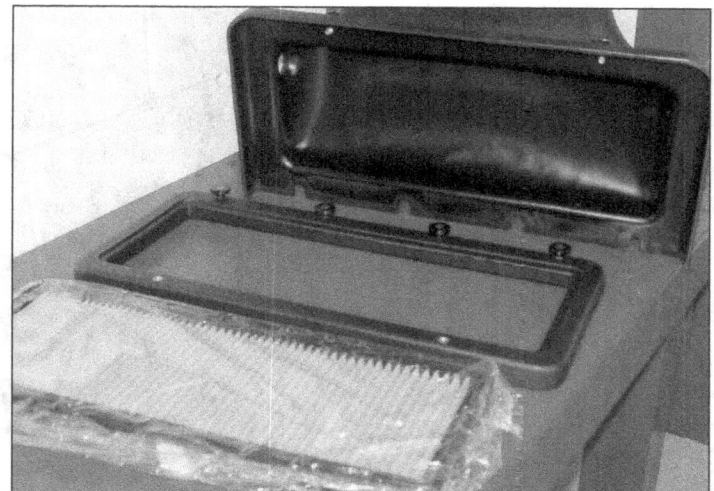

The "green filter" is a popular European performance item that is utilized in Callaway's intake system.

The Honker is delivered in a well-packaged box, with instructions and all the necessary installation hardware.

European performance cars. The filter media is combed-cotton cloth for high flow and has excellent filtration, as opposed to other filters. Additionally, stainless-steel wire is used for durability instead of aluminum. After MTI removed the old air filter, they used a #30 Torx to remove the bumper beam air cleaner bolts. A Honker test fitment was made to determine if the car needed to be modified. No changes were necessary.

During the test fit, masking tape was attached to the radiator shroud to mark the filter opening. Next, seven 7-mm shroud bolts were removed from under the car. Two metal retainers were also removed to completely loosen the shroud. Four 10-mm radiator cover bolts were removed, and the cap was taken off the car. Once the radiator cover was off, the shroud was gently pulled from the car. Care should be used during this step to avoid damaging the radiator. I noticed a lot of road debris on the evaporator and radiator, so this was a good time to clean the radiator with a Shop-Vac.

Next, the template that Callaway provided was located on the shroud. The opening was cut, and 12 template holes were drilled with the provided #4 drill bit that was part of the kit. The filter base was clamped to the topside of the shroud. The 12 template holes were used as guides to drill into the filter base. Twelve pop rivets secured the filter base to the shroud. The pre-lubricated filter element was attached to the filter base. The other part of the Honker package included the relocation of the MAFS. All C5s have their MAFS located near the filter. When the C6 was introduced in 2005, its MAFS was relocated next to its 90-mm throttle body. This relocation is another reason the Honker produces more power. The completed Honker

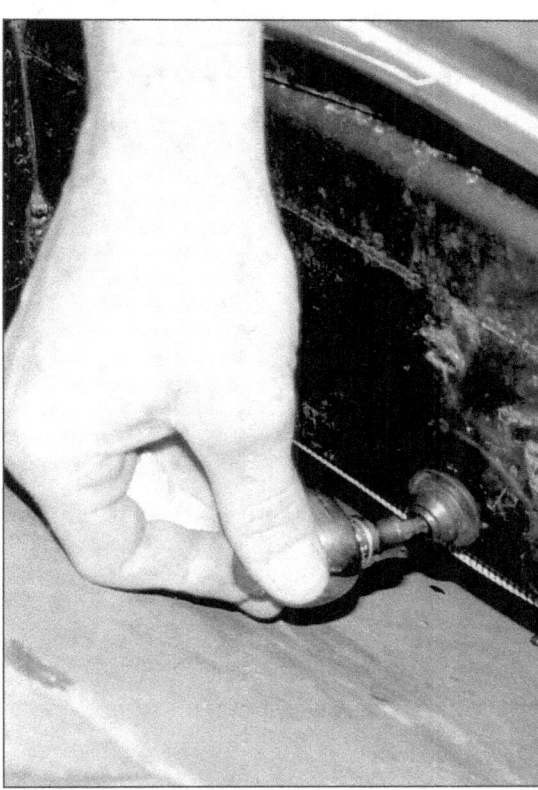

The two #30 Torx bolts must be removed prior to installation of the Honker.

CHAPTER 7

During the test fitting of the intake, tape was used to mark the location of the radiator shroud opening that must be cut.

C5s receive their air under the chin of the front fascia. It is not unusual for their radiators to get packed with road debris, as shown in this photo. When your car is on a lift, it is a good idea to check this area and clean it if necessary.

Once all of the radiator shroud bolts are removed, the shroud is carefully taken out of the car.

and MAFS was a perfect fit and looks like a factory installation.

Removing the radiator shroud was a little tricky and time consuming, but the clear Callaway instructions helped complete the job in less than two hours. The C5 started on the first try, and the LS1 settled to an even idle. Back on the dyno, the first dyno pull, with the hood closed, produced 419.4 hp and 402.1 ft-lbs of torque. Next, with the hood open, we got the same results. This was a gain of 19.5 hp and 15 ft-lbs of torque.

We cannot guarantee that your car will gain the same horsepower as mine did, but adding the Honker adds horsepower. The engine response really improved above 3,500 rpm. I learned that systems that draw air from the engine compartment do not make as much power as those that utilize outside air. So, if you are checking the efficiency of your air intake on the dyno, close the hood for real-world results. The Callaway C5 Honker air intake is 50-state legal. Since this installation, I have observed many Honkers being added to C5s with similar results. This is a great way to increase your engine's air intake.

BASIC ENGINE BOLT-ONS

This is what the installed Callaway system looks like in a C5. We saw no difference in the dyno results with the hood opened or closed.

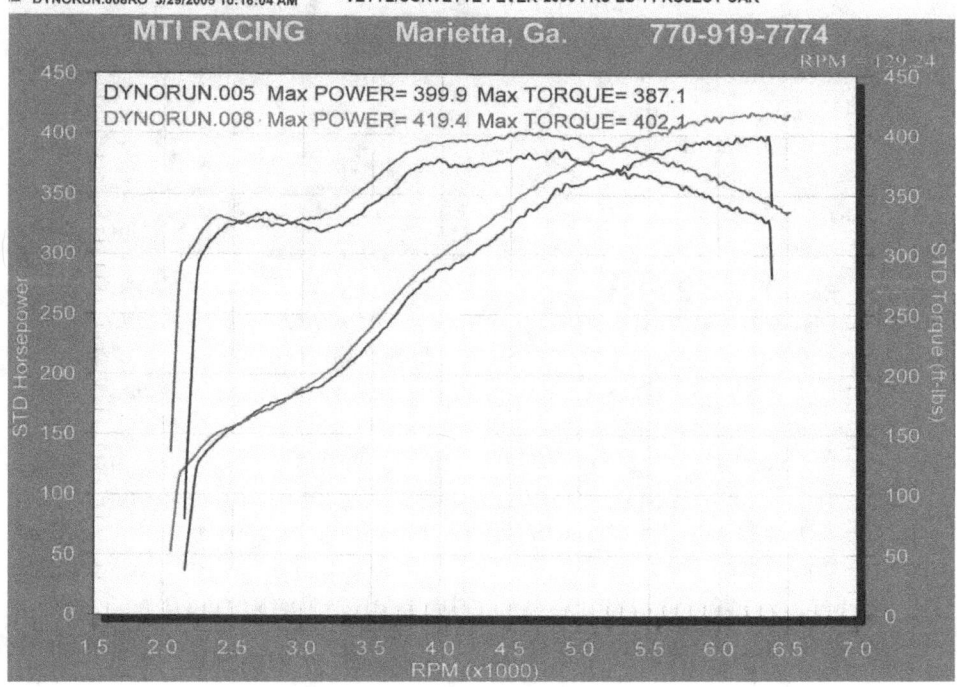

This LS1 test car produced 19.5 horsepower and 15 ft-lbs of additional torque on the dyno. The engine in this car had an MTI Racing head-and-cam package with long-tube headers prior to installation of the Honker.

Throttle Body Change-Out

My C5 had two remaining stock components left in the air intake system: the Throttle Body (TB) and the MAFS. The factory 57-mm throttle body has a butterfly mechanism that opens and closes with the help of a small motor. The motor gets its throttle position signal from the throttle actuator control (TAC). The TAC receives its signal from the gas pedal electrical actuator. A small amount of radiator water is piped into the underside of the throttle body to help cold-weather performance. Many aftermarket vendors make modified throttle body assemblies. However, since I have had good experiences with Callaway Cars, I ordered a new throttle body from them. I received their CNC-machined, 78-mm, blue-anodized 6061-aluminum BigBoreBillet Throttle Body unit. It has the name "Callaway" machined on its face. The MAFS is assembled as a sandwich of three parts held together with four Torx screws. The center section of the MAFS has small wires built into the part that senses air flow and air temperature. The two outside parts are made of aluminum. MTI makes these outside parts larger with poly, which makes the MAFS run cooler and flow more air. The replacement pieces are a direct bolt-on to the factory centerpiece.

Installation was pretty straightforward. MTI used a 10-mm extension to loosen the two bellows clamps on the air intake. Once the clamps are loose, the factory throttle body and stock mass airflow sensor are removed. Next, a radiator hose tool was used to remove the throttle actuator connector on the left side of the throttle body.

CHAPTER 7

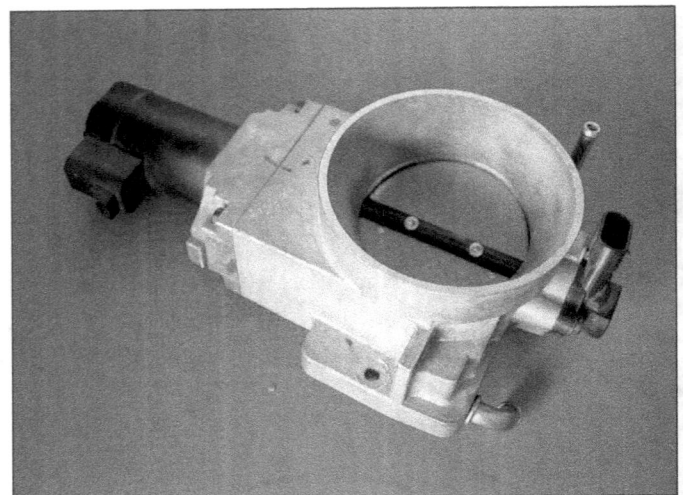

The motor on the side of the factory 57-mm throttle body gets its throttle position signal from the Throttle Actuator Control.

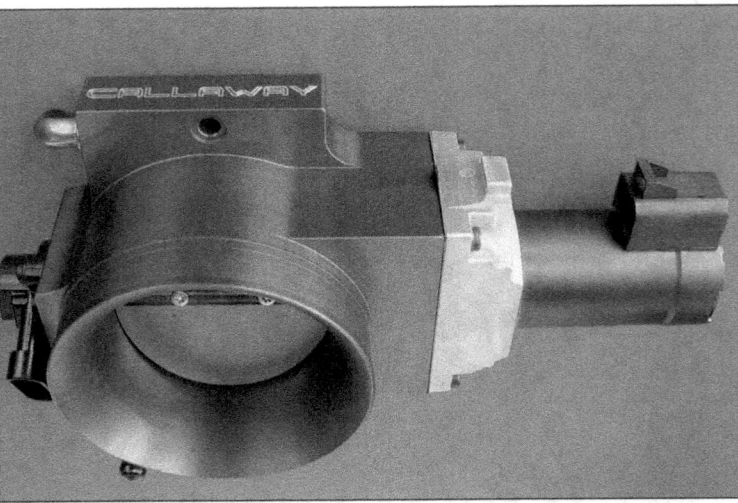

The 78-mm Callaway Big-Bore-Billet throttle body is a direct bolt-on to the factory LS1 or LS6 intake.

The positive crankcase ventilation (PVC) hose and the throttle position sensor connector on the right side of the unit were removed. The two throttle coolant hoses from under the throttle body were removed and plugged. A small loss of coolant is normal during this step. Next, the three 10-mm bolts were removed from the throttle body, and it was lifted from the car. This car lives in a warm climate, so we elected to bypass the throttle coolant lines. I do not recommend this procedure in cold climates. The removal procedure was reversed to install the new Callaway unit. Next, the car was tuned and dyno-ed, and measured a 5-hp and 8.90-ft-lbs rwhp increase in torque. Then, the lightweight, composite MAFS was modified. The air-temperature sensor and mass airflow connectors were unplugged and the unit was removed. To modify the MAFS, dismantle the factory unit by removing the four Torx screws and place the center section from the factory unit into the two MTI parts. Reassemble it with the four original screws, and you are finished.

The modified MAFS sensor was reinstalled by reversing the removal procedure. When the MAFS installation was complete, the car was tuned and dyno'ed again. We gained 4.9 hp and 6.20 ft-lbs of torque at the rear wheels. These two additions netted us a 9.90-hp and 15.10-ft-lbs of torque increase over the stock units. This bumped our output to 429.30 hp and 417.20 ft-lbs of torque, compared to 419.4 hp and 402.1 ft-lbs of torque rwhp on our base run. Not bad for bolt-on parts!

Spark Plug and Spark Plug Wires

The LS1 and LS6 engines were introduced with a new plug wire and coil system, called a coil pack, in which each cylinder has its own individual coil that is attached to a plug wire and connected to a spark plug. This system provides a hotter and more evenly distributed ignition source for each cylinder. Each cylinder head is covered with a plastic fuel rail cover. These covers dress up the engine compartment, but they do

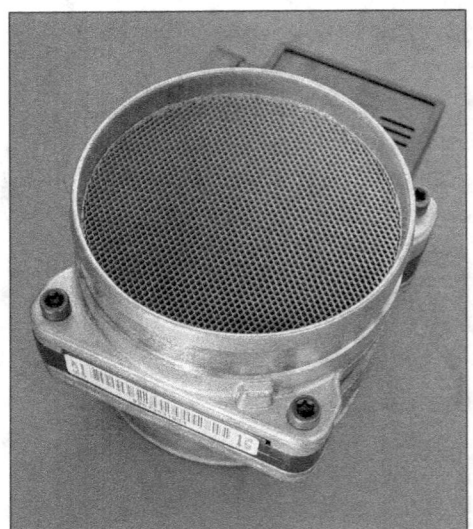

The factory MAFS is made with three pieces of aluminum. The unit also includes a debris screen to protect the small wires in the middle.

not allow heat to escape from the coil packs. I recommend removing these if you are going to run the engine really hard. The wires provided by the factory work well, but I recommend installing aftermarket wires after about 20,000 miles of use. High-quality aftermarket plug wires are thicker and are less prone to power leakage, which reduces engine power.

BASIC ENGINE BOLT-ONS

The factory throttle body is shown being removed from the stock LS6 intake.

Headers

Performance engines thrive on air—if you add lots of air on the intake side that means you need to reduce or eliminate restriction on the exhaust side. When it is mixed with fuel and burned, it moves out of the heads through the exhaust system and out of the car. Modified engines require higher volumes of air and fuel to make horsepower. Stock exhaust usually robs horsepower from the engine because of excessive backpressure. Headers are designed to minimize backpressure and improve the flow of exiting exhaust gases. Building headers is a science, but if done right, they make a huge performance difference.

High-quality headers are formed out of individual tubes welded to a round collector. In the case of the Corvette, each side of the engine has four tubes, welded to a flange, that come together into a collector. The collector connects the headers to the exhaust system. On street cars, high-flow catalytic converters usually come next, and, near the rear wheels, the left and right exhaust pipes are connected with an X-pipe. The X-pipe reduces resonance inside the car and balances exhaust flow. To complete this system, a high-flow cat-back muffler system is attached to allow the exhaust to exit the car.

Aftermarket companies offer three types of headers: short tube, mid tube, and long tube. Tuners select the appropriate length header based on the customer's driving

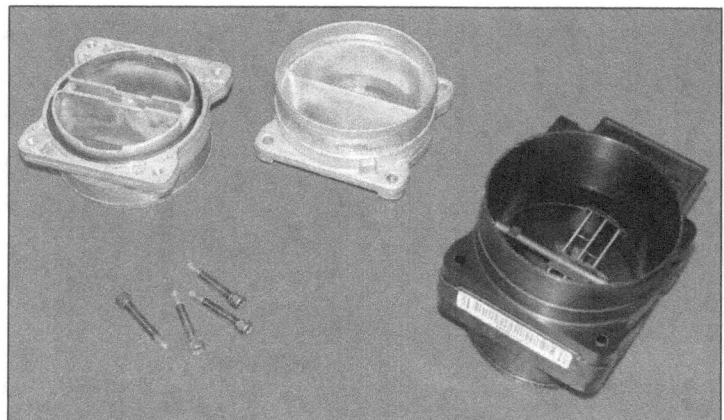

The factory center of the MAFS has been sandwiched between two poly MTI Racing replacement units, and the debris screen has been removed. Back on the dyno, the LS1 gained 4.9 horsepower and 6.20 ft-lbs of torque with this MAFS.

LS engines are fitted with individual cylinder coil packs, as indicated by the Xs on this photo. This provides a more even ignition source for each cylinder.

CHAPTER 7

The black fuel rail covers improve the look of your engine, but they do trap heat. I recommend removing them if you are drag racing or running your car on a road-racing circuit.

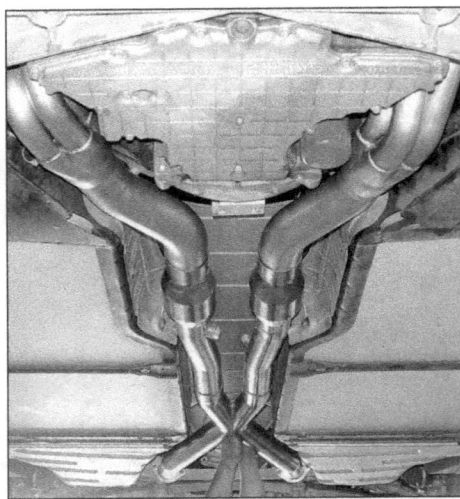

High-quality headers are designed to fit within the confines of the smooth C5 underbody. This photo shows how the headers, cats, and X-pipe flow into the mufflers.

requirements. The three header types are: shorties—easy to install, small power gain; mid length—not too small, but not so long as to scrape if your car is lowered; and longtube—maximizes power as well as exhaust noise.

What To Look For

Decide which header is right for you. If you want to stay 100% smog legal, stay with shorties only and make sure they have a California Area Research Board (CARB) number. If you have a 2000–2004 car, do not bother with shorties. These cars received a better-designed manifold and flow quite well for what they are. Switching to shorties nets minimal gain, if any. If you have a 1997–1999 car you'll gain some rwhp from shorties but it won't be much, either. If you decide on shorties, work your other modifications around your cam's design aspect, meaning if you

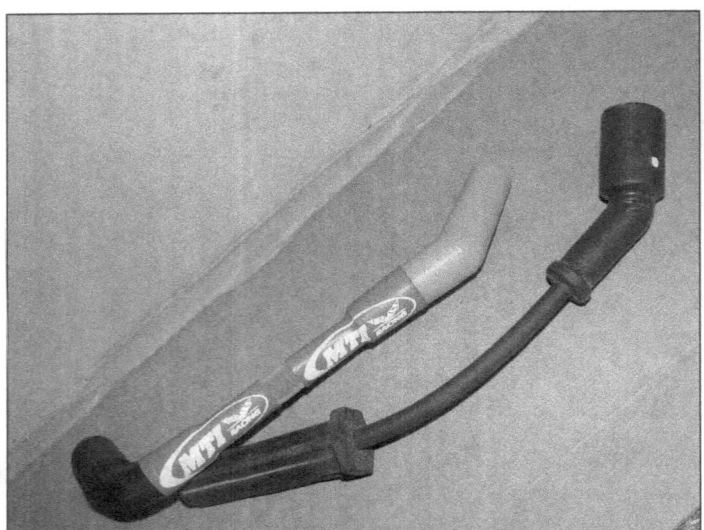

MTI Racing offers these custom-built spark plug wires (top). The smaller factory units can be seen below.

Long-tube headers flow into a collector that fits onto high-performance catalytic converters.

BASIC ENGINE BOLT-ONS

High-flow (low back-pressure) aftermarket mufflers like this Callaway Double-D system maximize the efficiency of good headers.

decide for a future cam, keep it small (220 duration or smaller).

Headers other than shorties require a new Y-pipe. Mid length versus long tube debates continue to go on, but mid lengths can produce great numbers and are a viable option for most people. Mid lengths are available for 1997–1999 and 2001–2004 cars; if you have a 2000 car, you need the EGR pipes from a 1997–1999 car, or you need to remove your EGR system. When buying long tubes, what you are paying for is fitment, quality, fit, and finish. All LTs are dyno'ed to produce similar net power gains. The 1-3/4-inch primaries are more than adequate for stock cubes. If you have an engine that has been stroked, shop for larger, 1-7/8-inch primary headers.

If you have a high-power, stock cubed setup, you might want to look into a 1-3/4 inches stepped to 1-7/8 inches. Buy your headers with some kind of ceramic coating or get stainless steel. If you can't afford coated headers, hold off until you can. If your car sees a lot of winters (real winters, i.e., East Coast, Midwest, etc.) you might want to seriously consider the stainless-steel headers; they are more expensive than ceramic-coated headers, but the chance of rust is greatly diminished.

Long Tubes

Since long tubes are by far the most popular headers, here are some of the more popular choices.

Pacesetters: Extremely popular due to price, and they are coated for under $400. Quality is very good for what you're spending your money on; welds and collectors are good. If you're on a budget and want long tubes, then Pacesetters should be at the top of your list.

Jet Hot/Hookers: The Hooker and Jet Hot long tubes are of the same design; jet hot took the hooker design and improved upon it a bit by moving the O2 bungs on the inside of the headers. They use a thicker tubing and have thicker flanges. Both are great long tubes and cost $500 to $600.

QTP/Kooks: Both Kooks and QTP are made with stainless steel, and are regarded highly. Quality is top notch and they can be polished for that "bling" look, if you'd like. Their only drawback is the price, at $700+, they are not for everyone.

SLP: SLPs make great headers; they are stainless steel *and* ceramic coated. Their major drawback is

These MTI Racing headers, cats, and X-pipe are sitting beside the company's Z06 427-cubic-inch development car.

price, installation, and lack of ground clearance. If you want to lower your car, pass on the SLPs. They are priced at $700+.

Others available but not reviewed:
Flowtech
Thunder Racing Headers
Dynatech
Stainless Works
PPC
SuperMaxx
TTS
LG Pro Long Tube Headers
MTI Racing

Cat-back Exhaust Systems

Cat-back exhaust systems are used with or without aftermarket headers. If you are adding headers, I strongly recommend adding a high-quality, cat-back system to complete your project. Most people do not add headers to their cars; they just bolt on cat-back systems. Owners usually just want to improve their car's appearance and sound their exhaust makes. Cat-back systems are available from a variety of aftermarket manufacturers. Major companies such as Corsa, B & B, Borla, Bassani, Callaway, etc., all offer specialized cat-back systems for C5 Corvettes.

You can buy your exhaust directly from the manufacturer or order them through Corvette supply houses. Some of these suppliers are Mid-America Motorworks, Corvette Central, West Coast Corvettes, etc. Each manufacturer produces its own unique sound and exhaust tip design. Sound and style are really a personal choice. My recommendation is to listen to and look at different exhaust systems before deciding on buying one for your car. If possible, talk to the owners about their experience with installation and quality of their particular system. Most importantly, ask them about cabin noise at cruising speeds. Some systems have so much negative resonance that you cannot hear yourself think on the highway. These cat-back systems are expensive, so it's best to take your time shopping for the sound and a look that puts a smile on your face.

This is exactly what I did before installing a Callaway Double-D cat-back on my C5. After looking and listening to a number of exhausts, I decided the Callaway was perfect for my car. One of the features of this particular system was how Callaway eliminated interior exhaust resonance without reducing efficiency. Their engineers spent a lot of time eliminating this common exhaust annoyance. I first heard this system on their C5 Z06 development car. From the rear, the exhaust produced a hearty note, but inside it was very quiet. Callaway Cars have been adding their distinctive Double-D tipped exhaust systems to custom-built Corvettes for many years. The one I selected (PN 208.50.4800) included polished, CNC Mandrel Bent 2.75-inch stainless-steel tubing that flows into their signature Double-D tipped outlets.

My C5 was already equipped with an aftermarket exhaust from another company. I decided to compare the power output of both systems. MTI Racing put the car on their Dynojet for a base run. Again, at the time of this test, the car was equipped with a stock displacement LS1 engine with a head-and-cam package. The engine pulled a respectable 429.30 hp and 417.20 ft-lbs of torque at the rear wheels. Next, the car was put on the lift and the old cat-back exhaust was removed in about 15 minutes. Installation took a little more time; still, everything was secured and ready for startup in about 45 minutes. Before installation, we pre-painted the optional Callaway Tip Surround Panel. The new painted panel was secured with screws to the fascia. The panel really finished off the project.

Back on the Dyno, the car was tuned and gained 7.70 hp and 6.10 ft-lbs from the previous system.

This B & B cat-back exhaust system is just one of the many different designs available in the aftermarket.

BASIC ENGINE BOLT-ONS

Vendors like Corsa often set up booths at major Corvette shows like Corvettes at Carlisle to let customers listen to their systems. Vendors also sometimes install the system you purchase at the show.

The LS1 now produced 437 hp and 423.30 ft-lbs of torque at the rear wheels. I was pleased with the performance gain. From the outside, the car produced an exhaust note with an authoritative rumble; inside, the car was very quiet. Even when we pushed the throttle, we did not experience any annoying resonance inside the car. MTI liked the sound this system produced, compared to the one that was removed. Overall, this installation was a homerun—it sounds better and produces more power!

Power Tuning

Tuning one of today's computerized engines has become a highly technical skill. Tuners use computer software programs to "re-map" the car's computer. During the installation of our bolt-on products, the car was dyno tuned when each job was completed. Every bolt-on part you add to your engine changes the computer's air/fuel ratio. Only computer tuning can maximize the performance improvements of each bolt-on part. One of the popular re-mapping programs is LS1 Edit. Power tuning is done on a rear-wheel dyno with the engine running and the tuning computer hooked up to the car's system.

The car is run up to fourth gear (for a 6-speed) and then accelerated from 20 mph to 140 mph, usually three times. Before any changes are made to the car's computer, a snapshot is made of the previous settings and saved to a file. That way, they can always come back to the original setting. Next, the tuner begins altering the previous settings in 100-rpm increments, adjusting the fuel and air mixtures all the way across the rev range. Power tuning usually extracts extra horsepower without changing any mechanical part of the engine.

This is why each time a part was added to the car, MTI owner Reese Cox retuned the engine to maximize each change. He did this after we installed the Honker, throttle body,

Here is the complete Callaway Double-D cat-back system with the optional (unpainted) insert that I installed on my car.

After any new item was installed on my car, it was put on the dyno before and after to determine what gain, if any, resulted from the change.

HIGH-PERFORMANCE C5 CORVETTE BUILDER'S GUIDE 87

CHAPTER 7

Reese Cox, owner of MTI Racing, power-tunes this C5 with his computers. He verifies each change he makes to a customer's engine on his in-house Dynojet dyno.

Here is another view of how Reese's computer power-tunes a customer's car on the dyno.

and cat-back exhaust. I watched as the horsepower and torque started to climb because of our new parts and power tuning. Our final run at the end of our bolt-on project was an impressive 437 hp and 423.30 ft-lbs of torque! We received an overall gain of 32.3 horsepower and 28 ft-lbs of torque with our new parts and power tuning.

Intake Manifolds

The C5 was totally redesigned in 1997, on the outside and the inside. Mechanically, there were very few carryover parts from the fourth-generation Corvette. The C5 was not only lighter, it was stronger, thanks to its new Hydro-formed tube frame rails. Die-hard Corvette fans bemoaned the end of the old, faithful small-block engine that traced its roots back to 1955. A new LS1 engine was all aluminum and displaced 348 cubic inches. Sitting on top of the engine was a high-tech, poly plastic intake manifold.

Aftermarket companies attempted to improve on this part, but mostly failed. When the LS6 engine was introduced in 2001, it featured a revised intake manifold, which produced about 10 to 15 more horsepower if bolted onto an LS1. The most favored aftermarket LS1 and LS6 is the FAST intake offered by the COMP Performance Group. The FAST is priced around $900 and usually produces around 20 extra horsepower on a car with a head-and-cam and headers.

All three manifolds are tricky to replace. The C5 engine sits partially under the dash, with little room to maneuver the units off the engine. Removal process starts by removing the fuel rail and the injectors. All of the electrical leads and vacuum lines are unhooked. The vacuum lines are mostly located, unseen, at the rear of the manifold. The manifold includes many small parts that need to be carefully stored and reinstalled in the correct order. A quality shop can usually complete this job in about 30 to 45 minutes; a weekend mechanic might take 3 hours. It is not a job for the faint hearted, but the FAST does produce power and allows you to bolt on a 90-mm throttle body to your engine.

Nitrous Oxide

Nitrous oxide, also known as dinitrogen oxide, is a chemical formula, N_2O. Under room conditions, it is an odorless, non-flammable gas with a pleasant, slightly sweet odor.

BASIC ENGINE BOLT-ONS

This poly-plastic LS6 intake manifold is standard on all 2001–2004 Z06 engines.

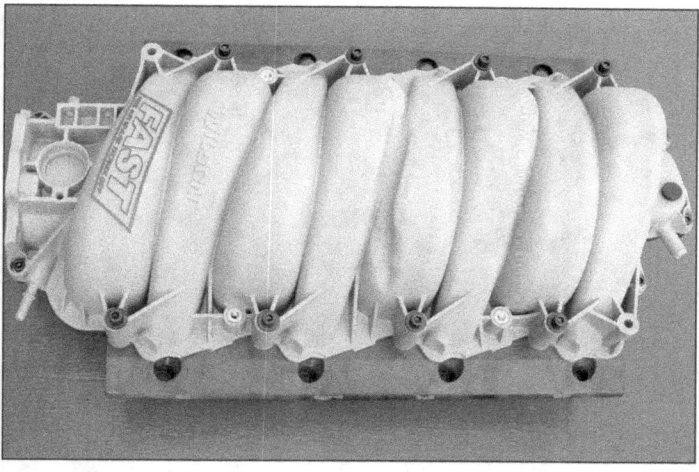

Wilson offers this poly FAST intake manifold that is a direct bolt-on to all LS engines.

It is commonly known as laughing gas, because when inhaled it can cause spontaneous laughter in people. Nitrous is used in racing applications because it increases a car's horsepower. Nitrous oxide is injected into the intake manifold to increase power. The gas delivers more oxygen, allowing the engine to burn more fuel and oxygen. Additionally, since nitrous is stored as a liquid, the evaporation of nitrous in the intake manifold causes a large drop in intake charge temperature. This results in a smaller, denser charge, and increases power to the engine.

One of the major problems using nitrous in a reciprocating engine is that it can produce enough power to destroy it. Power increases of 100 to 300% are possible. Unless the mechanical structure of the engine is reinforced, most engines do not survive this kind of operation. Nitrous can be introduced into a motor in several different ways. Nitrous kits such as BOSS, NOS, Nitrous Express, and Nitrous Direct all offer nitrous kits. Dry kits, wet kits, and direct port kits are available from aftermarket suppliers. Again, talk with people using these systems to determine which one is right for your application. It is very important when using nitrous in your engine to maintain proper water temperatures and fuel levels to avoid pre-ignition or detonation. This condition destroys your engine. Nitrous is a compressed, liquefied gas. While normally inert in storage and fairly safe to handle, nitrous can detonate under the wrong applications. Contamination with fuels has been implicated in a handful of accidents. Carefully follow your manufacturer's safety guidelines when using nitrous.

Nitrous is brought into the engine via an electric solenoid and can be designed as a single-shot or multiple-stage system. A three-shot system, for example, can introduce power to your engine in 50-hp gains, for a total boost of 150 hp. Each system can be custom tailored to fit your needs. Nitrous bottles are usually stored in your luggage compartment, and braided lines are run to your engine. It's a cheap way to get horsepower, but an easy way to destroy your engine. So be careful and have fun.

Do Bolt-on Products Really Work?

Now that we have reviewed some of the available bolt-on products you can put on a C5, I want to take a minute to share a secret experiment that GM performed on C5s in 1998. This experiment was actually part of the Z06 and SCCA T-1 showroom stock-racing development program. Its primary purpose was to determine what changes were required to make the Corvette competitive with its chief rivals, Viper and Porsche. GM noticed that after owners purchased their Corvettes, they began non-factory modifications aimed at better handling or quicker acceleration. So, GM conducted their own tests to determine the most effective ways to improve the C5 Corvette. They wanted to accomplish this by using aftermarket parts and established hot-rodding procedures. Corvette engineering developed the Corvette's engine, suspension, and structure with ample potential for higher performance.

These engineering experiments provided enterprising owners with a menu of sure-fire modifications they

CHAPTER 7

Nitrous oxide systems are an inexpensive way to bolt on horsepower. This photo shows the parts of a typical, 150-horsepower, electronic-fuel-injected, nitrous-oxide system. Remember, the power only lasts as long as you have nitrous in the bottle.

could do to their cars. They also offered a realistic look at the types of improvements GM was required to make for the T-1 and Z06 programs. Chevrolet's Specialty Vehicles Department used test methods that were very familiar to car magazine journalists. Standard 1998 coupes equipped with F45 (adjustable ride control) and Z51 (performance handling package) suspensions were hot lapped on the 2.25-mile road course at Moroso Motorsports Park in Palm Beach, Florida. To set appropriate performance benchmarks, test driver Andy Pilgrim flogged a Dodge Viper GTS and Porsche 911 Turbo.

Baseline tests placed the Corvette about five seconds per lap behind the Viper and four seconds behind the Porsche. The challenge faced by the Specialty Vehicles Department was to close that gap as affordably as possible, without reinventing the Corvette. In other words, make the Corvette run harder and faster, using parts and procedures that could be duplicated by a clever tuner at home. Phase I focused on handling improvements. Goodyear supplied some of the stickiest original-equipment rubber in its inventory—Eagle F1 Fiorano tires in sizes appropriate for the Corvette.

Fikse 18-inch aftermarket wheels were used all around, with a 9.5-inch rim width in front and a 10.5-inch rim in back. With even a modest increase in section width (to P295/35ZR-18 size radials), the Z51- equipped Corvette jumped a significant 0.10g in skid pad cornering tests—from 0.90 g to over 1.00 g. Various sway bars were also evaluated to balance the car and achieve best results, not only on the skid pad, but also in flat-out, road-course lapping. The best combination of skid-pad stick, road-course speed and open-road tractability came from a combination of P265/35ZR-18 tires in front, and P295/35ZR-18 rubber in back. Upsizing the stock front sway bar with an aftermarket part available from Hotchkiss Performance helped dial in the optimum handling balance. With the Corvette's adjustable suspension set in the Performance mode, the Viper's lap-time advantage was chopped in half. The beauty of simple wheel, tire and sway-bar modifications is that there's no loss of ride quality. Switching the adjustable suspension to the Tour position yielded a comfortable ride perfect for everyday commuting or cross-country excursions.

Phase II addressed the power disparity between Corvette and the Moroso pace setters. Specialty Vehicles technicians began with a standard hot-rodding trick: cylinder-head modifications. Milling 0.030 inch from the head's deck surface delivered a nominal increase in compression ratio—from the stock configuration's 10.1:1 to 10.9:1. The second step was what tuners call "pocket porting," improved airflow through intake and exhaust ports by opening up the bowl areas just below the valve seats. The required hand grinding isn't difficult, but expertise is required. So, these head modifications were assigned to an established machine shop and performance engine builder. The final step was swapping the factory camshaft for one with longer duration and higher lift. Three external alterations helped the engine's volumetric efficiency. In lieu of the factory air cleaner, Chevrolet Specialty Vehicles fitted

BASIC ENGINE BOLT-ONS

dual K&N conical-type filters (keeping the standard throttle body, mass-airflow sensor, and intake air duct). The stock, double-wall exhaust manifolds were replaced with single-wall designs fabricated from larger-diameter, stainless-steel tubing. A low-restriction Corsa tail pipe and muffler assembly was added downstream of the standard Corvette catalytic converter.

Dyno tests revealed a healthy 105-hp boost in output. The torque peak climbed by 69 ft-lbs, yet the curve was still flat; there's an energetic response when the throttle is nailed at any RPM. More than 100 extra horsepower is a very worthwhile improvement. The reasonable cost of the modifications that Corvette owners could make without removing the block from their car was a huge plus. The stopwatch told the most convincing story: the combination of extra power with improved handling was more than enough to advance the Corvette to pole position at Moroso, ahead of both the $68,000 Viper and the $106,000 Porsche.

Jim Campbell, former Corvette Brand Manager, was quoted after the test, "Our Corvette Super-car test demonstrated that there was plenty of potential untapped in the Corvette that allowed it to take on true super-cars. What was also amazing was the modest investment required to reach those performance improvements. Specialty Vehicles' menu of bolt-on modifications provided Corvette owners ample inspiration for tuning their own cars."

This test confirmed that the T-1 and Z06 program was on track. They were right; GM development engineer John Heinricy won the SCCA National T-1 championship four years in a row driving a Z06.

A Dodge Viper GTS (left) was compared to this red, pre-production FRC Corvette. Racecar driver Andy Pilgrim drove the cars at Moroso Motorsports Park in West Palm Beach, Florida, in 1998.

After a series of bolt-on modifications, which are discussed in this book, the FRC set the fastest time of the day at Moroso.

GM Development Dngineer John Heinricy drove this 1999 Phoenix Racing FRC to several SCCA T-1 national championships.

HIGH-PERFORMANCE C5 CORVETTE BUILDER'S GUIDE

CHAPTER 8

SERIOUS ENGINE MODIFICATIONS

The stock LS1 is rated at 345 or 350 horsepower (2001 and newer) and produces around 295 horsepower at the rear wheels.

The LS6 is rated at 385 horsepower (2001) or 405 horsepower and features revised heads, intake, and block. This engine produces around 335 rear-wheel horsepower.

In the last chapter, I reviewed some of the common bolt-on items owners can put on their C5s to improve power without disturbing the internals of their engines. Stock LS1s are rated at 345 or 350 hp (depending on year) at the crankshaft. What that means is that just the engines are bolted to a stationary dyno. During this type of test, the engine is not hooked to a transmission or differential. Putting a C5 on a rear-wheel chassis dyno is more real world. Rear-wheel dynos measure what the engine puts to the ground. They use large drum rollers turned by the rear wheels, and a computer measures RWHP and torque. For example, a stock LS1 rated at 345 hp usually produces between 292 to 297 rwhp. An LS6 rated at 405 hp at the crank produces 336 to 345 rwhp. Adding a good air-filter system, revised throttle body, and cat-back exhaust bumps a stock LS1 up to around 330 rwph. An LS6 with the same modifications usually produces around 355 to 365 rwhp. If you are searching for more horsepower, you must decide what to do to your car's engine next. Each choice costs you money and time away from your car.

In my view, the road to more horsepower in your Corvette leads down three different roads. I am going to attempt to discuss each of

SERIOUS ENGINE MODIFICATIONS

these three options to allow you to make an informed choice. The first is internal engine modifications, second is supercharging, and third is turbocharging. Selecting one of these choices should be made after carefully researching your driving requirements. Drag racing, road racing, Autocrossing, street driving, and weekend track events all require different kinds of engine performance and reliability. Each of these choices has benefits and drawbacks.

Internal Engine Modifications

Production road racers that use American cars like Corvette and Viper prefer internal engine modifications versus turbocharging or supercharging. Big-bore American street engines have a lot of untapped power potential that can be mined by modifying the heads and adding a better camshaft. These are called head-and-cam packages. By changing the head and cam, the engine usually has a lot more power. This is particularly important coming out of a slow-speed corner where you need instant power. Usually, a head-and-cam package increases the rev range of the engine. Again, this might make the difference between being able to avoid making a shift in a corner to gain speed. Another common road-racing modification is increasing the engine's cubic inches via boring or changing the entire block to a larger one. A road racer knows that minimizing complexity is a key to finishing a race. Turbochargers and superchargers add complexity and heat, which are enemies to engine endurance. Porsche is one of the few manufacturers that have successfully used turbochargers in their production racecars. Turbos are a great way to make small-displacement engines competitive against larger-bore engines like the Corvette or Viper.

Head-and-Cam Packages

The most common internal engine modification C5 owners can make to their cars is installing a head-and-cam package. They can opt to install polished and ported LS6 heads, which have bigger ports and flow more efficiently. Intake port volume on an LS6 head is 210 cubic centimeters (cc), compared to 200 cc on the LS1. The exhaust port volume for the LS1 is 70 cc, and 75 cc for the LS6. The combustion chamber on an LS6 is tighter at 64.45 cc, compared to 66.67 cc on the LS1 head. Both LS1 and LS6 heads use 2-inch intake and 1.55-inch exhaust valves. Some aftermarket suppliers prefer to port and polish the LS6 head because of

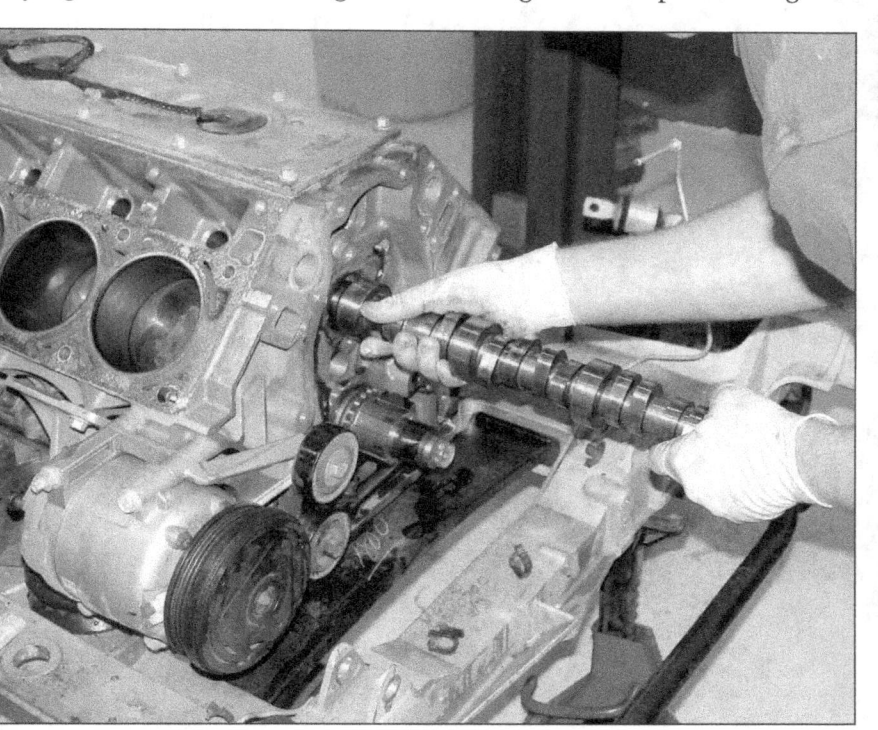

A head-and-cam package requires disassembling the engine to install the new parts.

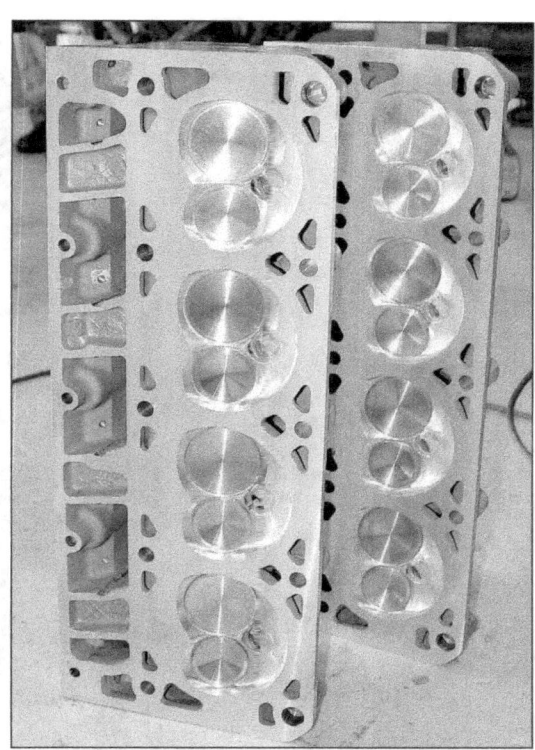

New heads usually include larger ported and polished combustion chambers and larger valves.

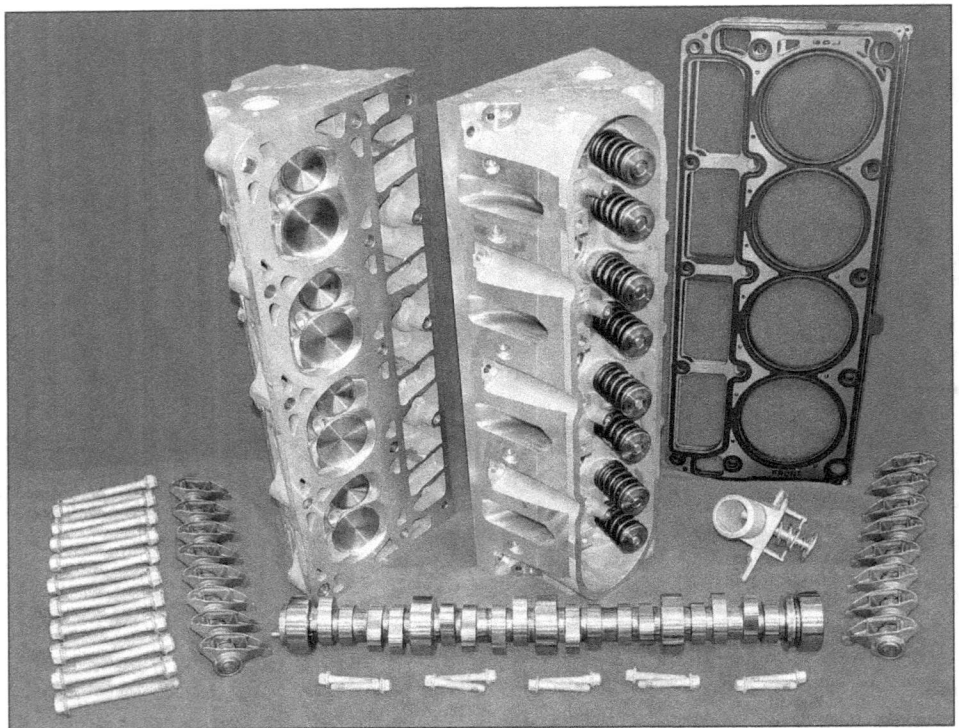

This Callaway Power Group II head-and-cam package includes the typical parts for this upgrade.

Reese Cox of MTI Racing installs a new cam into a stock displacement LS1 engine.

its improved port flow and combustion chamber characteristics. Typically, they usually increase the valve size to 2.02 inches intake and 1.57 inches on the exhaust.

When tuners select a cam for a street head-and-cam package, they look for more lift and a mild increase in duration. This helps keep emissions levels low, while providing the customer with good driveability, a broader power band, and increased peak power. The LS6 cam has a duration approximately 0.050-inch lift of 204 degrees intake and 218 degrees exhaust. With the stock 1.7:1 rocker arm, it produces 0.555-inch intake lift and 0.551-inch exhaust lift at the valve. The lobe separation angle is 116 degrees. A good street camshaft should have duration at 0.50-inch valve lift of just under 220 degrees on the intake and 230 degrees exhaust. An ideal lift at the valve is around 0.600 inch (with proper valve-springs) and a lobe separation angle of 114 degrees. Prices vary for this upgrade, but plan on spending $10,000 to $15,000 for this modification. Depending on the extent of other modifications done to your car, such as free-flowing air inlets and exhaust systems, you can expect to add 70 to 80 hp. This moves an LS1 from 295 rwhp to around 375 to 385 rwhp. An LS6 should produce around 400 to 410 rwhp.

Tuners are a secretive lot. They generally don't like a "fender lizard" (someone looking over their shoulder) while they turn your Corvette into a rice rocket eater. Modifying a car correctly is an art, and every tuner thinks his approach is the best for making horsepower. I have always looked for opportunities to look behind the scenes at what it takes to transform a C5 into something

SERIOUS ENGINE MODIFICATIONS

The head bolts are torqued and the valves are adjusted during this part of the engine rebuild.

special. After all, tuners are not inexpensive and if your performance goals are not met, getting them corrected is timely and costly. Before you decide to turn your keys and money over to a tuner, it is nice to know what to ask and what's involved. While writing this book, I decided to shadow a Corvette tuner during the modification process on my Corvette. I searched for an experienced tuner willing to let me watch his operation.

As you know by now, I have a good relationship with MTI Racing, especially with owner Reese Cox. When I asked about shadowing him during a head-and-cam install, he agreed. We used my stock 2000 FRC to document MTI's installation of their Stage I and II packages. Stage I includes: cold-air induction, air bridge, ported throttle body, ignition wires, Denso spark plugs, low-temp thermostat, X-pipe, and stainless-steel exhaust. The Stage II LS1 package requires installation of the Stage I package. Stage II LS1 upgrade includes: modified cylinder heads, custom grind cam, custom pushrods, double roller timing chain, modified oil pump, underdrive pulley, new head gaskets, new belts, new engine bolt kit, and Stage II computer reflash. Reese recommended adding a set of his long-tube headers, SPEC 3 pressure plate, clutch, and Fidanza flywheel—I agreed.

My car was delivered to MTI Racing's shop in Marietta, Georgia, to begin the transformation. There are several ways to complete this job. The head-and-cam package is installed by removing the hood and the engine accessories, including the radiator. This allows you to install the new parts from the top of the car. Another method is to remove just the engine and complete the project away from the car. The final way (the one MTI chose) is to remove the entire drivetrain from underneath and install the head and cam on the shop floor. Each has its advantages and disadvantages, and Reese chose the last method. Their first stop was putting the car on the dyno to get a baseline starting horsepower. The FRC produced 331.3 hp and 333.3 ft-lbs of torque. This is higher than a stock LS1, because the car had a Stage I package. MTI started the project by first removing the FRC's shifter.

Next, all of the chassis wiring was unplugged and the supporting attachments were removed. This included brake lines, shocks, water hoses, etc. Once everything was loose, the drivetrain was supported under the front and rear cradles with safety stands. Eight cradle bolts were removed, and the body was lifted clear of the drivetrain using a vertical lift. The front and rear cradles were left supporting the car's drivetrain. This included the rear end, transmission, torque tube, engine, and front and rear suspension components. This process took MTI four hours. Now the engine was completely exposed, which allowed MTI to remove the engine accessories and the steering rack. Next, the lifters and lifter buckets were removed. The LS engine design allows a camshaft change without removing the heads; however, these heads were going to be modified.

A vacuum pump was used to remove any anti-freeze that might have seeped into the engine's water passages and cylinders during disassembly. Next, a custom wrench was used to loosen the crankshaft pulley nut, which is torqued to 350 ft-lbs at

CHAPTER 8

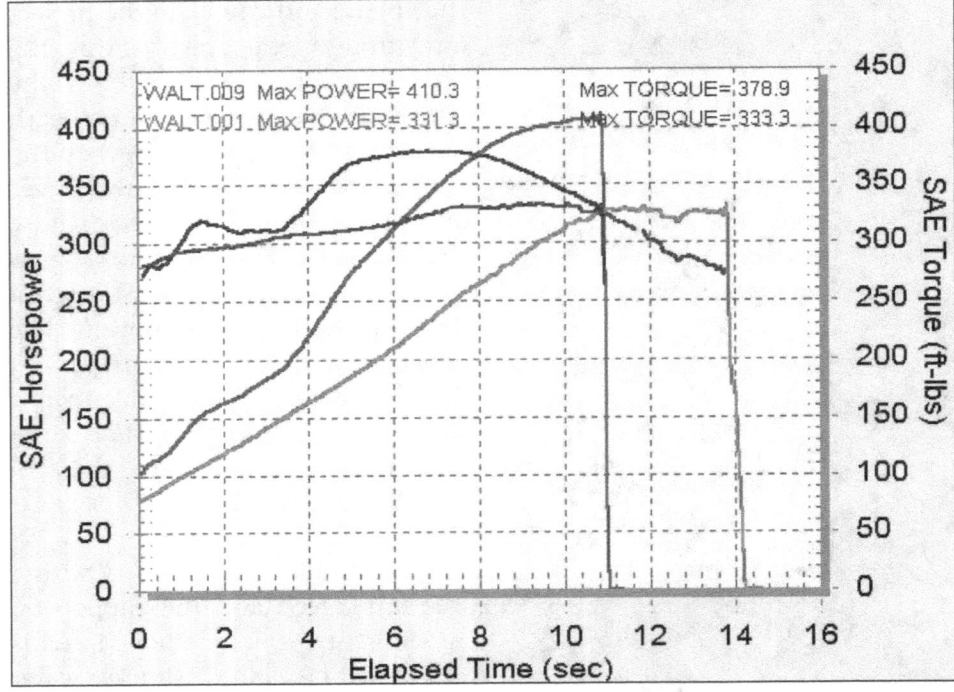

The LS1 produced 331 horsepower and 333.3 ft-lbs of torque at the rear wheels before the head-and-cam were installed. The car had a modified throttle body, air intake, and high-flow cat-back exhaust. After the installation, power increased to 410.3 hp and 378.9 ft-lbs.

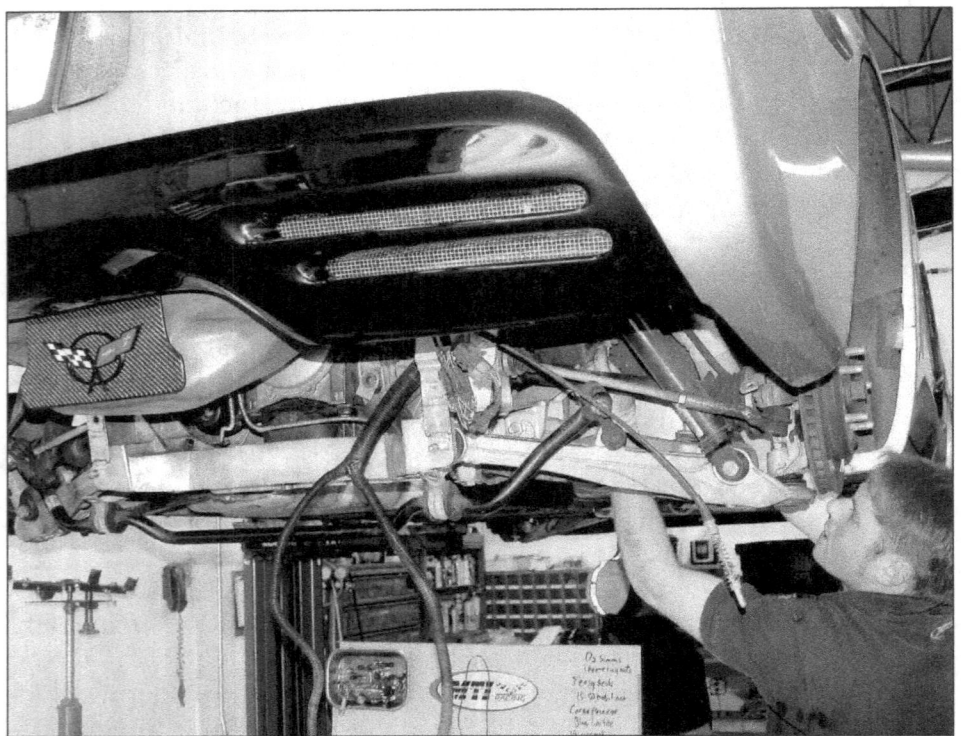

MTI Racing Technician David Munder begins disconnecting the wiring and bolts in order to remove the drivetrain from the body.

the factory. Then the oil pump, timing chain, and pulley were removed. The engine was ready for cleanup and new parts. This completed day one of the project.

On day two the team removed the torque tube, transmission, and rear suspension from the engine. This was done to allow installation of a new flywheel, clutch, and pressure plate. Next, Reese and his team prepared the car for reassembly. First, he checked the new cylinder heads, to verify the size of the combustion chambers. He checked the volume of the combustion chamber on each head to calculate compression ratio. He installed the camshaft. Then the cam was degreed for two reasons—to verify the cam specs and to measure the opening and closing event of the engine's intake cycle. This was done to get the phasing of the cam and crankshaft correct. Next, the deck height of the piston was checked to ensure correct compression ratio. The MTI Gen III cylinder heads are CNC ported and include a 2.02 intake and 1.60 exhaust valves. The intake and exhaust ports are hand blended to ensure optimum flow. After the heads were installed, the bolts were tightened to 37 ft-lbs. Next, MTI Racing's long-tube headers were installed. The SPEC 3 pressure plate and clutch were mounted to the Fidanza lightweight flywheel that was bolted to the crankshaft.

On day three the engine and driveline were completed and readied for reinstallation. MTI Racing utilized three sets of eyes during the reassembly process. After someone completed a task, two others reviewed the work to ensure proper completion and quality control. Slowly, the FRC was reunited with its drivetrain, and it took about two

SERIOUS ENGINE MODIFICATIONS

The drivetrain is being slowly removed from the body. The process takes about four hours for a competent shop to perform this task.

David Munder uses a custom wrench to remove the crankshaft pulley bolt.

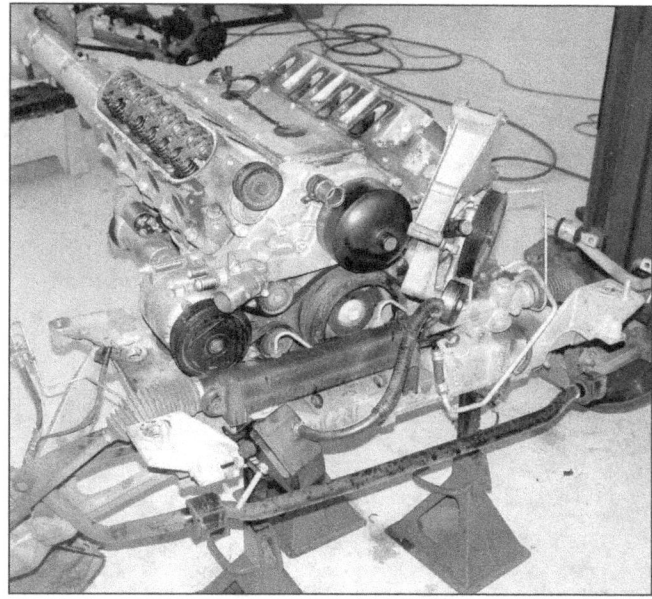
The engine is now being stripped of its major components.

MTI Racing Technician Jesus Garcia cleans the fluids and oil from the block prior to installation of the head-and-cam package.

hours to complete. At the end of the day, the engine was started for the first time. It was allowed to sit overnight to seal the special head gaskets.

On the final day, the car was computer tuned and road tested before going back on the Dyno. The MTI Racing headers and exhaust system fit nicely under the car. When the project was complete, the car was broken in and put back on the dyno. My best dyno run was 410 hp and 378.9 ft-lbs of torque versus the previous best run of 331.3 hp and 333.3 ft-lbs of torque at the rear wheels. That put this car close to 500 hp at the crank, pretty amazing for starting with a 345-hp car. As you read earlier, a Callaway Honker, a Callaway 78-mm throttle body, an MTI MAFS, and a Callaway cat-back exhaust were added after this project was completed. These changes brought the power up to 437 hp and 423.30 ft-lbs of torque. The car ran exceptionally well on the street and did not exhibit any bad behavior. Water temperatures remained stable with or without the air conditioning running.

CHAPTER 8

The stock pressure plate, clutch, and flywheel were replaced during this job. This is why the driveline was removed from the engine.

Because of its light weight (around 25 lbs compared to stock units' 60 lbs), the SPEC required more revs to start, but the engine revved quickly to its 6,500-rpm redline. If you use the car for daily driving, I recommend installing a heavier SPEC 1 or 2 clutch and pressure plate. It is easier to drive day in and day out. What you sacrifice in performance is gained in comfort. On the road, I found that first gear pulls so hard that it overcomes the car's traction control. First gear produces a lot of wheel spin even with 315/30 ZR17-inch tires mounted on 11-inch rims at the time of this project. The rumble of the cam and the

MTI Racing is checking the cubic-centimeter (CC) measurement of each combustion chamber prior to installing the new head onto the engine.

A lightweight SPEC 3 pressure plate and clutch are being mounted to a Fidanza flywheel. This combination weighs a total of 25 lbs.

The work is completed and the drivetrain is being reunited with the body.

SERIOUS ENGINE MODIFICATIONS

Back on the dyno, the completed LS1 head-and-cam package produced 410.3 horsepower and 378.9 ft-lbs of torque at the rear wheels.

sound of the exhaust made the price of admission very worthwhile. I punched the throttle while cruising and the car leapt forward and quickly headed toward its new redline.

With all this newfound power, I was glad my C5 was equipped with upgraded rotors and Hawk Plus HP brake pads. MTI not only improved my C5's performance, but they exceeded all of my project goals.

Note: Prior to making this upgrade, LS1 owners should switch to an LS6 intake manifold.

LS2 Block Change

Horsepower, horsepower—can we ever get enough horsepower? Well by now you may have figured out that I am addicted to *usable* horsepower. Throughout my writing career in the Corvette hobby, I have only ridden in or driven four fast Corvettes. They are: 1969 L-88 Rebel Corvette roadster (finished fourth overall at the 1972 12 Hours of Sebring, naturally aspirated), 1988 Callaway Sledgehammer (254.6-mph street car, twin turbocharged), 1989 ZR-1 SnakeSkinner (640-hp, 2,700-lb GM Prototype test car, naturally aspirated), and Chuck Mallett's 1996 One Lap of America Racer (1,050-hp, 250-mph street car, supercharged).

All of these cars had a common thread: not only were they blindingly fast in a straight line, they cornered and stopped with the best sports cars in the world. Each received their power from different methods, naturally aspirated, supercharged, or turbocharged. I enjoy watching single-purpose racecars like dragsters burn up the quarter mile, but I admire tuners who can make all of a car's driving components (power, handling, and braking) work together in one package. The four cars that I mentioned above accomplished that goal.

As I have continued on the journey of modifying my own C5, I have kept that goal in mind. I wanted a fast car that had a suspension and braking system that could safely handle the power. When MTI completed my head-and-cam package, I upgraded my shocks and installed more aggressive brake pads in the car. But after driving the car awhile, I felt that the head-and-cam package lacked torque. When the LS2 engine was introduced in 2005, the engine was expanded from 5.7 liters (346 cubic inches) to 6 liters (360 cubic inches); I wondered if

This English Racing 1969 L-88 Corvette finished a remarkable fourth overall and first in the GT class at the 1972 12 Hours of Sebring. This record remained unbroken for 32 years, until a factory C5R Corvette matched this finish in 2004.

CHAPTER 8

Talk about fast! This 1988 990-horsepower, twin-turbo Callaway Corvette was driven at 254.6 mph by the late John Lingenfelter on an Ohio test track. This street-able, air-conditioned, full-interior Corvette is still among the fastest street-able cars in the world.

In 1991, GM Development Engineer John Heinricy converted this 1989 prototype ZR-1 into the SS or "Snake Skinner." The car's weight was reduced to 2,700 lbs by deleting many accessories and adding lightweight body parts. The 600-horsepower LT-5 engine helped make this car go well over 200 mph.

Tuner Chuck Mallett built this 1,050-horsepower supercharged Corvette for the 1996 One Lap of America. One Lap creator Brock Yates called this 240+ mph monster the "Corvette from Hell!"

this engine might hold the answer to more torque. Shortly after the LS2 was introduced, tuners began offering engine packages that included a 4-inch stroke and a 4.010 bore. This translates into 6.6 liters or 404.1 cubic inches. During the installation of my head-and-cam package, Reese mentioned that he was going to offer this engine to his customers. I was very happy with the added horsepower, but I still felt it needed more torque. One thing led to another, and once again my C5 visited MTI Racing to get one of his LS2 engines installed.

MTI Racing's 6.6 package consists of an LS2 block with a 4.010-inch bore and 4.000-inch stroke that equals 404.1 cubic inches! It fits both C5 and C6 Corvettes. The heart of this new beast is a new, GM Performance LS2 short block, which received a 4.010-inch bore before assembly. The bottom end includes a Callies 4340 Racemaster forged crankshaft. The crank for this application weighs 52 lbs and has all forging lines removed to improve aerodynamic penetration through oil. The counter weights have an airfoil shape to also improve oil penetration. The engine uses Compstar 4340 forged I-Beam connecting rods mounted to Mahle F1 Teflon skirted dished pistons.

Each piston is coated with hard-coated aluminum for heat protection. These parts are held in place with H-11 lightweight, tapered wrist pins. These wrist pins weigh 103 grams each, compared to 147 grams for the stock pins. The engine is topped off with LS6 MTI modified heads and an MTI cam. This is a good camshaft for street and track use. With duration measured at 0.50-inch valve lift, the cam is just under 220 degrees on the intake and 230 degrees exhaust. Reese told us to expect a nice bump in torque.

SERIOUS ENGINE MODIFICATIONS

You know the old saying: "There is no substitute for cubic inches!" Since our LS1 benefited from many MTI Racing upgrades, it was decided to reuse some of our previously installed parts on the new engine. This included the heads, Z06 intake, and 78-mm Callaway throttle body. The MTI Racing long-tube headers, Callaway exhaust system, Fidanza flywheel, and SPEC pressure plate and clutch were set aside during disassembly for reuse. MTI Racing elected to remove my old LS1 engine from the top rather than the bottom. Removal from the top allowed the car to be moved around the shop more easily. MTI quickly removed the usable parts from the old engine. The team installed a Callies 4340 Racemaster crank, Mahle F1 pistons, and Compstar connecting rods into the new LS2 block. Once the lower end was assembled, the pan and oil pump were installed.

MTI Racing Technician Mason Harris begins dismantling this C5 for an engine upgrade. The new, bare, LS2 block sits beside the car.

Next, an MTI Racing spec hydraulic roller cam was installed, along with the timing chain and sprockets. The timing chain cover and external cam sensor wiring connector were also installed. Next, the cam buckets, intake valley pan, head bolt studs, and gaskets completed the short-block assembly. The heads, valvesprings, and crank pulley completed the engine. The team then mounted the Fidanza flywheel and SPEC pressure plate and clutch. The engine was now ready for installation.

During installation, it was discovered that the LS2 has one extra stud on the right side of the block that interferes with the C5 motor mount. Part of the stud had to be removed to clear the mount, but everything else fit perfectly. The two knock sensors located in the intake valley on the C5 were relocated to each side of the LS2 block. Also, the LS2 cam sensor is now located on the front instead of the back of the block. Reese built new wiring harnesses to accommodate these changes.

New, larger 32-mm injectors were installed to feed the increased

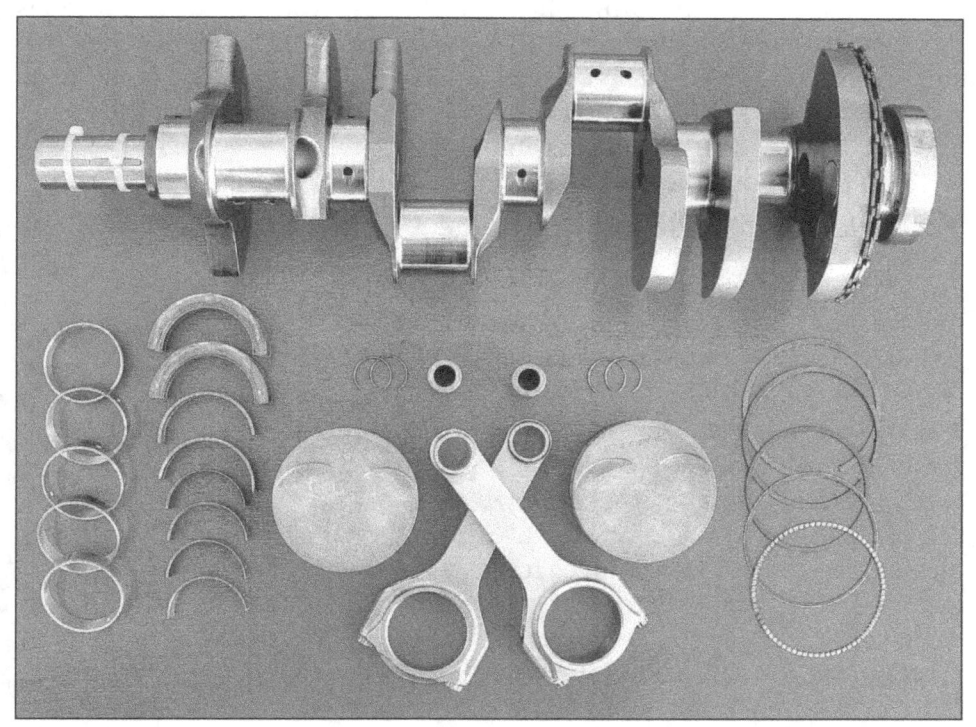

The engine was bored to 4 inches to make room for the Mahle F1 pistons and the Callies 4340 Racemaster forged crankshaft. Compstar connecting rods were used for this engine build.

The lower end of the new LS2 engine is being completed. By adding the windage tray to the bottom of the block, the rod and main bolts can be installed and torqued to proper specs.

The cam buckets, intake valley pan, head bolts, and gaskets have been installed onto the new engine.

cubic inches. The finishing touches included adding the headers, intake, radiator, cooling fans, and hood. The car was ready for its first startup. Reese checked the computer with his laptop and it started on the first try. After we completed a trouble-free, 500-mile break-in run, we returned to MTI Racing and hooked the car up to the dyno. Our best pull was 477 rwhp and 464 ft-lbs of torque. If you apply 16.5% for driveline losses, this rounds out to 556 hp at the crankshaft! The best thing about this 6.6 package is that it produces this power without adding turbos, superchargers, or nitrous to the engine.

On the road the car is very docile, almost a sleeper. The car lopes along with no stumbles or bad manners and it even has power in sixth gear. We no longer have to watch the tach to make sure the motor is turning above 3,500 rpm to get maximum performance. Now you can punch it at 2,500 rpm and have all the power you need. This is not a cam motor—it's a torque motor. We averaged 27.6 mpg on a 7-hour trip with the air conditioning running. But the remarkable thing is that even at 2,000 rpm, the LS2 produces well over 350 ft-lbs of torque. When you punch it, hang on—it turns from a kitten into a tiger. The change in the car's personality is pretty amazing. In its former life, the 2000 FRC was a quiet, comfortable cruiser. The added 40 hp and 50 ft-lbs of torque to the rear wheels over the head-and-cam package can really be felt. Before, the car came on really strong above 3,500 rpm; now, the power curve is very flat, which gives you power whenever you push the pedal. After the engine was installed, new front/rear springs, bigger sway bars, and Wilwood brakes were installed to cope with the increased power (see Chapters 3 and 5). Reese is a former Speedvision GT competitor and a very accomplished road racer. He arranged to compare my completed car to a stock 2006 Z06 at Road Atlanta's 2.54-mile 12-turn road course. With Reese driving, my car lapped 1.1 seconds faster during its six-lap comparison. So the proof of all these changes is in the pudding!

C5-R Block Change

The basic LS1 engine block architecture is used in the LS2, LS-7, LS-9, C5-R, and C6-R engines. The C5-R and C6-R blocks feature stronger webbing, but unless you are adding serious horsepower (+800 to 1,500 hp), the LS-7 or LS-9 blocks should be adequate

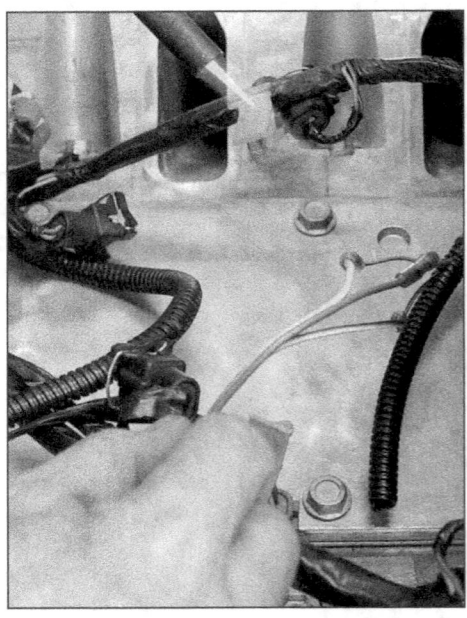
Reese Cox built a new wiring harness for the LS2's relocated cam and knock sensors.

SERIOUS ENGINE MODIFICATIONS

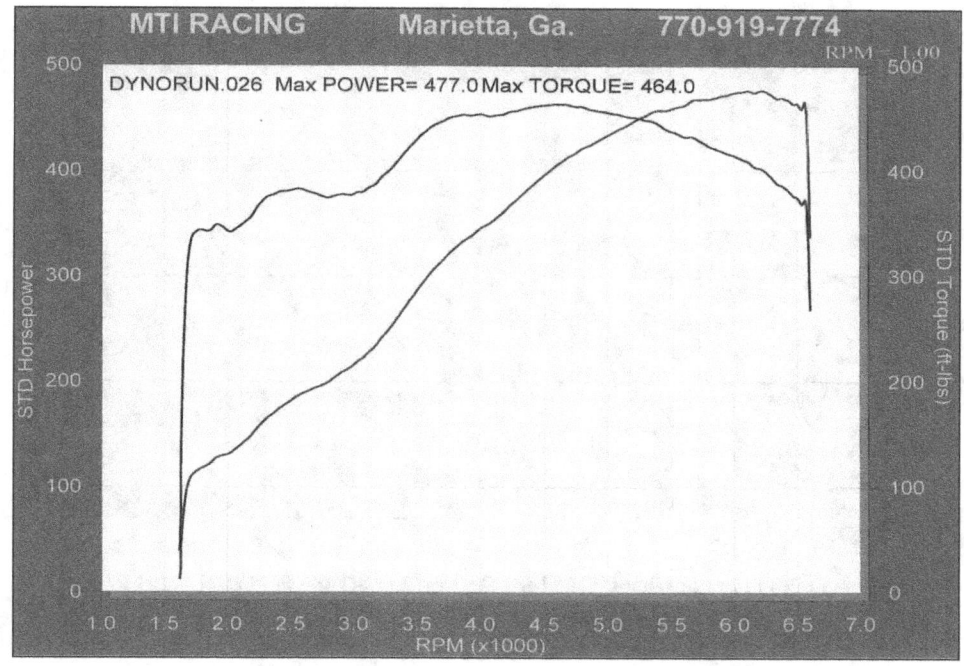

When the job was completed, the car went back onto the dyno and produced 477 horsepower and 464 ft-lbs of torque at the rear wheels. This is around 556 horsepower at the crankshaft.

for your needs. Many tuners offer packages with 427 cubic inches, and so far I have resisted the temptation to put one of these motors into my car. Again, these engines do produce more torque and serve as an excellent foundation for turbocharged and supercharged engines. But so far, I am happy with my car's total performance. Maybe I will change my mind if I sell one million copies of this book!

Turbochargers

Turbochargers have been used as a performance enhancement on many different kinds of vehicles for years. Their popularity really got a big boost during World War II, when they were added to Allied fighter planes and bombers as a way of allowing them to fly at much higher altitudes. The war helped advance the turbocharger technology, and today they are fitted to many different kinds of vehicles, airplanes, trucks, and small-displacement cars. Indy cars have used turbos to boost power in their engines for many years, and Porsche is a heavy user of turbos in their racecars. Reeves Callaway broke new ground with Chevrolet in 1986 when he offered a twin-turbo package for the C4 Corvette. The twin turbos boosted the L-98's output from 230 hp to 345 hp. That was a big number in 1986.

Turbos lost favor with GM with the introduction of the 375-hp LT-5, the 405-hp LS6, the 505-hp LS-7, and the 650-hp supercharged LS-9. Corvette has relied on making horsepower with naturally aspirated and supercharged engines. Naturally aspirated Corvette engines with large displacement and high compression can muscle their way to the top of the hill. This is why Corvettes and Vipers trounce competitors with great big engines under their hoods.

However, some tuners love turbocharging. In the Corvette community, Callaway and Lingenfelter are well known for their turbocharging experience. Callaway's 254.6-mph Sledgehammer was powered with a twin-turbocharged, 990-hp small-block. Lingenfelter Performance Engineering (LPE) is a multiple winner of *Car & Driver*'s Supertuner shootout with a twin-turbo C5.

Turbos use wasted exhaust gases to turn the turbine located inside the turbo unit. The effect is

The car was taken to the 2.54-mile, 12-turn Road Atlanta racetrack and was compared to a 2006 Z06. The C5 was consistently over 1 second per lap faster than the Z06 during the test.

This twin-turbo Lingenfelter Corvette won the Car & Driver Supertuner shootout.

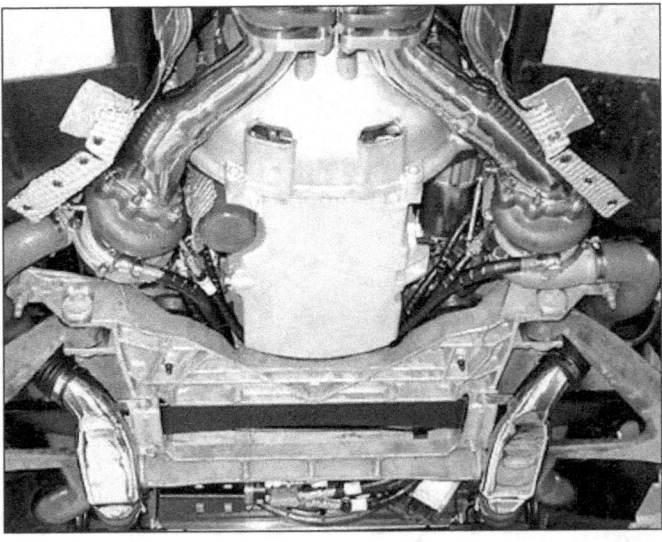

The twin turbos on this C5 are tightly packed behind the front engine cradle. Turbos produce a lot of heat and this is why you see heat shielding placed around the turbos.

not unlike a water wheel. When using a water wheel to power a wheat-grinding mill, no water gets into the mill because it is separate. The same goes for a turbocharger. No exhaust gas bleeds to the intake charge because the power source is separate. The exhaust gases enter and exit turbine enclosures—exhaust gas goes in radially, turns a wheel, and exits axially. On the other side of the turbo, work gets done in the opposite direction. The rotating impeller shaft powered by the exhaust moves air, which enters the center (axially) and exits the side (radially). So, a turbocharger simply uses leftover power in the exhaust to pump more air directly into the engine for increased boost or power. Boost controls determine the right amount of boost sent to the engine.

More boost produces more power, but reduces engine life and durability. Because turbos are powered by exhaust, they become very hot under extreme use. Heat is the enemy of a car and the downside of turbos is that they must be carefully protected from a car's vital operating parts. Anything that is located near a turbo tends to overheat, fail, or melt. My advice is that if you want to add turbos to your car, have it modified by an experienced vendor like Lingenfelter or Callaway.

Superchargers

Let's start with the similarities between turbochargers and superchargers. Both use forced-induction systems to compress the air flowing into the engine. The advantage of compressing the air is that it stuffs more into the cylinders. More air means more fuel can be added, so you get more power from each cylinder explosion. A turbo or supercharged engine produces more power overall than does the same engine without the charging. Typical boost provided by a supercharger is 6 to 8 lbs per square inch (psi). Since normal atmospheric pressure is 14.7 psi at sea level, you can see that you are getting about 50% more air into the engine. Therefore, expect to get 50% more power. However, it's not perfectly efficient, so an improvement of 30% to 40% is more likely.

The key difference between a turbocharger and a supercharger is the power supply. Something has to supply the power to run the air compressor. In a supercharger, a belt connects directly to the engine. It gets its power the same way that the water pump or alternator does. A turbocharger, as we discussed above, gets its power from the exhaust system. Both systems have tradeoffs. In theory, a turbocharger is more efficient because it is using the "wasted" energy in the exhaust stream for its power source. On the other hand, a turbocharger causes some amount of backpressure in the exhaust system and tends to provide less boost until the engine is running at higher RPM. This is known as turbo lag.

Superchargers have become popular in recent years for several reasons, including cost, efficiency, reliability,

SERIOUS ENGINE MODIFICATIONS

Superchargers are belt driven and produce full power under full throttle conditions. They usually add 125 rear-wheel horsepower to an LS1 engine.

and performance. Supercharging an engine often results in power increases in the range of 50% to 100%. Although superchargers are expensive, nothing provides more horsepower for your dollar. They provide power only when the engine is under full throttle or under load, not under normal cruising conditions. This means that the supercharger does not affect the engine's reliability, longevity, or fuel economy under normal driving conditions.

Most superchargers sold today are centrifugal style. This means they are internal-compression superchargers. This style creates boost (compresses the air) inside the supercharger head unit (blower) before discharging it into the engine's air intake. External compression superchargers (roots or screw-type superchargers such as those offered by Whipple, Kenne Bell, Jackson Racing, Eaton) have become less popular as centrifugal superchargers have evolved. Centrifugal superchargers (Vortech, Paxton, Powerdyne, ATI ProCharger) are more reliable, especially at higher boost levels. They are capable of creating more boost than external compression superchargers while creating a much cooler intake charge. Boost is created when the supercharger's internal impeller pushes air through the blower. This push overcomes the vacuum force naturally created by the engine's air intake. This allows air to be forced, rather than pulled, into the air intake. Boost is measured in pounds per square inch, or PSI. More boost equates to a denser air charge into the engine's combustion chamber. This allows the engine to burn more air and fuel and create more horsepower. Most street superchargers produce somewhere in the range of 6 to 9 psi, meaning they produce 6 to 9 additional pounds of pressure over the atmospheric pressure at that elevation (at sea level, atmospheric pressure is 14.7 psi).

Supercharger impellers on centrifugal superchargers are spun via an external pulley that is normally driven from the engine's accessory belt. Because the supercharger pulley needs to spin at very high RPM, an internal step-up causes the impeller to run at substantially higher speeds than the input pulley. The speed that the impeller spins determines how much boost the supercharger develops. Changing the input pulley size can have a large effect on the amount of boost put out by the supercharger. Smaller pulleys produce more boost. This is why having a selection of pulleys is so popular with supercharger owners. This selection allows owners the ability to squeeze every bit of power from the engine. Because pulleys only cost around $70, they are an inexpensive way to test and tune your supercharger at different boost levels.

Many people assume that running a supercharger, and hence added intake boost, puts added strain on an engine's parts. This is not necessarily true, because engine damage is almost always caused by high RPM. Because a

The supercharger's compressor head is what makes the power for the engine.

This ProCharger supercharger is being installed onto the 427-cubic-inch engine. It sits beside the engine and requires an oil supply to keep it lubricated.

tems) use engine oil to lubricate the step-up gears and keep heat and friction to a minimum.

While this lubrication is the most common and works well, it does require the engine's oil pan to be tapped so the supercharger can draw engine oil from the engine. The ATI self-contained systems use oil to provide lubrication, but they use proprietary oil that stays inside the supercharger head unit and never requires changing. This system is efficient and does not require the engine's oil pan to be tapped, but it is noisier than Powerdyne's belt drive system. Typical superchargers bolted onto a stock LS1 or LS2 engine add about 120 hp to the rear wheels.

supercharger helps the engine produce more power at lower RPM, a supercharged engine makes the same horsepower as its naturally aspirated counterpart at substantially lower engine RPM. Many of today's street engines are designed to run up to 6,000 rpm. Some people think that a supercharger increases the engine's compression to the point of detonation. Detonation exists when the combustion pressure is so high that the inlet charge ignites before the spark plug fires. When this happens, combustion takes place while the piston is still traveling up the cylinder bore. This puts tremendous loads on the piston, rod, and crank. Most supercharger kits include a boost timing retard chip that retards the engine's ignition timing to prevent detonation.

Because superchargers spin at such high speeds, they often create a substantial amount of heat and require lubrication to keep friction to a minimum. Different supercharger companies have combated heat and friction in different ways. While no single method is the best, each has advantages and disadvantages. Powerdyne uses an internal belt to spin internal gears (step-up drive), which minimizes heat, is very quiet, and lasts for over 50,000 miles. This internal belt never slips, and does not require your engine's oil supply for lubrication. It is one of the easiest superchargers to install. Vortech, Paxton, and ATI (except ATI's self-contained sys-

Intercoolers

Both turbochargers and superchargers can utilize intercoolers to improve performance. Intercoolers cool the air after it has been discharged from the turbo or supercharger before it enters the intake manifold. The cooler air provides a denser air charge, which can make added horsepower, especially under higher boost conditions. Intercoolers are popular for racing applications, but are not normally needed for street drivers running 6 to 9 psi of boost.

Intercoolers work well for turbocharged and supercharged engines by cooling the charged air before it enters the engine.

CHAPTER 9

DRAG RACING

Drag racing is a sport for everybody. Here, two friends are racing against each other to see who has the fastest ride.

Corvette owners are very proud of how well our cars handle and accelerate. The rush of speed that they can provide is hard to describe. Unfortunately, at every traffic light you pull up to, someone invariably wants to "race" you. It's tempting to go for it, but if you do it routinely, the long arm of the law will eventually catch you. Illegal "street racing" probably still occurs in your town, usually late at night on some deserted back street. However, this type of unsanctioned racing is dangerous and sometimes fatal. So what can you do? Well, if you like drag racing, I recommend taking your C5 to one of the many hundreds of drag strips located around the country.

Top-flight drag-racing cars are usually trailored to events, because they are so highly modified. In building a competitive drag-racing Corvette, owners spend a lot of time and money shifting weight over the rear wheels. This ensures that the rear tires get maximum traction as the car leaves the starting line. This re-engineering usually makes these Corvettes more difficult to use as everyday drivers. Unlike a front-wheel-drive car, a Corvette benefits from this weight transfer because the drive wheels are in the back. Power increases vary, depending on the extent of the engine and chassis modifications the Corvette receives. A stock LS1 6-speed runs the 1/4 mile around 13.3 at 109 mph, and an automatic LS1 runs the 1/4 mile around 13.8 seconds at 103 mph.

With proper preparation, a C5 LS1 automatic has the potential to turn the 1/4 mile in a little over 10 seconds. The path to that goal is not cheap, but if you are a dedicated drag racer like Paul Smith, it is well worth the investment. Paul purchased a red, automatic LS1 Corvette coupe new in 1998. Paul originally had Mallett Cars in Berea, Ohio, modify it for drag racing, including installing a roll bar.

The LS1 automatic was a consistent winner in bracket races. With constant tweaking, Paul got the car to move from the low 13-second 1/4 mile times to the low 12s. Paul wanted his LS1 to break the 10-second mark. To do this, he

CHAPTER 9

Many one-make drag races are held at local racetracks. This Corvette-only event at Beach Bend Raceway in Bowling Green, Kentucky, is very popular.

turned to MTI Racing to work out a plan to modify his car. Owner Reese Cox put together a modification plan that Paul accepted for this car. The MTI Racing team added more bracing to the roll cage to strengthen the chassis.

Next, they massaged the LS1 motor with a set of Air Flow Research heads and a more radical cam. The stock 346-cubic-inch LS1 is now producing 415 rwhp. MTI Racing also installed a Callaway Honker air intake and new set of headers. Next, a 4,500-rpm high-stall converter was inserted into an MTI-modified automatic transmission. The transmission was installed with no lockup. The new torque converter produces 520 ft-lbs of torque.

Serious drag-racing enthusiasts who want to be competitive usually modify their cars to the point where they are no longer street-able.

This West Coast Corvette-sponsored Black Attack 427 FRC produces so much rear weight transfer that it requires "wheelie bars" to keep it on the ground.

The consistency of an automatic pays off in drag racing. The green automatic has put a half a nose on this yellow Z06.

DRAG RACING

Paul Smith got this Mallett-prepared 1998 coupe into the low 12s.

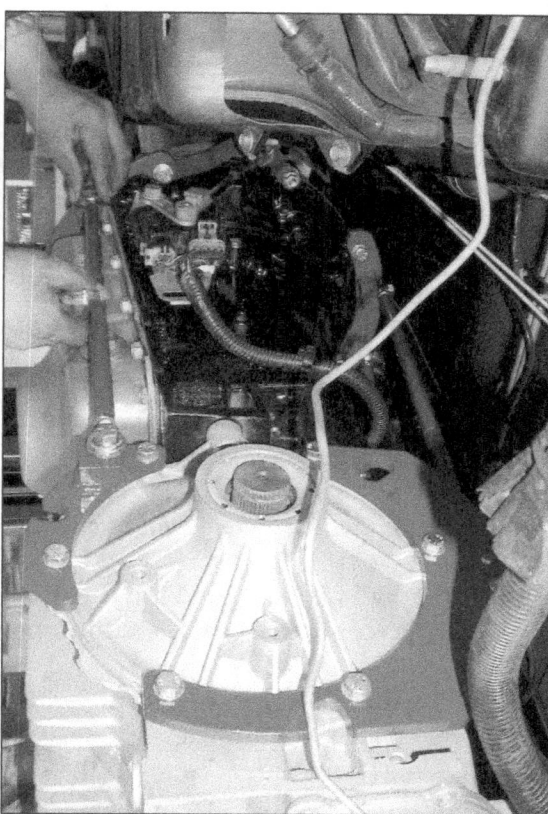
MTI installed this Dyno Tech rear-end cradle to help strengthen the GM gear case. The rear end is attached to a modified automatic transmission.

When Paul agreed to let MTI Racing use his car for a drag-racing development ride, the first thing they did was reinforce the roll bar.

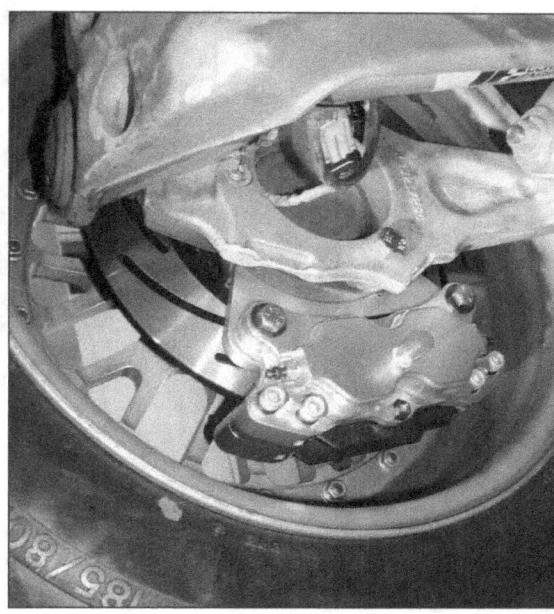
Standard factory front brakes were replaced with these lightweight Strange calipers and rotors.

MTI installed strengthened DynoTech Engineering rear axles and a rear-end cradle to prevent torque from shattering the axle case.

The front sway bar was removed from the C5 to reduce weight. The standard front factory brakes were replaced with lightweight Strange calipers and rotors. These lightweight units work well, while saving a lot of front-end weight. Low-resistance front shocks were installed to help shift weight to the rear on the starting line. The

HIGH-PERFORMANCE C5 CORVETTE BUILDER'S GUIDE

CHAPTER 9

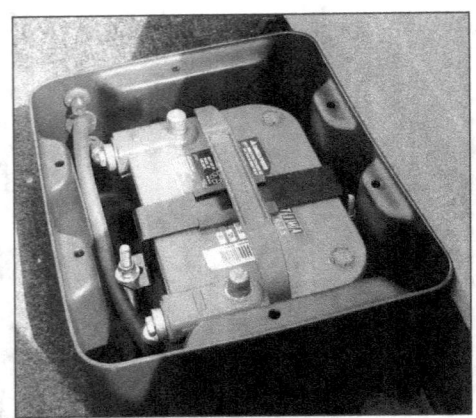

The battery was relocated from the engine compartment to the rear cargo area for better weight transfer.

Mickey Thompson 275/55R16 drag radials are fitted onto Complete Custom Wheels.

battery was relocated to the back cargo compartment for additional weight transfer.

Base front and rear springs remained in the car. These soft springs help the car squat in the rear and rise in the front under hard launches for good weight transfer. The headlights were removed and the covers were fixed into a non-opening position.

Lightweight, M&H Skinnie tires (P185 x 16 inch) were mounted on Complete Custom Wheels (CCW) 5.5-inch rims. On the rear, M&H 275/55R16- inch drag radials were mounted on 11-inch CCW wheels. Finall,y an MTI heat-treated rear axle with 4:10 gears was installed. Paul was happy with MTI Racing's completed work. The real proof to see if the car improved was on the track. Well, it did. Paul's son, Paul Jr., routinely clocks a 1.373 60-foot time, which really helps get this car to the timing lights quickly. Paul Jr. launches the car between 1,800 to 2,000 rpm, and the red C5 usually lifts both front tires 6 to 10 inches off the ground. Paul Jr. runs consistent 10.58s at 125+ mph. This car is strictly a bracket racer and, with his amazing 1.373-second 60-foot time, Paul's red C5 takes home a lot of bacon. Paul runs his C5 in the Sportsman Pro ET class with great results. 90% of today's drag racing falls into the bracket category. In Chapter 2, I told you that almost 119,000 C5 coupes were built from 1997 to 2004. This is a great car to look for if you want to go drag racing. I recommend finding a car with minimal accessories for weight reasons. These are great cars to take to the weekend drags.

Here is another example of a stock C5 that is used for drag racing. This car is a 2002 Z06 6-speed, and

Another weight-saving MTI trick was eliminating the pop-up headlight units and motors. The covers are permanently fixed in the closed position.

These Complete Custom 5 -1/2-inch front wheels are another weight-saving trick used to extract more performance out of the Corvette.

You can see the full effect the MTI weight-transfer program had on Paul Smith's car on the starting line. His son Paul Jr., pulled his best 1.373 60-foot time with this setup.

Paul and his son have been very successful drag racing this 1998 automatic C5 coupe.

the times are shown with stock tires and a new air intake and Drag radials.

Stock Engine, Stock Tires: 11.81, 117.26, 1.78, 60-foot times. Non-factory air intake and Drag Radials: 11.52, 120.21, 1.64, 60-foot times.

2002 Z06

The drag radials and the air intake make this a worthwhile change to improve this car's performance. Again, as we have mentioned in other parts of this book, C5s respond well to bolt-on additions to its engine and drivetrain. If you really need a fast C5 drag Corvette, call Lingenfelter. I witnessed an automatic 2000 Lingenfelter twin-turbo 427 FRC turn an 8.89 @156.5 mph. The late John Lingenfelter started out his career in drag racing and he was hard to beat. A 1,000-hp twin-turbo Lingenfelter Corvette retails for over $225,000! It's only money.

The National Hot Rod Association (NHRA) and the International Hot Rod Association (IHRA) both offer sanctioned drag races at approved racetracks. Sanctioned racetracks have to follow the rules of their governing body to hold events. These rules typically cover registration, track safety, emergency medical personnel, car classification, protests, and timing equipment.

These tracks also must provide competitors with properly designed racetracks that include adequate stopping areas. A drag race is an acceleration contest from a standing start between two vehicles over a measured distance. The accepted standard for that distance is either a 1/4 mile (1,320 feet) or 1/8 mile (660 feet). NHRA tends to support 1/4-mile racing and IHRA supports 1/8-mile events. Drag racing is a series of two-vehicle, tournament-style

I witnessed this innocent-looking, 1,000-horsepower Lingenfelter twin-turbo 427 FRC make an 8.89 @ 156.5 mph pass down the 1/4 mile.

CHAPTER 9

The late John Lingenfelter (left) and tuner Chuck Mallett were swapping stories at a Corvette event. John drove the Callaway "Sledgehammer" on its 254.6-mph record run.

A five-point NHRA roll bar is required for any car that turns an 11.49 or faster elapsed time.

These two Corvettes are jumping off the starting line in a head-to-head race.

Both drivers must trip the starting photocells to light up the Christmas tree to activate the starting lights.

eliminations. The losing driver of each race is eliminated, and the winning drivers progress until only one, the winning driver, remains. Each race is started by means of an electronic device commonly called a "Christmas Tree." It was given this name because its multicolored starting lights resemble a Christmas Tree. On each side of the Tree are seven lights: two small amber lights at the top of the fixture, followed in descending order by three larger LED lights, a green bulb, and a red bulb. Two light beams cross the starting-line area and connect to trackside photocells. These photocells are wired to the Christmas Tree and electronic timers in the control tower.

When the front tires of a vehicle break the first light beam, called the pre-stage beam, the pre-stage light on the Christmas Tree indicates that the racer is approximately seven inches from the starting line. When a competitor rolls forward into the stage beam, the front tires are positioned exactly on the starting line

HIGH-PERFORMANCE C5 CORVETTE BUILDER'S GUIDE

and the stage bulb is lit on the Tree, which indicates that the vehicle is ready to race. When both vehicles are fully staged, the starter activates the Tree, and both drivers focus on the three large amber lights on his or her side of the Tree. All three large amber lights flash simultaneously, followed 0.4 second later by the green light; or, the three bulbs flash consecutively 0.5 second apart, followed 0.5 later by the green light. Two competitors are monitored for their elapsed time and speed on each run. Upon leaving the staging beams, each vehicle activates an elapsed-time clock, which is stopped when that vehicle reaches the finish line. The start-to-finish clocking is the vehicle's elapsed time (ET), which serves as a performance measure. Each lane is timed independently. The first vehicle that crosses the finish line wins, unless, in applicable categories, it runs quicker than its dial-in (dial) or index. A racer also may be disqualified for leaving the starting line too soon. This could also occur if a competitor leaves his or her lane by crossing the track centerline or hitting anything such as a wall, guardrail, or track fixture.

Another action that could lead to disqualification is failing to stage properly, or failing a post-run inspection. Some sanctioning bodies weigh each car and check their fuel after each run. They also do a complete engine teardown after a victory. Both NHRA and IHRA use a handicap starting system to equalize competition in certain categories. This system enables vehicles of varying performance levels to compete against each other on an equal basis. The estimated elapsed times for each vehicle are compared, and the slower car is given a handi-

This MTI Racing LS1 engine produces 410 rwhp and 565 ft-lbs of torque.

cap head start. By using this system, virtually any two vehicles can be paired in a competitive drag race.

Here's how it works. If car A chooses a dial of 16.00 and car B chooses a dial of 14.50, car A gets a 1.5-second head start. If both vehicles cover the 1/4 mile in exactly the predetermined elapsed time, the win goes to the driver with the best reaction time, or whoever reacts quickest to the green "go" signal on the Christmas Tree. If a driver runs quicker than his or her dial, he or she is said to break out and is disqualified. If both drivers run quicker than their dials, the win goes to the driver who breaks out by the least. A foul start, or red light, takes precedence over a breakout, so a driver who red-lights is automatically disqualified even if his or her opponent breaks out. If both vehicles cover the 1/4 mile in exactly the predetermined elapsed time, the win goes to the driver who reacts quickest to the starting signal. Reaction to the starting signal is called "reaction time." Both lanes are timed independently of one another, and the clock does not start until the vehicle actually moves. Because of this, a vehicle may sometimes appear to have a mathematical advantage in comparative elapsed times but can actually lose the race. This fact makes starting line reflexes extremely important in drag racing.

The drag-racing fraternity has increased tremendously in recent years, with more and more people converting their everyday street cars into 1/4-mile rockets. Modifications to a Corvette can be anything from just changing the intake and exhaust to a full, twin-turbo conversion. This could include turbos, nitrous oxide,

CHAPTER 9

This 2001 convertible and 1996 Corvette just got the green light to start a heads-up race.

bigger engine capacity, or replacing standard body panels with aftermarket lightweight products. For many, drag racing is just a hobby, but others, like Lingenfelter, have turned their hobby into a successful business.

As we have said before, drag races are conducted in heats over a distance of 1/4 or 1/8 mile. The driver with the best time wins and goes on to the next heat. This continues until a final winner is achieved in the class. Cash prizes and trophies are awarded to the winners, but most compete for the fame achieved and the pure thrill of going at such high speeds. A well-tuned Corvette street car can run a 12-second ET and reach a speed of 115 mph on a 1/4-mile track. The times you achieve are also based on the height above sea level of the racing track. Drag Racing has become a way of life for many competitors. People still like to race illegally on the street rather than on a drag strip. Some feel the danger makes it more thrilling. I think you not only endanger yourself by doing this, you also endanger innocent people.

There are some things to remember the first time you attempt to race your car at the drags. The race winner is determined when the elapsed time is scored by two lights. The first is when the light turns green at the start, and the second is when the front end passes through the traps at end (far end) of the track. In practice, it is necessary for the driver to "jump the gun" by a fraction of a second, starting the car during the split-second interval between when the yellow light goes out and the green light goes on. However, if the car crosses the electric eye (beam) in front of it before the green light comes on, the driver has red-lighted and is disqualified. (If both cars red-light, only the first car to cross is disqualified.) A driver who gets a substantial lead at the start is said to have gotten a holeshot. The driver's reaction time (like Paul Jr.'s 1.373, 60-foot time) is crucial to winning a drag race. Timing lights also record the car's top speed, in addition to the ET that is shown on the timeslip. The car that crosses the finish line first wins. A car can actually blow an engine part way down the strip and coast to the end of the track at a (relatively) lower top speed than the competitor, and still win with a lower elapsed time. This is called "heads-up racing," and is used in all professional classes.

In the common Eliminator racing format, the losing car and driver are removed from the contest, while the winner goes on to race other winners, until only one is left. In some instances, there are three cars remaining. In that case, one car—either chosen at random or the car with the fastest elapsed time at that point—gets a "bye run," where his or her car goes down the track by itself (in order to at least partially eliminate the advantage that otherwise comes from the engine having one less run on it) and then awaits the winner of the other two for the title. However, in most Eliminator formats, the bye runs take place only in the first round. Drivers are equally divided between making an easy pass on the bye run so as not to stress the car unduly, or making a real effort for the benefit of the spectators.

As I mentioned before, the NHRA oversees the majority of drag 1/4-mile racing events in North America. The next largest organization, the IHRA, is about one-third the size of the NHRA and conducts a majority of 1/8-mile events in North America. Nearly all drag strips associate and select one or the other of these sanctioning bodies. The NHRA is more popular because of its large, 1/4-mile, nationally recognized tracks, while the IHRA is a favorite of smaller, 1/8-mile, local tracks. One reason for this (among others) is that the IHRA is less restrictive in its rules and less expensive to be associated with.

There are literally hundreds of different classes in drag racing, each with different requirements and restrictions on things such as weight, engine size, body style, modifications, and many others. The NHRA and IHRA share some of these classes, but many classes are only used by one sanctioning body or the other. The NHRA boasts over 200 classes, while the IHRA has fewer. Both organizations even have a class for aspiring youngsters—Junior Dragster. During a race, vehicles are classified based on the extent of modifications that have been made to a car. Classifications take into account engine capacity, number of cylinders, and if it is turbocharged or supercharged or has nitrous oxide installed. These classifications are in place to ensure that all of the cars are evenly matched. To allow different horsepower cars to compete against each other, some competitions use a handicap system. This system delays faster cars on the starting line long enough to even things up with a slower car. This may be based on rule differences between the cars in Stock, Super Stock, and Modified classes, or on a competitor's chosen dial-in in bracket racing.

The victory goes to the driver who is able to precisely predict elapsed time, whether it is fast or slow. This, in turn, makes victory much less dependent on large infusions of money, and more dependent on skill. Therefore, bracket racing is popular with casual weekend racers. Many of these recreational racers drive their vehicles to the track, race them, and then simply drive them home. Most tracks do not host national events every weekend, so they host events for weekend racers. Organizationally, however, the tracks are run according to the rules of either the NHRA or the IHRA (for the most part). Even street vehicles must pass a safety inspection prior to being allowed to race.

Paul Smith, Jr., heats up the rear tires before starting another bracket race.

Blown-alcohol and nitrous-oxide-injected Pro Modifieds with 2,000 horsepower engines are capable of running in the low 6-second range at over 230 mph. The IHRA Pro Stocks are just behind, running in the 6.3-second range at over 210 miles per hour, while the NHRA Pro Stocks run in the high sixes at over 200 miles per hour. Top Sportsman and Dragsters, the two fastest sportsman classes, run a bracket-style race and can range from the 6.4-second range at 210 mph to the high sevens at over 170 miles per hour. Cars in Super Comp/Quick Rod are either dragsters or doorcars, but run with a throttle stop. Some of these cars can run as low as a 7.50 at around 180 mph without a throttle stop. Recent NHRA rule changes have been making Pro Stock cars smaller. Engines have been changed from 500 cubic inches (8.2-liter V-8s) to factory-modified 4- and 6-cylinder double overhead camshaft engines. Competitors are allowed to convert a Pro Stock car to a Sport Compact Pro Rear Wheel Drive car. Corvette tuner John Lingenfelter, driving a Chevrolet Cavalier, lost his life driving one of these compacts.

The Burnout

When approaching the starting line (also known as the staging area), most racers apply water (formerly bleach) to the rear tires, either by backing into a small puddle (the water box) or having it sprayed on. The car then exits the

This 550-horsepower Callaway Z06 is able to produce spectacular burnouts.

water and does a burnout to heat the tires, making them even stickier. Some cars have a mandatory line-lock that prevents the rear brakes from engaging when the brake pedal is depressed (which can be toggled on and off). This allows the car to remain stationary (with the brakes applied) without burning up the rear brake pads while doing a burnout. Cars in street classes (must be street legal) are the only exception to this pre-race ritual, as the grooved tires tend to retain some of the water.

Staging

After the burnout comes the staging phase, where the cars pull up to the starting line. Each lane has its own string of lights on the Christmas Tree, with two small orange lights on top. These are the pre-staged and staged lights. The two cars slowly creep forward until the first (pre-staged) orange light is lit. This means they are very close to the actual starting line (a mere 7 inches). Then the cars nudge forward until the second (staged) light is lit. This indicates they are at the starting line. When both cars have lit both bulbs, the starter begins the Christmas Tree.

The Nitrous Purge

Only cars running nitrous oxide can do this. The driver pushes a button that activates a solenoid called a purge valve, which clears the gaseous nitrous oxide in the line out into the atmosphere without entering the

The Christmas tree on the right is showing green lights to these two Corvettes as they start their race.

DRAG RACING

These two supercharged C5s are having a close head-to-head race. The yellow coupe is an automatic and the Z06 is a 6-speed. The automatic won this race.

These same two cars switched lanes for another run against each other.

disqualification. In the case of a double disqualification in which one driver commits a foul start and the second driver crosses into his opponent's lane, the driver who committed the foul start wins. Another important consideration is when to shift gears. Most drag cars are shifted manually by the driver, and there are optimum times for shifting that vary with each car. Typically, power increases as the engine RPMs increase, but only up to a point before power begins to taper off. The ideal time to shift is at the peak power point. Most drag racers use a tachometer to judge shift points. In Fuel classes especially, pedalling the car (adjusting the throttle) to prevent loss of traction is often important and is one measure of how good a driver he or she is. Strategies for crossing the finish line usually only involve bracket racing. If one car has a huge lead, it may slow down before crossing the finish line to prevent a breakout. Especially in bracket racing, it is not uncommon to see the leading vehicle's brake lights come

motor. This brings the liquid nitrous oxide towards the motor, ensuring a correct mixture of nitrous oxide and fuel when the system is activated. Motors that utilize nitrous oxide are generally built with stronger internals to facilitate the increased combustion temperatures and pressures seen in a nitrous-injected (sprayed) powerplant.

The Race

Several things are important on the way down the track in drag racing. First, do not cross into your opponent's lane, as this results in

Gate attendants determine which class you will run in when you enter the track.

HIGH-PERFORMANCE C5 CORVETTE BUILDER'S GUIDE

CHAPTER 9

Safety equipment is mandatory if your car turns an 11.49 or faster ET.

This car passed tech inspection and is getting its number put on the rear window with shoe polish.

on briefly before the finish line. If both cars break out, the car closer to their dial-in wins.

While the professional and other faster classes get all the attention on television and in the press, there are far more casual and weekend racers, like Corvette owners, to whom it's just an enjoyable hobby. Many potential first-time amateur drag racers are put off by their lack of knowledge as to what to do. Even if you have a 13.0-second or slower car, it is relatively easy to have an enjoyable weekend at the track.

Other cars run at the sportsman level and are usually not street driven. They are Super Comp/Quick Rod cars, Top Dragster vehicles, Top Sportsman cars, cars that run in Super Gas/Super Rod and Super Street/Hot Rod, and vehicles built specifically for bracket racing. Each track usually has three car categories and a Super Pro Bike category. The car categories are Super Pro (any electronic devices are allowed, from 7.00 to 12.99 or depending on the track), Pro (door-cars with no electronics except for a transbrake, 9.00 to 14.99), and Street (no electronics allowed, full street equipment, must be street legal, 12.00 to 17.99).

When You Arrive

If you are racing, most of the time you need to have your Corvette tech'ed, which means inspected. Gate attendants (where you enter and pay) are used to this question, and know whether a street car needs to be tech'ed or not. Two things can happen here. First, you need to have the car tech'ed and should go to this area. Second, street classes have no tech requirement (mostly IHRA tracks), so you simply head for the pit area. In the case of a tech requirement, you need an official to look over the car and be sure there are things such as seat belts, a correct helmet (if required), street-legal tires, a correct exhaust, and other street-legal items. The tech official (assuming the vehicle passes) then uses his white shoe-polish to paint

DRAG RACING

Competitors like to talk "trash" with each other between runs in the pits.

an identifying number on your upper-passenger windshield, and possibly on a side window as well. The official then gives you a slip verifying you have been tech'ed, and you may then proceed to the pit area. In the case of no tech requirements, be sure to save the stub you got at the gate, since you need it before being allowed to race.

The Pits

Unlike NASCAR, the pit area in amateur drag racing is a huge parking lot. If your car didn't need to be tech'ed, you need a number on your windshield. Although most tracks have an official who supplies the number, not all do. Use the shoe polish up high on the passenger side, then draw a line under it. The pit area is where everyone in amateur drag racing walks around and enjoys talking to other people, seeing similar cars, and generally just talking trash with others over performance.

Arriving early, as mentioned, means you can get in line to do a few practice runs down the track. During these runs, it's only practice, so you could conceivably be paired up with a much faster car. The object here is not to win, but to simply get a feel for how your car performs. All tracks have a place back around the pits where you can get a timeslip after a run.

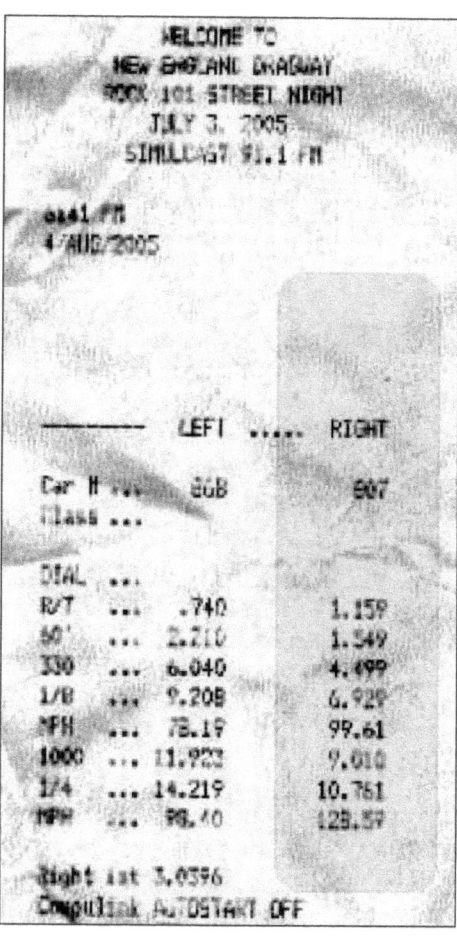

This Callaway Corvette driver had a 60-foot time of 1.549 seconds and ran a 10.761 @ 128.59 mph. The timing slip provides the owner with a lot of information.

Timeslip

Years ago, timeslips were written out by hand, but now they are computerized. A quarter mile is a fair amount of distance, and after slowing down the car needs to turn around (not on the track—there are roads leading back to the pit area, called return roads). A small building or other place is where you get a slip of paper with your number at the top (and the one you raced against as well).

Paul Smith has decided to run his 1998 automatic coupe with an 11.10 dial-in time. If he runs faster than the time posted, he will break out and lose the race.

HIGH-PERFORMANCE C5 CORVETTE BUILDER'S GUIDE

During the 1997 One Lap race, Jim Minneker lines his C5 up next to a twin-turbo Porsche in a bracket race at Memphis Speedway. Jim never broke out and won this event against all competitors.

Aside from winning or losing, practice runs are the same as the real thing. You get your ET, your average speed through the final 66 feet of the track (MPH at finish, or trap speed), and your reaction time. Most tracks also include your time at various intervals on the way down the track. One of the most common is the 60-foot time. The 60-foot time is a good indication of how quickly you got off line.

Dialing In

Before actual racing begins, drag racers need to dial in, or put their estimated time on their windshield underneath the ID number. The time is to the hundredth, as in "14.55." After a couple of practice runs, most racers have an idea of how his or her vehicle is going to perform. It is worth noting that the time you post is an estimate of your car's quickest time, since going faster than your dial-in results in disqualification, called a breakout. You are allowed to change this number as many times as you like, right up until you actually stage for the race. Shoe polish is easily removed with Windex and a few paper towels. A common ego trip for many weekend racers is to paint a ridiculous dial-in (say, 8.45) on a car that can barely do 17s and watch as people walk by and wonder what you have under the hood.

Smart racers dial in closer to their real times. For example, a Super Comp/Quick Rod Corvette in Super Pro ran two practice runs of 8.18 and 8.16, so the driver believes an 8.17 dial-in is good. His opponent in a 1967 Mustang ran times of 11.13 and 11.16, so he believes that an 11.14 is a good dial-in. The driver in the Mustang leaves three seconds before the Corvette. So there you have it, probably more than you ever wanted to know about drag racing. But trust me, it takes a lot more skill to be a 1/4-mile winner than most people think and, as in any other sport, winning is sweet glory.

This white light is what you want to see at the end of the 1/4 mile. It tells who the winner of the race is and it also gives you your speed and elapsed time.

CHAPTER 10

AUTOCROSSING

An autocross is a safe, low-cost driving competition where drivers navigate through a temporary course marked by traffic cones. Corvettes are perfect autocross cars because of their awesome handling and excellent power-to-weight ratio. Autocross events place more emphasis on car handling and driver skill than on sheer horsepower, but horsepower helps. Speeds are slower when compared to other forms of motorsports. Autocross is a national-level sport, which makes it a great way to get started in competition driving. Autocross events are usually held in large paved areas, like parking lots or

Autocross encourages both sexes to compete for fastest honors. Here, a B Street Prepared Ladies Z06 is having its tire warmers removed. The driver is getting ready to make another run at the SCCA Solo Nationals in Topeka, Kansas.

Multi-time Solo II champion Danny Popp practices his autocross starts with his 480 rwhp, A Street Prepared Z06.

HIGH-PERFORMANCE C5 CORVETTE BUILDER'S GUIDE   121

CHAPTER 10

Studying the course before an event helps a driver set a winning time. Here, Danny Popp closely inspects the course he ran later in the day.

This regional SCCA Solo II autocross event always attracts a large field of competitive cars. Competitors are very friendly and love to glean any fast secrets they can from fellow drivers.

Very little equipment is required for an autocross event. However, many competitors always bring driving shoes and gloves, a tire pump, tire gauges, and comfort items such as water and a cooler.

airfields. Drivers must learn a new course each time they compete. Prior to driving, a competitor walks the course, taking mental notes and developing a strategy for their upcoming runs. Organizations such as the Sports Car Club of America (SCCA) and the National Auto Sport Association (NASA) sponsor events throughout the United States. Local Corvette clubs sometimes hold events sponsored by their club. This chapter reviews the more popular of the two organizations that support autocross, the SCCA.

Solo Events

SCCA Solo events are all about a driver's ability to accurately and precisely maneuver around a pylon-marked course in the fastest time possible. If you think you have what it takes to beat the clock and your fellow drivers, then show up at an SCCA Solo event. SCCA Solo eventsare low-cost, low-risk, motorsport events. No competition license or roll bars are required—just add a helmet. With over 1,500 SCCA Solo events each year, you can gauge

AUTOCROSSING

Courses are marked with pylons and races are usually held in a large parking lot or a deserted airfield. This Corvette driver is negotiating an extremely tight right-hand turn on this course.

and modifications). Corvette racecars run in the Modified class. The SCCA-sanctioned events are self insured, and are conducted under the watchful eyes of their safety stewards. This is why this is one of the safest motorsports. Approximately 1,100 sanctioned Solo events, totaling more than 10,000 competitors, are held each year throughout the country. More people compete in Solo competition than in any other motorsport, save drag racing.

yourself against Corvette drivers. Each driver is individually timed to the thousandth of a second, over a short, miniature road course clearly defined using traffic cones.

Cars compete one at a time, hence the name "Solo," in a class with similar cars. Solo II emphasizes driver skill and vehicle handling rather than just speed. The corners are tight, and there are lots of them, so the driving is exciting and challenging. Speeds do not exceed those normally encountered in highway driving. The skills you learn and practice here—smooth transitions, enhanced braking, and skid correction—have an immediate impact on improving the safety and skill of your street driving. Solo is an excellent way to teach car control to young drivers in a safe environment.

Stock or Modified Class

Obtaining an official SCCA rule book is a good investment. It tells you about legal modifications, rules, and many other topics. Unmodified Corvettes are placed in the SS (Super Stock) category. Modified Corvettes are placed in A Street Prepared or B Street Prepared (depending on year

This Phoenix Racing Z06 was competing in the SS class at this autocross event. Phoenix Racing later converted this car to a T-1 racer. John Heinricy won the 2005 T-1 National Championship driving this car.

This modified B Street Prepared Z06 was driven very competitively at the Solo II Nationals in Topeka, Kansas.

HIGH-PERFORMANCE C5 CORVETTE BUILDER'S GUIDE

CHAPTER 10

- Your goal for the first run is to avoid getting lost on the course.
- Your goal for the rest of the day is to improve your time on each run.
- Your goal for the rest of the season is to beat somebody (anybody!) and continue to make each run faster than the last.

At this point, you are learning a lot on each run, and you may be 10 seconds behind the class leader. That's not unusual—you're still doing okay. Generally speaking, the veteran drivers like to help the novices. The magic words, "I am a novice," will get you extra instruction from other competitors, who can critique your run.

What to Bring to an Event

- A safety helmet (safety requirement)
- Extra air in your tires (for better handling)
- A folding chair (for comfort)
- Thermos of water (for comfort)
- Cooler (for comfort)
- Windex and paper towels (to clean your windows for best visibility)
- Caulk (to mark your tires to determine the correct air pressure)
- Shoe polish (used to mark your class and car number)
- Tire gauge (to determine the correct air pressure)
- Portable air tank (to adjust your tire pressure)

Registration

To register, you must have a valid driver's license and an entry fee ($15 to $25). Fill out the information card at the registration area. You are assigned a car number for the day. At registration, you are asked to sign the insurance waiver. You must do this to compete. Once your class and car number have been assigned, mark your car using white shoe polish on the window (it comes off with Windex).

Tech Inspection

Your car must pass tech inspection before you can compete. Read the tech inspection chapter in the rule book to see what you need to do. The tech inspector signs your card if you pass, or recommends changes to make the car pass, such as additional tie-downs for the battery or removal of loose items or center caps if you've forgotten.

Course Walking

After tech, you need to walk the course. Occasionally, course maps are available at registration. If you are a novice, a novice chief can take you on a guided walk after the drivers meeting. Try to have the course memorized before you go on the guided walk.

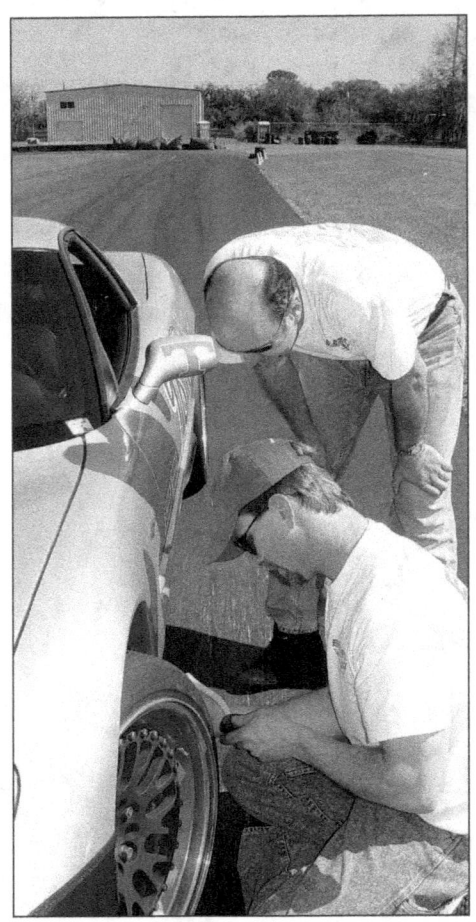

Safety is a big concern with the SCCA. Every competitor's car gets a thorough safety and technical check before it is allowed to compete in an event.

Every event starts with a driver's meeting that is followed up with a walk around the course. This group is finishing up their driver's meeting and will soon walk the course.

Drivers Meeting

The driver's meeting is *mandatory for all drivers*. The event chair holds the meeting approximately one-half hour before the first car starts. Be sure to attend. This is where you find out information about the course conditions, number of runs, particular safety concerns, and how penalties are assessed.

AUTOCROSSING

Lining up behind the competitor in front of you helps keep the event moving smoothly and quickly.

If you spin out or get lost during your run, don't panic: straighten your car out and complete your run.

This is a typical starting gate at a small parking lot autocross. The cones placed on the left of this photo tell the driver that he or she needs to turn left at the end of the short straight.

Your Runs

You usually have a minimum of three timed runs. Find out who is running before and after you, so you know where to line up. Running in order makes the timing people's job easier, and keeps the event running smoothly. The event chair calls out which classes are to come to the grid. Once you are on the grid, wait for the cars in front of you to launch, and then move up until you are on the start line.

A starter waves a green flag when it is okay for you to start. The green flag means go as soon as you are ready—the timer does not start until you pass through the lights. If you get "lost" on course, take the time to orient yourself and continue. Don't head back to the start line, because you may be pointed toward another car. Times are posted after each run. Your fastest run of the day is used to determine your finishing position.

The Awards

After the event, everyone meets for the trophy presentation. The location for the presentation is usually announced at the driver's meeting. The event chair and his/her assistants give out results and present trophies to the top third of each class, plus a trophy for Fastest Time of the Day (FTD).

Penalties

A penalty is given if:
- A cone is knocked over and is out of the box.
- A cone is knocked over and is in the box.
- A cone remains standing but is out of the box.

A DNF is given if:
- You spin out of control and cannot continue.
- Your car experiences mechanical failure.
- You get lost on the course.
- You disobey the track marshal's instructions.

A penalty is NOT given if:
- The cone remains standing and is touching the box.
- The cone remains standing and is partially in the box.
- And, of course, if the cone remains standing within the box.

Car Setup Tips

You may want to put more go-fast goodies on your Corvette, but make sure to read the rule book, and stay legal for your category. But keep in mind, at this point you can go faster sooner by working on your driving skills instead of on the car. The 2001–2004 Z06 is a top choice among SS autocross competitors. It offers the best standard suspension, tires, and engine components for the class. If you want to run in a Modified class, the 1999–2000 FRC and the 2001–2004 Z06 are top choices. The FRC is less expensive to purchase, especially if you are going to modify the car for a street prepared category.

National Solo II Champion Jerry Onks checks his tire pressure before and after each autocross run.

Tires

Remember to put extra air in your tires. The reason for this is to keep your tires from rolling under during hard cornering. But how much is too much? Put chalk on the edges of your tire, in three places around the diameter, and you can see how far over the tire was going during your runs. Bleed out a little air if the chalk is still showing on the tread, or add a little more if the chalk has been worn off down the sidewall. The line of worn chalk remaining should be right at the corner of the tread and sidewall. Keep notes on how many PSI you ran and where the chalk line was for your next event. Remember, as you get better and corner harder, you'll need more air to compensate, so keep using the chalk at every event.

Driver Restraint

In order to have good car control in driving, you have got to stay put, so make sure your seat belt is

The 2001–2004 Z06 is very popular in the SS class. The car is fairly inexpensive to purchase and is a fast and nimble autocross competitor.

Jerry uses a high-quality, six-point seat belt attached to a bar behind the seats. These belts keep him securely fastened to his seat during violent turning maneuvers.

AUTOCROSSING

tight and firm. Some people like to tug hard on the shoulder strap to engage the lock on the seat-belt reel. Highly modified cars sometimes use a six-point seat belt for added safety.

Driver Location

Most experienced drivers agree that the best place for your seat—to give you the best control—is forward far enough to have your leg slightly bent when the clutch is all the way to the floor, and to have the seatback reclined or upright to a position that allows you to rest your wrists on the steering wheel when your shoulders are firmly against the seat. This position allows you to run the full range of steering inputs and foot motion without stretching or moving in your seat, and can have a huge impact on your driving skill.

Alignments

If you're looking for a cheap way to improve your Solo II setup, this is a good one. Corvette factory specs are established for everyday street driving. Improving your car's turn-in for autocross may make your car twitchy on the street, so use your own discretion. To get some suggestions, ask a driver who has a car similar to yours.

Course Walking

Your first walk gives you the general layout. Walk the course alone, concentrating on memorizing the layout. Think of it in sections, with key cones marking the turns, such as start straight, slalom (enter on right), decreasing sweeper to the left, right-hand curve, thread-the-needle section, and finish. Stop every now and then and run through the course in your head, from the beginning to where you are. Get down—the course looks different from a seated position. This gives you a better picture of what the course looks like at speed.

Pace off the distance between cones in a slalom. Some course designers vary the distance, and it's good to know before you arrive whether you need to vary your speed in a slalom. Take a notepad if you like, and make notes such as pavement changes, camber change, bumps, sand, etc. Make a mental note to yourself (or write it down) how far ahead to look. This helps you to remember to look ahead while you are driving. There is no need to memorize *every* cone on the course, only the ones you plan to be near—the "important" ones. Look from one important cone to the next in your plan.

In Grid

Before you run, while you are in grid, go over the course again several times in your head, executing the plan you made.

Correct alignment settings are an autocross driver's secret weapon. Here, MTI technician David Munder checks this C5's alignment before heading to the racetrack.

Champion Danny Popp spends a few minutes going over his car before he starts another run.

HIGH-PERFORMANCE C5 CORVETTE BUILDER'S GUIDE

CHAPTER 10

After Your Run

Sit in your car and go over your run. Figure out where you didn't execute the plan. If the plan was to be near a particular cone and you were five feet from it, then you didn't execute the plan correctly. This should have made a red light go off in your head. Maybe you need to adjust the plan because you were going too fast in the slow parts.

Driving Tips

Look Ahead

I can't emphasize this enough. It's so easy to forget, but it makes such a big impact on driving. It all relates to hand-eye (and eye-foot) coordination. Look where you want your hands to drive you, and look far enough ahead to take advantage of the feedback. If you're looking at the outside cone that you're afraid of hitting, well, you'll hit it. If you're looking 10 feet in front of the bumper, the turns will keep surprising you. Imagine looking at your feet while you are running on foot! You won't be very coordinated, and you won't have a good sense of distance or speed. The same goes for driving hard corners in autocross. Look ahead. You may be astounded at your performance the first time you remember to do this all the way through a course.

Slow Down to Go Fast

A common problem when you're starting out is trying to take the tight sections too fast, and not staying in control. Just be patient in the slow spots. They're slow spots, after all.

Danny Popp is on his way to a class victory on this run. He is a master at properly using his brakes and throttle to swiftly get him through the cones.

Brake Hard in Corners

Go ahead, squeeze the brakes hard. There's no morning coffee on your dashboard, or eggs in the front seat. Once you decide to slow down for the corner, don't waste any time. If you find yourself at a crawl and you're not at the corner yet, you've just found out that you can brake later. Locking up your tires does not make you stop faster, so squeeze the brakes and let them do the work, not your tires.

Adhesion

Don't ask too much of your tires. For any tire/pavement pair, there's only a certain amount of traction. You can use up that traction

This SS Corvette driver is braking very hard in a straight line before sweeping through this next set of cones.

with your throttle, your brakes, or your steering wheel. So if you're going into a corner using 100% of your traction to make the turn, what happens when you ask for more traction by applying the brakes? Either you won't brake or you won't turn. Or both. Same goes for accelerating out of a corner. Ease into the throttle as you ease out of the turn. So use full throttle and full braking only in a straight line. This goes back to slowing down to go faster, and brings us to...

Smooth Inputs

You may have noticed that I used the phrases "squeeze the brakes" and "ease in the throttle." This is where you have to change your mindset about inputs to controlling your car. You need to convince yourself that you can make your car respond better by squeezing the brakes hard instead of standing on the brakes, by rolling in the throttle rapidly instead of stomping on the gas, by turning the wheel quickly instead of cranking it around. Subtle, but it shows up in how often your car is in control instead of scrubbing off speed pushing around a corner. And it takes a lot of practice to become second nature.

Shift Near Redline

On the street, we don't usually shift near redline (high RPM). But in autocross, you want to be making the most of the power available to you. You'll learn to hear the motor as you drive and to stay in a lower gear longer. Most courses are in second or third gear for Corvettes.

Launch

Each car varies, but try to start at higher RPM (usually 2,500 rpm). Don't dump the clutch, or you'll find your wheels spinning. Let it out rapidly and find the right RPM to maintain traction. Higher horsepower cars want to use lower RPM than do less powerful cars.

Always remember to have fun, even when you are being stomped by some national hot-shoe. You'll never stop learning—the best drivers tell you this still applies after 10 or 20 years! Remember, seat-time, seat-time, seat-time. Nothing makes you go faster sooner. And nothing is less expensive in improving your times.

The Nationals

The SCCA Solo National event is held each year in September. Its current home is Topeka, Kansas. This is the Mecca of autocross, and a must-see for any car enthusiast. Each driver

Danny tests his launch procedure with every set of new tires. He wants to avoid wheel spin, while not bogging the engine at the start.

Jerry Onks is hard on the throttle after clearing this set of cones. He will use his brakes at the next gate to set up his proper entry speed.

CHAPTER 10

The SCCA Solo Nationals that are held each September in Topeka, Kansas, usually have over 900 competitors racing at this abandoned airfield.

This Corvette-powered sprint car ran in the top autocross A-Modified class. A-Modified cars usually set the event's fastest time of the day (FTD). Danny Popp came within 3/10 second of setting the FTD at this event in his A Street Prepared Corvette.

Danny Popp won several of his SCCA National Pro Solo II championships driving his father's immaculate 1972 LT-1 small-block Corvette.

competes over two days, but, if you have the time, stay for the whole show, as it takes four days to get through over 900 drivers. Corvettes are multi-year champions in SS, A, and B Street Prepared. Top Pro Solo II champion Corvette driver Danny Popp has been competing in these events for many years. He learned how to autocross from his father Herb Popp, who is also a multi-time autocross champion.

Herb Popp spotted his first Corvette in 1953 and was captivated with the styling of this new American sports car. He vowed to own a Corvette one day. His dream came true in 1960 when he took delivery of a black-on-red, 270-hp 1960 Corvette. One of the first things he did was join the Queen City Corvette Club. It didn't take Herb long to become a charter member of the National Council of Corvette Clubs. Today, he is one of the club's original 16 charter members. In 1960, Herb decided to take his new ride racing. His racetracks consisted of local Cincinnati, Ohio, parking-lot autocross events. Herb took the hubcaps off the wide-whitewall-tired Corvette and headed to a local race.

It took him several years to start winning trophies, but eventually he won so many events that he became a local legend for his autocross skills. In 1965, he took delivery of a 327/350-hp silver coupe. He bought this car because it came equipped with the new four-wheel disc brakes. Herb thought the new brakes would give him a competitive edge for autocrossing events. Sadly, he had to make room for his new purchase, so he sold his faithful 1960 Corvette. His trophy-winning ways continued with this car for seven years. His fondest memory was running the high banks of Daytona at a National Council of Corvette Clubs (NCCC) event in 1971. By then, Herb was married to Judy, his career at General Electric was firmly established, and his first child, Danny, was born. The family gave Danny his first plastic toy Corvette at Christmas when he was two. This started Danny's lifelong passion for Corvettes. Herb and Judy took their son to every weekend event, and it didn't take long before Danny was helping Dad wrench his racer.

In 1972, Herb did the only thing a new family person could do. He put more excitement into his life by buying another Corvette. His dark-blue 1972 coupe came equipped with the high-revving LT1 small-block. Of course, Herb started racing and winning with his new ride in autocross events. Upgrades included bigger wheels, tires, and side pipes. Herb's pit crew grew when son Adam came along. His wife Judy and the boys continued to attend autocross events on the weekends. While Danny and Adam were growing up, more Corvettes entered the family. A 1986 L-98 C4 joined the LT1, and both cars continued to be upgraded for autocross events. The boys drove the LT1, while Herb competed in the L-98.

Today, his son Danny competes in Solo II events with a McCluskey Chevrolet-sponsored Z06, and Adam races the L-98. The family travels to the events and serves as pit crew. Herb has passed on a good legacy for his sons to follow, and the Corvette community is better off!

Danny throws his 500+ hp Z06 around the track like a go-kart. He has amazing car control. Even if his car gets sideways, he knows how to power it out of trouble.

Danny's father Herb is standing proudly beside his new 1960, 270-hp Corvette. Herb autocrossed this car for five years.

Herb and his wife Judy have just arrived at another autocross event in Ohio. He has already removed his hubcaps. Notice the vintage 1957 fuel-injected roadster parked in the back of the photo.

CHAPTER 10

This 2003 Z06 is undergoing a tire-testing session with Danny at a private racing facility.

Danny is an ASE-Certified Corvette Specialist at McCluskey Chevrolet in Cincinnati, Ohio. McCluskey is a long-time sponsor of Danny's autocross activities.

After several hot laps on a new set of tires, Danny is shown using a pyrometer to take tire temperatures across the entire tread area of the tire. This temperature information is useful for alignment settings and tells the driver how well each corner of the car is performing.

Danny has won four SCCA Solo II and two Pro Solo II national autocross championships driving, what else? Corvettes. Like many successful champions, the spark that stirred his Corvette passion started when his parents presented him with a plastic Corvette replica at age two. At an early age, Danny started working on Dad's 1965 silver coupe and his 1972 LT1. This experience taught him the basics of being a mechanic. Dad also let Danny drive his Corvettes in autocross events. Slowly, the trophies started piling up. Dad's LT1 netted Danny five of his championships, and the blue rocket is still in the family garage.

I caught up to Danny in 2005 as he was preparing to compete in a Pro Solo National Series event. McCluskey arranged to have Danny spend two days testing at a private race facility. He was working on car setup and testing a new autocross tire for a major manufacturer. Danny did not let a minute go to waste. He ran several timed hot laps, checked the tire temps and tire pressure, and then let the car sit before the next run. Danny and his crew changed to a different tire compound and repeated the test. Everything was written down for future documentation. This testing went on from morning to night, with a short break for lunch. Danny continued to demonstrate passion, intensity, and tenacity during the busy testing session. Pleased with their results, the group packed up and headed to their Pro Solo event.

Five cars were entered in A Street Prepared, including Danny's blue Z06. The course was held at a former World War II air base. Two different courses were used during the event, one on Saturday and a different course on Sunday. Every time a competitor hit a cone, one second was subtracted from the time. Each day, each class was allowed to run the course three times, and the best time was used for a total score. This type of racing is serious. We watched Danny prepare for his run by observing other competitors on the course and placing tire warmers over all four tires to maintain their heat.

Before each run, Danny sat at the starting line, eyes closed, as he

AUTOCROSSING

moved his hands over the steering wheel like he was driving the course. How did he do? Danny negotiated the tricky one-mile course in 49.880 seconds with his Z06 and didn't hit one cone. He won his class by 4.078 seconds and missed setting the fastest time of the day over all the entered cars, including racecars, by 3/10 second! Danny left the event with a good start towards his next championship, and, from what we saw, he is truly a champion. After watching his performance, I know why he won the BSP Solo II championship in 1994, 1996, and 1999, and won two BSP Pro Solo titles in 1997 and 2000. He also won an ASP Solo II national championship driving a Z06 in 2003, and an ASP Pro Solo national championship in 2004. Danny also finished third overall in the 2005 *Car & Driver* One Lap of America. His electron-blue McCluskey-sponsored Z06 is capable of mid-11-second quarter-mile times. Car control is the key ingredient to a successful autocrosser. Solo II events are very serious affairs for the top-running competitors, and Danny Popp is among the best.

When a driver is able to master a tight corner like this, they know they have the right setup to miss pylons in a real race.

Five cars were entered in ASP on the day Danny won his class by 4.078 seconds.

Danny and teammate Jerry Onks use tire warmers before each of their runs. These warmers help make the tires stick during their hot laps.

Danny pushed his Electron Blue Z06 through the pylons at an incredible rate. He missed the FTD by 3/10 second.

CHAPTER 11

ROAD RACING

Early Corvettes (1953–1962) were ideal drag cars. In the 1950s, Corvettes were difficult to beat in stoplight races. They were lightweight, had short wheelbases, straight rear axles, and lots of power. All of these advantages helped put America's sports car ahead of the competition. This drag-racing advantage changed when the 1963 model was introduced. Chief Engineer Zora Duntov was a road racer at heart. He wanted Corvette to become the dominant production sportscar racer and pushed to have an independent rear suspension added to the car. He succeeded in 1963, when the new Stingray was introduced with an independent rear axle. This new design allowed for better cornering speeds on road courses, but it was not as effective on the drag strip. The Stingray was a great design, but suffered from excessive weight and poor brakes. When Carroll Shelby introduced the Ford Cobra in 1962, Zora Duntov knew Corvette was in trouble. He set to work on building a lightweight Corvette to compete with this new production supercar. The Cobra weighed 1,000 lbs less than the Corvette and produced close to the same power with its small-block Ford engine. Zora's answer to the Cobra was the Grand Sport. It weighed 2,000 lbs and its 388-cubic-inch engine produced close to 500 horsepower.

However, GM instituted a racing ban on all corporate products in the summer of 1963. The ban halted Grand Sport development, and GM told Zora to destroy the five prototypes that had been constructed. Zora ignored the order and sold them to private teams. Without factory support, the Grand Sports were raced for a short time and soon became uncompetitive. Meanwhile, the Ford Cobras continued to win every production race they entered.

The 1963 Corvette coupe/convertible was a startling design departure from the 1962 version. It was a hit with buyers, but had poor results on the racetrack due to its weight and poor brakes.

Only five 1962 Grand Sports were built by Zora Duntov and his engineering team. Duntov originally planned on building 100 examples of the 500-horsepower, 2,000-lb SuperVette until GM stopped production. The five remaining examples are the most valuable Corvettes ever built.

ROAD RACING

Zora Duntov sold this 1966 prototype L-88 coupe to Roger Penske in November 1965. The car won its class at the 1966 Daytona 24 hours and the 12 Hours of Sebring. Roger sold the car after Sebring.

Zora really wanted to beat the Cobras, so he continued working to improve the production Corvette's road-racing abilities. In 1965, Corvettes were equipped with four-wheel disc brakes and a big-block, 396-cubic-inch engine. In 1967, the limited-production, "off-road" L-88 427-cubic-inch-engine option was introduced. In spite of the car's weight, the L-88 had enough power to overtake the lighter Cobras, and soon Corvette was the king of the hill.

The L-88 continued to be the engine of choice through the 1960s and 1970s and was always very difficult to beat.

The fourth-generation Corvette was only available with a small-block engine. However, the new car was equipped with sophisticated electronics and a state-of-the-art lightweight aluminum suspension system. What the car lacked in straight-line acceleration was made up with racecar-like handling and braking. The new Corvette became unbeatable in showroom stock racing, and, from 1985 to the end of 1987, was never beaten in a showroom stock race.

Other manufacturers complained so loudly about Corvette's dominance that the SCCA banned them from racing in showroom stock

Crew Chief Dana English (left), John Greenwood, and Burt Greenwood work on this fourth-generation Corvette in the Nelson Ledges pits. This was the C4's debut race in June 1984 at the 24-hour showroom stock race.

Dave Heinz and Bob Johnson finished the 1972 24 Hours of Le Mans driving this English Racing L-88 Corvette. This was the first Corvette to finish Le Mans since 1960. It took 23 more years (in 1995) until a Callaway Corvette finished this grueling race.

CHAPTER 11

The 1988 and 1989 Corvette Challenge series produced very close and exciting races. The cars were colorful, loud, and fast, much to the delight of the race fans.

events in 1988. To soothe Corvette fans, the SCCA introduced the "Corvette Challenge" series in 1988. This was the first time Corvette produced a racecar at the factory.

The cars were built in Bowling Green with race-prepared engines before being sent to Protofab to have their race equipment installed. The series was cancelled after running for two years. However, the Challenge produced some of today's best drivers, including Boris Said, Andy Pilgrim, Paul Tracy, and Stu Hayner. The Challenge cars continued to be raced successfully throughout the 1990s. However, a new Corvette was beginning to emerge from the design studio that was going to replace the C4.

The fifth-generation, or C5, was introduced in the fall of 1996. During this time, another program was given corporate approval. This program authorized an outside vendor, Pratt & Miller, located in Wixom, Michigan, to design, build, and test a new production racecar called the C5-R. The car was scheduled to debut at the 1999 24 Hours of Daytona. The C5-R was tested secretly around the country at small, unknown racetracks, and was finally spotted by spy photographers in mid 1998. In the meantime, Corvette engineers were working hard on a new production C5 called the fixed-roof coupe (FRC).

This car was a less expensive version of the coupe and convertible, but also stronger and lighter than its cousins. The hardtop was non-removable, and this strengthened the entire car. Corvette engineer and race driver John Heinricy extensively tested this car in 1997 and 1998, as mentioned in Chapter 4. By the time the car was introduced as a 1999 model, a GM-approved T-1 package was available for the 1999 Corvette. Race teams bought the FRCs and began preparing them for road-racing events.

Heinricy and fellow racer and Corvette engineer Jim Minneker supported a limited-production run of 20 boxcars, available to approved race teams. The boxcars were designed to run in races for modified production cars such as the Speedvision GT series. The rules for this series allowed racers to strip the interiors, and add fuel cells and different brakes to their boxcars.

So, by the beginning of the 1999 season, Corvette had competitive racers running in three series. The first was the international endurance series with the Pratt & Miller C5-R. Next, Corvettes were competing and winning in the SCCA T-1 production-car category.

Many of today's top drivers got their start driving Corvette Challenge Corvettes. Boris Said, Andy Pilgrim, and Paul Tracy are still racing today.

ROAD RACING

GM Racing and Pratt & Miller secretly tested the new C5R for two years before it ran its first race at the 1999 24 Hours of Daytona.

Finally, Corvette boxcars were competing and winning races in the Speedvision GT pro-racing series. This was a major change for Corvette, and flooding the world with competitive racecars soon proved to be a very wise marketing decision.

Corvette engineering learned a lot of lessons with C5 racing on three very different racing venues. These lessons were used to develop a new hot-rod Corvette called the Z06. The Z06 was an improved version of the 1999 and 2000 FRC and included more horsepower and a revised suspension. Owners drive these cars during the week to work and go to track events on the weekends. The high-revving LS6 engine and crisp, nimble handling made quick work of its competition. Several high-performance driving schools opened using Corvettes. The Justin Bell Driving Experience, Bragg Smith, and Bob Bondurant driving schools all offered Z06s to their students. While Justin Bell and Bragg Smith schools are no longer available, check around for a similar type of school if you want to learn how to drive your car well.

Tuners such as MTI Racing also offer weekend driving schools.

Amateur Track Events

Some tuners participate in amateur track days at various racetracks around the United States. Tuners can prepare your car for these events for a fee. This includes car preparation, transportation to the track, driving instructions, and mechanical support for your car. In addition, tracks charge you by the day to use their facilities. Amateur events usually have three racing categories for you to enter.

These classes (usually A, B, and C) help track operators determine your skill level for safety reasons. New drivers are put into the beginner class and are forced to follow a pace car with no passing allowed. Drivers usually have to do this for at least one day. Each higher class is less supervised, until you reach the A class. In this class, you are allowed to

GM extensively tested a new version of the Corvette called the Fixed Roof Coupe (FRC) before it was introduced. This former fastback coupe was converted to the new FRC body and was undergoing aerodynamic testing by Powell Motorsports at Daytona Speedway.

This Les Stanford-sponsored FRC started life as a 1999 Boxcar. Corvette Chief Engineer Tom Wallace helped build this car. Veteran Corvette driver Bill Cooper drove it successfully during the 1999 season.

CHAPTER 11

GM Engineer John Heinricy drove this Danny Kellermeyer-prepared 1999 boxcar. John is shown on his way to victory at the last race of the year at Laguna Seca, California in 1999.

Corvettes also found numerous victories in SCCA's T-1 amateur racing series. This Jim Rathmann-sponsored T-1 Corvette was a good example of a competitive T-1 racer.

John Heinricy demonstrates how hard a competitive driver uses his brakes.

The Z06 can be driven to work during the week and then driven to the track on weekends—it is that good.

The former Justin Bell Driving Experience used Z06s and standard coupes at the driving school in Florida. This school closed, but Corvettes are still being used as school cars by Bob Bondurant's driving programs.

run your own pace and pass other cars on the straightway. Passing in the corners in any class is never allowed for safety reasons.

What You Need

Most times, 16-year-olds or older can attend (16/17 require parent's signature) a track event. A clean, maintained street vehicle (okay to trailer) is required, as is a Snell 85+ helmet (loaners usually available). The standard belt that

ROAD RACING

MTI Racing offers its customers trackside support during weekends at racetracks. It offers mechanical assistance and provide drivers with feedback on their driving style.

came with your car is approved for these events. All convertibles must be equipped with a roll bar that is above the driver's head. Vehicles with factory hoops or pop-up rollover systems are not allowed.

Driving Schools

A high-performance driving school is not a competition event. The instructors teach the basics of car control, from experienced road racers at non-racing speeds in a safe, closed-course environment. At no point should you go faster than you feel is comfortable. At no point should you go faster than your instructor feels is comfortable. There is nothing to prove. The point is to learn.

Insurance

Damage to your car is not covered by any insurance at the track. It is between you and your insurance company. Track Insurance is liability only, typical of racetrack and racing-event insurance.

When You Arrive

Complete the registration process. Complete the safety review of your car. Secure your gear in your pit area. Be at the mandatory driver's meeting on time.

Car Setup

Any C5 automatic or stick can be taken to a track event. No matter what options are on your C5, taking your car to the track can teach you valuable driving lessons in a safe, controlled environment. Participating in track events does not make you into a racecar driver; it does, however, teach you the limits of your car's suspension and braking system. Track events also teach you the difference between over-steer and under-steer and how to correct for it. Most importantly, it helps you become a better driver because you have learned what your car can and cannot do in emergency situations.

The biggest change you can make to a stock car's handling at a track event is varying your tire pressures.

What a great place to pass a Porsche! Corvettes are very good track cars, and with very little modification they are among the fastest cars on the track.

Track events break drivers into three categories: A, B, and C. This is designed to keep the less-skilled or less-experienced drivers lapping at a slower and safer pace. This B-class driver is still able to turn some pretty quick laps in this 2004 automatic coupe.

With EMT run-flat original-equipment tires, a good place to start is to add air to each tire, 3 lbs over the factory recommendations. The stock Z06 F1 Supercar tires respond well to 32 lbs front and 33 lbs rear. If your car is over-steering (the rear swings out in a corner), lower the rear-tire pressure in one-pound increments after each session.

Drivers benefit from getting feedback from experienced race drivers. This is a big payoff for people attending these weekend track events.

If your car is under-steering (front wants to go straight in a corner), increase rear-tire pressure in one-pound increments after each session. Before any track event, make sure you check the condition of your engine's serpentine drive belt.

If any cracking appears on the top or underside, I recommend replacing it. Check the level of your brake fluid and its color. If it is dark and cloudy, you should have an expert bleed the system and install fresh brake fluid. Also check your radiator level (cold engine). Make sure your coolant is fresh and is not showing any signs of rust. I also recommend a fresh oil change and checking your transmission and rear-end oil levels. Tire condition, tread depth, and alignment should also be checked. Make sure your suspension's castor and camber are set to factory settings. Racers set their cars up outside factory specs to maximize their car's handling. But for normal, non-modified cars, I recommend staying with the factory settings.

Once you have completed your preparation, you are ready to head to the track. Remember, the more stock your car is, the less track time you get. Stock C5s without oil coolers tend to overheat their oil quickly. My advice is to closely monitor your oil temperatures when on course. When you see your oil temps approaching 280 degrees, it is time to come into the pits and cool your car down. Open the hood, turn off the engine, and check your car over while you wait for the temps to return to normal. If you have a portable fan and spot an electric outlet, direct the fan under the front of the car for faster cooling.

Once you have become comfortable driving road courses, you might want to begin thinking about

A track event has a wide variety of cars, and it is a great way to learn the limits of your car.

This Ferrari is sliding backwards down the hill. The track is a much safer environment when you make a mistake versus the highway.

Passing is only allowed on the straightaway. This MTI Racing-prepared Z06 is getting ready to pass this modified C5.

modifying your car to improve its reliability, performance, and safety. Oil coolers are an excellent investment for component reliability. I recommend frequent oil changes and paying close attention to all of the car's fluids. Performance improvements should not be restricted to the engine. Performance shocks, stiffer composite springs, and thicker sway bars all dramatically improve your C5's handling. I have found that C5s respond well to 35-mm, hollow-front sway bars and to 25-mm, rear-hollow sway bars.

Cars equipped with plastic sway-bar links benefit from the addition of metal sway-bar end links from a Z06. Stock LS1 engines produce 295 to 305 rwhp. LS6 Z06 engines produce 336 to 344 rwhp. With the addition of a top-level air intake like the Callaway Honker and a good cat-back exhaust system, a stock LS1 now produces around 330 to 335 rwhp. An LS6 with similar modifications produces around 360 to 365 rwhp. The horsepower is felt on the track coming out of corners.

The lead Corvette is running perfect tire pressure, while the yellow car in the back is badly under-steering and needs a tire-pressure adjustment.

If this power is not satisfactory, your next step could be installing a head-and-cam package or a supercharger. Head-and-cam packages usually add about 80 to 100 rwhp, and a Supercharger adds around 120 rwhp. The head-and-cam installation requires that the heads, intake, and engine-drive accessories be removed during installation.

A supercharger installation requires removal of the intake and the engine-drive accessories during installation. The pros and cons of each installation are: the head-and-cam package is more expensive and produces a little less power; the supercharger is a little less expensive, produces a little more power, but has more mechanical parts to maintain; a supercharger usually requires a higher hood, which needs to be repainted to match your color. The sky is the limit when you begin heading down the trail for more power. You can combine a supercharger with a head-and-cam package or convert your LS1/LS6 block into a 383-cubic-inch or 427-cubic-inch engine. Always remember, you have to get this power onto the track. A 500-rwhp provides a non-professional race driver with plenty of thrills on a racetrack. When adding extra power, don't forget to upgrade your car's brakes, wheels, tires, and suspension. I also recommend changing your automatic transmission's torque converter. If you have a 6-speed, add a high-performance flywheel, pressure plate, and clutch for better reliability.

Most tracks require safety equipment in the top classes such as a roll bar and six-point seat belts. In the case of an off-course excursion and your car flips, a roll bar will probably save you from serious injury. Six-

The serpentine belt runs most of the engine accessories. It is vital that you routinely check this belt for wear and cracking. Keeping a spare in the trunk is a good idea.

point seat belts hold you securely into your seat and allow you better car control, because they keep you from bouncing around during hard cornering. Another big safety item is brakes. Stock C5 brakes are very good, but under hard use, the pads wear out quickly and the rotors overheat and warp. I recommend adding a set of high-performance brake pads like Hawk Ceramic or HP Plus pads. The HP Plus gives you a very aggressive brake pedal, but leaves a lot of

Good tire alignment improves handling and reduces your tire wear. If you are going to a track event, a good alignment is highly recommended.

CHAPTER 11

After lapping at high speed, it is a good idea to bring your car in, open the hood, and let it cool down.

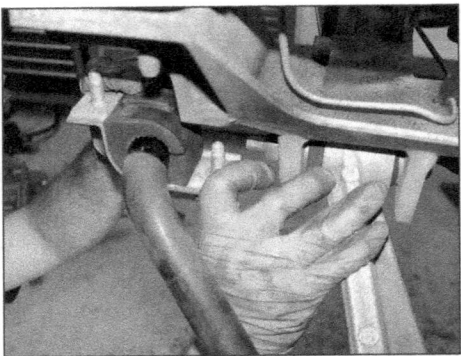

Changing to bigger front- and rear sway bars gives you much better car control in corners. This is a relatively inexpensive modification that pays big dividends on the track.

Many aftermarket vendors offer high-performance, lightweight flywheels, clutches, and pressure plates. The crankshaft weight reduction these parts offer gives your engine quicker response and improved driveline reliability.

This is a typical roll-cage arrangement in a showroom stock SCCA T-1 racecar.

brake dust on your wheels and tends to squeal during street use. The ceramic is not as dusty and is quieter on the street, but the brake feel is not as aggressive as the HP Plus. I also recommend cryo-treated slotted brake rotors.

If you are going to do a lot of weekend track events, I strongly recommend the HP Plus pads on a stock C5 brake system. If you are only going to do occasional events, then go with the ceramic pads. If you modify your car's engine to produce more power, then you need to do the same thing to your braking system. Aftermarket suppliers like Wilwood, Brembo, Baer, AP, etc., offer excellent aftermarket braking packages for your C5. Expect to pay $3,000 to $6,000 for a high-performance brake package. This might sound expensive, but if you want your car to stop from 160 mph, it is well worth it.

Driving Tips

As you head out onto the track, if it is your first time, you follow either a pace car or are placed into a line of fellow drivers. Things to look for are the lines or routes they take around each corner. It is also important to notice how they move as far to the left as possible before entering a right hand. Then notice how close they get to the curb on the right-hand corner. Coming into a corner, try to do all of your braking in a straight line. Braking in the corner upsets the car's suspension. Gently feed the car as much power as it can take as you exit the corner, until you are in a straight line.

The pace car has been around the track enough to know the best line. Learning its route helps you to quickly start turning good lap times. As you become more comfortable with your car and the track, your lap times drop. It's easy to become hooked on this kind of racing.

Equipment needed

When you go to the track, I recommend taking simple tools like screwdrivers, pliers, wire, wire cutters, electric tape, duct tape, flashlight, portable air pump, air gauge, small jack, and a lug wrench. This assortment of tools allows you to make minor repairs to your car that might prevent you from leaving the track. Track time is expensive, so you want to utilize every minute that is available to you. If you have room,

ROAD RACING

Good seatbelts keep you from bouncing around at high speeds. These are a good safety investment.

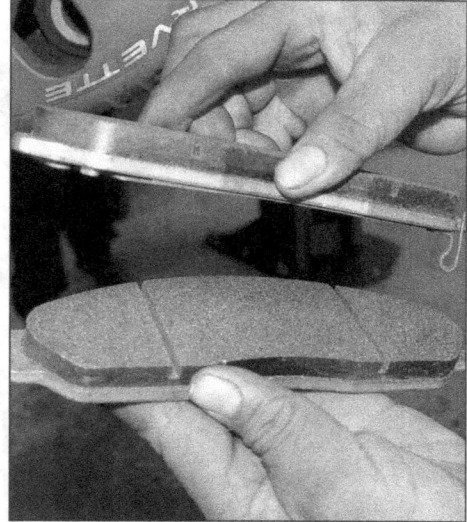

You can greatly increase the stopping power of your factory brakes by adding aggressive brake pads, like these Hawk HPs shown here.

pack a couple of one-gallon jugs of water. A ground cloth, small cooler with drinks, blanket, and portable chairs make waiting between track sessions more comfortable.

Event Selection

Check with your local Corvette clubs to determine what track events are scheduled for your area. Most of the major racetracks offer these events. I suggest using Google to search for events that might interest you. Good luck!

SCCA T-1 Amateur Racing

Participating in track-day events can sometimes give you enough confidence and desire to make you want to participate in an actual race series. The SCCA is a huge racing organization dedicated to amateur racing. The SCCA is divided into many regions around the country. Each region has a series of races covering multiple categories of production and all-out racecars. Each year, the competitors who finish in the top three in each of their regional categories are invited to the national runoffs. Corvettes that are less than 10 years old are eligible to race in the T-1 category. According to the SCCA rulebook, the T-1 category "is intended to provide the Membership with the opportunity to compete in commonly available, recently-produced automobiles in as near the legal, street-driven form of those automobiles as is practically and safely possible under racing circumstances."

John Heinricy, director of high-performance vehicles at General Motors, won his fifth consecutive SCCA National Championship in 2005. John won the Touring 1 race in his Phoenix Motorsports/Goodyear Chevrolet Corvette C5 Z06. His margin of victory was 1.649 over a Dodge Viper driven by Scotty White. The C5 Z06 continues to be very competitive in this category against the Vipers and Porsche GT3. The 2002 Z06 is the car of choice for a beginner building a T-1 racecar. The 2002 to 2004 cars have the same horsepower ratings (405) and the same mechanical specifications.

Car setup and construction have to be done according to the SCCA rulebook, which is found online at the SCCA website. The engine must remain stock, but can be blueprinted and balanced. Exhaust must remain stock from the engine to the catalytic. The exhaust can be changed from the cats to the

The best way to pull away from a competitor is to keep feeding the car power as it exits a corner, like Danny Kellermeyer is doing racing against this Viper.

Taking simple hand tools to the track like a jack, wrenches, etc., allows you to do some routine maintenance yourself.

HIGH-PERFORMANCE C5 CORVETTE BUILDER'S GUIDE

CHAPTER 11

Depending on the number of entries, regional SCCA events usually combine several classes of racecars to fill up the field.

rear of the car. Transmission, cooling system, brakes, and suspension must adhere to factory specifications. A full roll cage must be installed around the stock interior. You are allowed to change the driver's seat to a race seat, but the passenger seat must remain. The SCCA allows the installation of GM Motorsports T-1 suspension package (PN 12480062). This includes new springs, sway bars, and shock absorbers. In addition, GM Motorsports transmission cooler kit (PN 12480080) is permitted. The other good news is that the SCCA allows updating and backdating within models and years listed in this classification. Basically, you can install Z06 parts into a non-Z06 like an FRC.

Rules that govern this category are available from the SCCA. You can go online and print a copy or write the SCCA to ask for a hard copy to be mailed to you. T-1 races are usually 30 minutes in length. You need two complete sets of spare tires, plus the ones on your car. One set should have rain tires mounted in case of bad weather. You need a pit cart filled with tools and a proper tow vehicle and trailer to pull your racer to the track. An SCCA competition license is required to compete in T-1 races. The SCCA offers regional driving schools that you can participate in to get your competition license. Check with your local region for dates and times for these schools.

There you have it. These are a few tips if you want to road race your C5. It is a great foundation that lends itself well to this type of racing.

T-1 driver Jim Rathmann demonstrates how you should be belted into your racecar. If you look closely, you might notice the stock passenger seat.

John Heinricy is on his way to his fifth T-1 victory in this Phoenix Racing Z06.

SCCA allows very few modifications to a T-1 showroom stock racecar. This FRC's LS1 engine is a good example of how stock these cars must be to qualify for the T-1 category.

More great titles available from CarTech®...

S-A DESIGN

Super Tuning & Modifying Holley Carburetors — Perf, street and off-road applications. *(SA08)*
Custom Painting — Gives you an overview of the broad spectrum of custom painting types and techniques. *(SA10)*
Street Supercharging, A Complete Guide to — Bolt-on buying, installing and tuning blowers. *(SA17)*
Engine Blueprinting — Using tools, block selection & prep, crank mods, pistons, heads, cams & more! *(SA21)*
David Vizard's How to Build Horsepower — Building horsepower in any engine. *(SA24)*
Chevrolet Small-Block Parts Interchange Manual — Selecting & swapping high-perf. small-block parts. *(SA55)*
High-Performance Ford Engine Parts Interchange — Selecting & swapping big- and small-block Ford parts. *(SA56)*
How To Build Max Perf Chevy Small-Blocks on a Budget — Would you believe 600 hp for $3000? *(SA57)*
How To Build Max Performance Ford V-8s on a Budget — Dyno-tested engine builds for big- & small-blocks. *(SA69)*
How To Build Max-Perf Pontiac V8s — Mild perf apps to all-out performance build-ups. *(SA78)*
How To Build High-Performance Ignition Systems — Guide to understanding auto ignition systems. *(SA79)*
How To Build Max Perf 4.6 Liter Ford Engines — Building & modifying Ford's 2- & 4-valve 4.6/5.4 liter engines. *(SA82)*
How To Build Big-Inch Ford Small-Blocks — Add cubic inches without the hassle of switching to a big-block. *(SA85)*
How To Build High-Perf Chevy LS1/LS6 Engines — Modifying and tuning Gen-III engines for GM cars and trucks. *(SA86)*
How To Build Big-Inch Chevy Small-Blocks — Get the additional torque & horsepower of a big-block. *(SA87)*
Honda Engine Swaps — Step-by-step instructions for all major tasks involved in engine swapping. *(SA93)*
How to Build High-Performance Chevy Small-Block Cams/Valvetrains — Camshaft & valvetrain function, selection, performance, and design. *(SA105)*
High-Performance Jeep Cherokee XJ Builder's Guide 1984–2001 — Build a useful Cherokee for mountains, the mud, the desert, the street, and more. *(SA109)*
How to Build and Modify Rochester Quadrajet Carburetors — Selecting, rebuilding, and modifying the Quadrajet Carburetors. *(SA113)*
Rebuilding the Small-Block Chevy: Step-by-Step Videobook — 160-pg book plus 2-hour DVD show you how to build a street or racing small-block Chevy. *(SA116)*
How to Paint Your Car on a Budget — Everything you need to know to get a great-looking coat of paint and save money. *(SA117)*
How to Drift: The Art of Oversteer — This comprehensive guide to drifting covers both driving techniques and car setup. *(SA118)*
Turbo: Real World High-Performance Turbocharger Systems — Turbo is the most practical book for enthusiasts who want to make more horsepower. Foreword by Gale Banks. *(SA123)*
High-Performance Chevy Small-Block Cylinder Heads — Learn how to make the most power with this popular modification on your small-block Chevy. *(SA125)*
High Performance Brake Systems — Design, selection, and installation of brake systems for Musclecars, Hot Rods, Imports, Modern Era cars and more. *(SA126)*
High Performance C5 Corvette Builder's Guide — Improve the looks, handling and performance of your Corvette C5. *(SA127)*
High Performance Diesel Builder's Guide — The definitive guide to getting maximum performance out of your diesel engine. *(SA129)*
How to Rebuild & Modify Carter/Edelbrock Carbs — The only source for information on rebuilding and tuning these popular carburetors. *(SA130)*
Building Honda K-Series Engine Performance — The first book on the market dedicated exclusively to the Honda K series engine. *(SA134)*
Engine Management-Advanced Tuning — Take your fuel injection and tuning knowledge to the next level. *(SA135)*
How to Drag Race — Car setup, beginning and advanced techniques for bracket racing and pro classes, and racing science and math, and more. *(SA136)*
4x4 Suspension Handbook — Includes suspension basics & theory, advanced/high-performance suspension and lift systems, axles, how-to installations, and more. *(SA137)*
GM Automatic Overdrive Transmission Builder's and Swapper's Guide — Learn to build a bulletproof tranny and how to swap it into an older chassis as well. *(SA140)*
High-Performance Subaru Builder's Guide — Subarus are the hottest compacts on the street. Make yours even hotter. *(SA141)*
How to Build Max-Performance Mitsubishi 4G63t Engines — Covers every system and component of the engine, including a complete history. *(SA148)*
How to Swap GM LS-Series Engines Into Almost Anything — Includes a historical review and detailed information so you can select and fit the best LS engine. *(SA156)*
How to Autocross — Covers basic to more advanced modifications that go beyond the stock classes. *(SA158)*
Designing & Tuning High-Performance Fuel Injection Systems — Complete guide to tuning aftermarket standalone systems. *(SA161)*
Design & Install In Car Entertainment Systems — The latest and greatest electronic systems, both audio and video. *(SA163)*
How to Build Max-Performance Hemi Engines — Build the biggest baddest vintage Hemi. *(SA164)*
How to Digitally Photograph Cars — Learn all the modern techniques and post processing too. *(SA168)*
High-Performance Differentials, Axles, & Drivelines — Must have book for anyone thinking about setting up a performance differential. *(SA170)*
How To Build Max-Performance Mopar Big Blocks — Build the baddest wedge Mopar on the block. *(SA171)*
How to Build Max-Performance Oldsmobile V-8s — Make your Oldsmobile keep up with the pack. *(SA172)*
Automotive Diagnostic Systems: Understanding OBD-I & OBD II — Learn how modern diagnostic systems work. *(SA174)*
How to Make Your Muscle Car Handle — Upgrade your muscle car suspension to modern standards. *(SA175)*
Full-Size Fords 1955–1970 — A complete color history of full-sized fords. *(SA176)*
Rebuilding Any Automotive Engine: Step-by-Step Videobook — Rebuild any engine with this book DVD combo. DVD is over 3 hours long! *(SA179)*
How to Supercharge & Turbocharge GM LS-Series Engines — Boost the power of today's most popular engine. *(SA180)*
The New Mini Performance Handbook — All the performance tricks for your new Mini. *(SA182)*
How to Build Max-Performance Ford FE Engines — Finally, performance tricks for the FE junkie. *(SA183)*
Builder's Guide to Hot Rod Chassis & Suspension — Ultimate guide to Hot Rod Suspensions. *(SA185)*
How to Build Altered Wheelbase Cars — Build a wild altered car. Complete history too! *(SA189)*
How to Build Period Correct Hot Rods — Build a hot rod true to your favorite period. *(SA192)*
Automotive Sheet Metal Forming & Fabrication — Create and fabricate your own metalwork. *(SA196)*
How to Build Max-Performance Chevy Big Block on a Budget — New big-block book from the master, David Vizard. *(SA198)*
How to Build Big-Inch GM LS-Series Engines — Get more power through displacement from your LS. *(SA203)*
Performance Automotive Engine Math — All the formulas and facts you will ever need. *(SA204)*
How to Design, Build & Equip Your Automotive Workshop on a Budget — Working man's guide to building a great work space. *(SA207)*
Automotive Electrical Performance Projects — Featuring the most popular electrical mods today. *(SA209)*
How to Port Cylinder Heads — Vizard shares his cylinder head secrets. *(SA215)*

S-A DESIGN RESTORATION SERIES

How to Restore Your Mustang 1964 1/2–1973 — Step-by-step restoration for your classic Mustang. *(SA165)*
Muscle Car Interior Restoration Guide — Make your interior look and smell new again. Includes dash restoration. *(SA167)*
How to Restore Your Camaro 1967–1969 — Step-by-step restoration of your 1st gen Camaro. *(SA178)*

S-A DESIGN WORKBENCH® SERIES

Workbench® Series books feature step by step instruction with hundreds of color photos for stock rebuilds and automotive repair.

How To Rebuild the Small-Block Chevrolet — *(SA26)*
How to Rebuild the Small-Block Ford — *(SA102)*
How to Rebuild & Modify High-Performance Manual Transmissions — *(SA103)*
How to Rebuild the Big-Block Chevrolet — *(SA142)*
How to Rebuild the Small-Block Mopar — *(SA143)*
How to Rebuild GM LS-Series Engines — *(SA147)*
How to Rebuild Any Automotive Engine — *(SA151)*
How to Rebuild Honda B-Series Engines — *(SA154)*
How to Rebuild the 4.6/5.4 Liter Ford — *(SA155)*
Automotive Welding: A Practical Guide — *(SA159)*
Automotive Wiring and Electrical Systems — *(SA160)*
How to Rebuild Big-Block Ford Engines — *(SA162)*
Automotive Bodywork & Rust Repair — *(SA166)*
How To Rebuild & Modify GM Turbo 400 Transmissions — *(SA186)*
How to Rebuild Pontiac V-8s — *(SA200)*

HISTORIES AND PERSONALITIES

Quarter-Mile Chaos — Rare & stunning photos of terrifying fires, explosions, and crashes in drag racing's golden age. *(CT425)*
Fuelies: Fuel Injected Corvettes 1957–1965 — The first Corvette book to focus specifically on the fuel injected cars, which are among the most collectible. *(CT452)*
Slingshot Spectacular: Front-Engine Dragster Era — Relive the golden age of front engine dragsters in this photo packed trip down memory lane. *(CT464)*
Chrysler Concept Cars 1940–1970 — Fascinating look at the concept cars created by Chrysler during this golden age of the automotive industry. *(CT470)*
Fuel Altereds Forever — Includes more than 250 photos of the most popular drivers and racecars from the Fuel Altered class. *(CT475)*
Yenko — Complete and thorough story of the man, his business, and his legendary cars. *(CT485)*
Lost Hot Rods — Great Hot Rods from the past rediscovered. *(CT487)*
Grumpy's Toys — A collection of Grumpy's greats. *(CT489)*
Woodward Avenue: Cruising the Legendary — Revisit the glory days of Woodward! *(CT491)*
Rusted Muscle — A collection of junkyard muscle cars. *(CT492)*
America's Coolest Station Wagons — Wagons are cooler than they ever have been. *(CT493)*
Super Stock — A paperback version of a classic best seller. *(CT495)*
Rusty Pickups: American Workhorses Put to Pasture — Cool collection of old trucks and ads too! *(CT496)*
Jerry Heasley's Rare Finds — Great collection of Heasley's best finds. *(CT497)*
Street Sleepers: The Art of the Deceptively Fast Car — Stealth, horsepower, what's not to love? *(CT498)*
Ed 'Big Daddy' Roth — Paperback reprint of a classic best seller. *(CT500)*
Car Spy: Secret Cars Exposed by the Industry's Most Notorious Photographer — Cool behind-the-scenes stories spanning 40 years. *(CT502)*

CarTech®, Inc. 39966 Grand Ave., North Branch, MN 55056. Ph: 800-551-4754 or 651-277-1200 • Fax: 651-277-1203
Brooklands Books Ltd., PO Box 146 Cobham, Surrey KT11 1LG, England. Ph: 01932 865051 • Fax 01932 868803
Brooklands Books Aus., 3/37-39 Green Street, Banksmeadow, NSW 2019, Australia. Ph: 2 9695 7055 • Fax 2 9695 7355

Visit us online at www.cartechbooks.com for more info!

More Information for Your Project ...

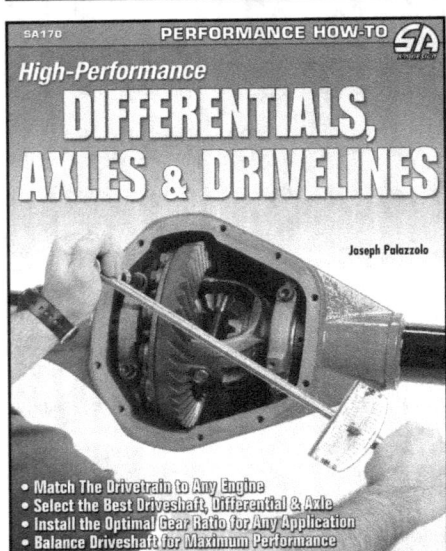

HIGH-PERFORMANCE DIFFERENTIALS, AXELS & DRIVELINES by Joseph Palazzolo This book covers everything you need to know about selecting the most desirable gear ratio, rebuilding differentials and other driveline components, and matching driveline components to engine power output. Learn how to set up a limited-slip differential, install high-performance axle shafts, swap out differential gears, and select products for the driveline. This book explains rear differential basics, rear differential housings, rebuilding open rear differentials, limited-slip differentials, and factory differentials. Ring and pinion gears, axle housings, axle shafts, driveshafts, and U-joints are also covered. Softbound, 8-1/2 x 11 inches, 144 pages, approx. 400 color photos. *Item #SA170*

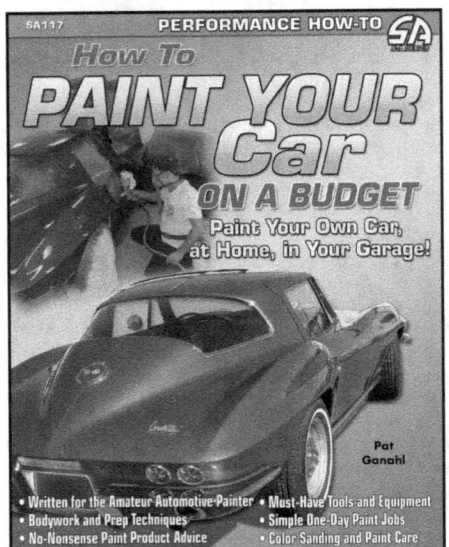

HOW TO PAINT YOUR CAR ON A BUDGET by Pat Ganahl If your car needs new paint, or even just a touch-up, the cost involved in getting a professional job can be more than you bargained for. In this book, author Pat Ganahl unveils dozens of secrets that will help anyone paint their own car. From simple scuff-and-squirt jobs to full-on, door-jambs-and-everything paint jobs, Ganahl covers everything you need to know to get a great-looking coat of paint on your car and save lots of money in the process. Covers painting equipment, the ins and outs of prep, masking, painting and sanding products and techniques, and real-world advice on how to budget wisely when painting your own car. Softbound, 8-1/2 x 11 inches, 128 pages, approx. 400 color photos. *Item #SA117*

THE STEP-BY-STEP GUIDE TO ENGINE BLUEPRINTING by Rick Voegelin this book is simply the best book available on basic engine preparation for street or racing. Rick Voegelin's writing and wrenching skills put this book in a class by itself. Includes pro's secrets of using tools, selecting and preparing blocks, cranks, rods, pistons, cylinder heads, selecting cams and valvetrain components, balancing and assembly tips, plus worksheets for your engine projects, and much more! Softbound, 8-1/2 x 11 inches, 128 pages, over 400 b/w photos. *Item #SA21*

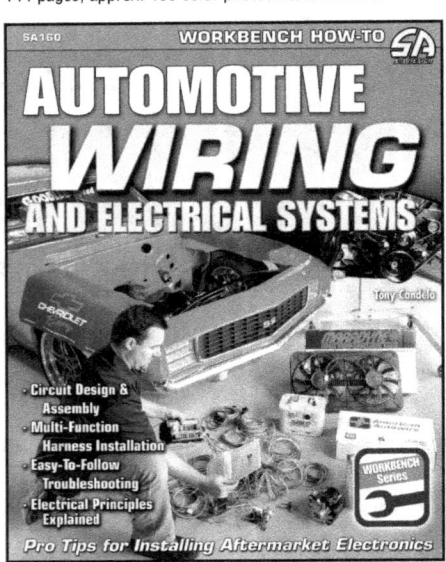

AUTOMOTIVE WIRING AND ELECTRICAL SYSTEMS by Tony Candela This book is the perfect book to unshroud the mysteries of automotive electrics and electronic systems. The basics of electrical principles, including voltage, amperage, resistance, and Ohm's law, are revealed in clear and concise detail, so the enthusiast understands what these mean in the construction and repair of automotive electrical circuits. Softbound, 8-1/2 x 11 inches, 144 pages, approx. 350 color photos. *Item #SA160*

AUTOMOTIVE BODYWORK AND RUST REPAIR by Matt Joseph This book shows you the ins and out of tackling both simple and difficult rust and metalwork projects. This book teaches you how to select the proper tools for the job, common-sense approaches to the task ahead of you, preparing and cleaning sheet metal, section fabrications and repair patches, welding options such as gas and electric, forming, fitting and smoothing, cutting metal, final metal finishing including filling and sanding, the secrets of lead filling, making panels fit properly, and more. Softbound, 8-1/2 x 11 inches, 160 pages, 400 color photos. *Item #SA166*

PERFORMANCE AUTOMOTIVE ENGINE MATH by John Baechtel When designing or building an automotive engine for improved performance, it's all about the math. From measuring the engine's internal capacities to determine compression ratio to developing the optimal camshaft lift, duration, and overlap specifications, the use of proven math is the only way to design an effective high performance automotive powerplant. This book walks readers through the wide range of dimensions to be measured and formulas used to design and develop powerful engines. Includes reviews the proper tools and measurement techniques, and carefully defines the procedures and equations used in engineering high efficiency and high rpm engines. Softbound, 8.5 x 11 inches, 160 pages, 350 photos. *Item #SA204*

www.cartechbooks.com or 1-800-551-4754